*In memory of
my Father and Mother
for whom Bromham
was home.*

BROMHAM

in

BEDFORDSHIRE:

a History

Roger W. Rideout

© Roger William Rideout 2002

All rights reserved. No part of this publication may be reproduced, stored in a retrieval system or transmitted in any form or by any means, electronic, mechanical, photocopying, recording, or otherwise without the prior permission of Roger William Rideout.

Published by
Roger William Rideout, 255 Chipstead Way, Banstead, Surrey SM7 3JW, England

ISBN 0-9544173-0-5

Printed in Great Britain by Ian Allan Printing, Hersham, Surrey KT12 4RG

ACKNOWLEDGEMENTS

I am indebted to the following for permission to reproduce copyright photographs: Bedfordshire County Council in respect of the Water Mill; The Bedfordshire and Luton Archive and Record Service in respect of the pictures of Major Hill's Garage and the Crown Inn; the Bedford Museum in respect of the Village Store in 1906; Richard Wildman of Bedford in respect of the Miss Rice-Trevor's Sunday School class.

The excellent photographs of the North and South porches of the Church are no longer subject to copyright but were obtained (in 1955) from the National Property Register. The copyright of the latter was then vested in P.H. Lovell of Harrow. Copyright has long since ceased to apply to Harvey's pictures and to Fisher's drawing of the Bridge in 1812. The Author holds the copyright of all other pictures.

CONTENTS

Preface — vi

Chapter I – Introductory Snapshots — 1
The Potters — 1
The last of the Romans — 2
The Gallant Horseman — 7
A Victorian Lady — 7

Chapter II – Early Landscapes — 10
Names — 10
The Domesday Survey – 1086 — 11
The Feudal Manor — 12
    Bowles ? — 17
Tenants in chief — 18

Chapter III – Religious Worship — 21
The Anglican Church — 21
    The structure — 21
    Monuments — 21
    History — 22
    Works — 24
The Parish Library — 25
The Chantry — 26
The Chapel — 27

Chapter IV – The People — 35
The Population — 35
Family names — 35
Their brushes with the law — 38
Notables — 41
Occupations and Possessions — 43
    Trades — 43
    Possessions — 43
Taxation and the poor — 46
    The Poor Law — 47
Education — 52
The Oakley Hunt — 58
Second World War evacuees and other wartime events — 59

Chapter V – Portraits 65
    The second Sir Lewis Dyve – his ancestors and family 65
    Thomas, Lord Trevor and sons 77
    The Rice-Trevors and the last flourishing of the estate 80

Chapter VI – Later Landscapes 88
    The End of the Estate 88
    The Mill 93
    Other Property 95
        Bromham Hall 95
        The Park 96
        Bromham House 97
        The Post Office 98
        The Village Hall 98
        The Cattle Pound 98
        A Nature Park 99
    The Waterways and Bridges of Bromham 99
        Rivers and streams 99
        The Bridges 101
        Springs 105
    Roads and Railways 107
        Roads 107
        Turnpike trusts 108
        Railways 110

Chapter VII – Wildlife 115

Appendices 128
    I   Tenants under the Crown 128
    II   Incumbents and Chantry priests 129
    IIIA Genealogy – The Dyves 131
    IIIB Genealogy – The Trevors and Rice-Trevors 132
    IV   The Bromham May Song 133
    V   Field Names 134
    VI   The 1844 Tithe Commission Valuation 143
    VII   The Rate Account Book for 1928 150
    VIII Teaching staff at Bromham School 153
    IX   Comparative populations 155

Index of Names 156

Illustrations

between pages 64 and 65
An Armorial
St. Owen's Church, Bromham
Harvey's etching of Bromham Church from the North
The South Porch
Memorial to the third Lord Trevor
The North Porch
The Dyve Brass
The Water Mill
Restored machinery in the Mill
Fisher's sketch of Bromham Bridge (1812)
The Chantry Spring
The old bridge
The Mill Stream
The School in 1942
A School Report
Harvey's views of Bromham Hall
Miss Rice-Trevor and her Sunday School class
Harvey's etching of the Vicarage from the South
Greenwood Cottages
The Smithy
The Crown Inn
Major Hill's Garage in the 1920s
The village store in 1906
The Stagsden Gate
Bromham House
One third of the population
The first Baptist Church and Sunday School
The Baptist Church
The Village Hall
The Jubilee of King George V
The End of the Rainbow
Erich, Carl and Franz
Woad

Maps
North West Bedfordshire
The growth of the village

PREFACE

I first attempted to write a History of the village of Bromham in Bedfordshire, where I was born and lived at that time, in 1953 for a school history essay prize. I won the prize not, I was told, for the beauty of my composition but because I was the only entrant to have done significant original research. That being so the prize should have been awarded to Ms Joyce Godber of what was then called the Bedfordshire County Record Office. She suggested, and brought to my table, all the original documents I then consulted. Looking back I realise that she was very wise because she appreciated the limitations on time and the task in hand and brought me enough, but not too much, to digest.

To my surprise, when, in 2002, I next visited what had become the Bedfordshire and Luton Archive and Records Service, after Ms Godber's death, I found the same attitude prevailing among the staff, with the exception of the restriction on what was supplied. The writing of local history with such a degree of assistance and such an extensive record as this service has is nothing but pleasure. Archivists appear to be an unusually helpful group and my second great individual debt is to Mr Collett-White, also of the Bedfordshire Records Service, who, among other useful material, supplied me with all his extensive notes on Bromham school. I am grateful to Mr Trefor Jones for useful information on publishing and also for directing me to his, and now my, printers. I am also greatly indebted, for information and comment, to my brothers John and David and my sister Rosemary Spencer. My wife has not only read the proofs but put up with long periods of my absence, punctuated by computerised panic.

Some of the original material from 1953 still appears in this much larger version. In the intervening years I added comments to the original manuscript and, inspired by the chance to purchase a then complete set of the Bedfordshire Magazine, I joined the Bedfordshire Historical Record Society and built up a considerable library, not only of its annual publications, but also of the surprisingly large number of texts available on aspects of Bedfordshire history. Finally, I resumed my original research and this volume is the result of that accumulation over a period of 50 years.

A long history of writing the results of research in other fields has taught me that whenever one takes one's hand off the keyboard one realises how much more there is still to write. This I know to be true of the history of Bromham. It is to be hoped that if this proves to be the first extensive general history of that village others, in the future, will add to, and improve, it.

R.W. Rideout
Woodmansterne, Surrey
November 2002

Prayer of Peace

Lord Jesus, enable us to receive the peace you offer us.
Help us to experience peace, in our bodies, in our minds,
in our emotions and in our feelings.
Strengthen us in times of worry, upset and fear,
so that we will not be afraid,
but place our trust in you.

(David,J. Merriman. Prayers for all Occasions, p.266)

Bromham Baptist Church
"church for all the family"

Chapter I
INTRODUCTORY SNAPSHOTS

The Potters

We are standing on a gravel bed. Much later, people will know that it is the year 50 BC. Behind us is the great loop of a slow flowing river, which has left this deposit as it has cut into the southern bank. There must have been a time when it flowed faster and cut more urgently for the gravel fills much of this end of the loop for at least half a mile in front of us. We shiver a little in a keen breeze from the south west, up the valley and across land which looks as if it floods in winter. Certainly it is now covered with lush grass and few trees.

We have walked north against the flow of this river on the opposite bank to this flood land and noted a surprising amount of clearance of the pervading forest to make room for numerous small agricultural settlements.[1] We have paused now to decide which route to take, for just in front of us there is a small, but quite busy, track running down from higher, and heavily wooded, land to the west, to cross the river at a ford made by a ridge of this same gravel. We can see that just over the river our track meets another running north and south and along this track there is moving what looks like an entire agricultural community of men, women and children, and their domestic animals laden with their possessions. They move purposefully as if their leaders have been here before and they turn to splash across the ford to congregate on our shingle. We realise that they are going to make a new settlement here. On this windswept gravel? Surely not? But the men are walking around excitedly raising hands to sense the direction and strength of the wind. Some, with their feet, are marking shapes in the gravel. Their women have moved to the edge of the gravel where trees begin and offer shelter but seem to be aware that it would be wiser to build their homes on the cleared land.

These people, however, are not native to this land. They are from Belgic Gaul where Rome has established its authority and from which Julius Caesar has recently conducted exploratory raids into this island. Their leaders, indeed, came as raiders but have settled and developed trade[2]. They already have a major centre, which the Romans will call Verulanium, but it is 30 miles south, so our group are somewhat adventurous. They are aware of a need to defend their new settlement with defensive ditches. Their settlement is to become highly successful and, indeed, almost industrial, for these people are potters, as well as farmers, and the principal attractions of this site are its exposure to the wind, which will serve to raise the temperature within their kilns to some 1000°C[3], and the clay from the river bank which, when washed, will make a rough domestic pottery, for which the

Roman conquest will considerably increase demand. A small flint napping industry will also be developed, probably to produce tools for the potters.[4]

They will, however, be a self sufficient community agriculturally. Close to their circular huts they will build a corn drier,[5] and food storage pits which they will even try to make waterproof.[6] They will grow prosperous here, although they scarcely use money, and will barter their products for finer pottery.[7]

The last of the Romans

After the Roman invasion and the suppression of the extremely bloody revolt of the Iceni under Boudicca (who objected to the reversion of her father's kingdom to direct Roman rule and who burned Verulanium and Londinium before a wild dash by Paulinus and the XIVth Legion from Wales led to her defeat and suicide) this area came under the Roman administrative division of the Catuvellauni. Our settlement of potters would have found trade possible over increasing distances, greatly extended by the 11900km of Roman road which existed in Britain by the end of the first century. They seem to have preferred barter. Very little in the way of coin was found on the site but they acquired a large number of pins for their garments as well as a better class of pottery than they produced, some of which may have come from Warwickshire. They may have dug a defensive ditch and they also dug drainage ditches. They had learned to domesticate animals and in their early days there they grew a sort of coarse barley. Sometime between 150 and 170 AD they built corn drying ovens (which they had ceased to use by 250 AD). They seem to have been forced to abandon their settlement by flooding of the valley from the south, but they did leave fifty years or so after the first signs of the collapse of Roman authority threatened their peace.

Under the Romans there were undoubtedly a number of villas in the area. One was excavated at Church End, Kempston in 1991.[8] The so called holy well at the western end of Bromham bridge may have been pre-Christian because early bishops frowned on them.[9] The Romans were quite keen on water gods and, of course, there would have been a spring there. But there were other springs in Bromham and since that was not a river crossing point it may be unlikely that this spring would have been singled out. There was a small Roman settlement at Biddenham around 170AD, where, in 1857, a 40 feet deep well or pit, dating from the Roman era, was opened one hundred yards from a supposed Roman road called Akeman Street which, if it existed, ran from Bedford to Irchester.[10] The pax romanum ensured peaceful development of such settlements for 200 years. But by the end of the third century Roman power was declining. One Carausius was in command of the British squadron of the Roman navy in about 293 when his execution was ordered on charges of corruption. Sensibly enough, he seized the province of Britain, but was murdered by his second in command who was, in turn, killed in battle against a Roman invasion force. Less than one hundred years later Rome would not have been in a position to send such a force and in 406 AD its troops in Britain again elected their own emperor Marcus. By then hordes of barbarians were streaming across the Rhine and some were threatening Britain. Marcus did not last long and the British appointed a soldier called Constantine to resist the invasions. He, understandably enough, thought he could best do so in Gaul and he took the British garrison there, leaving Britain defenceless. The British, seeing that nothing could be expected from Rome expelled the Roman administration, set up a local government and raised a defence force. The Emperor Honorius, therefore, merely stated a fact when, in 410, he told the British they must look after themselves.

Our second sighting of Bromham is almost five hundred years after the first. We are standing almost at the same spot but now the gravel expanse we knew is covered with a shallow lake. There has been widespread long term flooding in this part of the country and it seems that it was this which drove our potters away in the third century. Now the Roman order is threatened and the people, some of whom are the descendants of Roman soldiers who settled and stayed when the last official garrisons departed, must defend themselves. Once again it is bands of adventurers from the Continent that provide the threat. Roman power in Gaul is also declining and some of those coming to Britain are escaping from similar pressure at home. But the Romans are still recognisable here and one is approaching the lake. She is very richly dressed. We have not seen the direction from which she has come. There are villas across the river and she may have crossed at another ford a little lower down. The Roman dwellings we can see on our bank are less grand than that from which she must have come. She stands by the bank a long time in thought before she takes a ring from her finger and drops it into the water.[11] The breakdown of authority would give her much to worry about as travellers, or refugees, brought news of landings on the east coast. She is probably invoking the protection of the water god whom she has not deserted with the coming of Christianity, which she will also have added to her pantheon. We shall not see her like again.

The British leader Vortigen[12] allied with the Saxon mercenary Hengist, but these immigrant "English" (who had been glad to accept the invitation to help defend Britain rather that live under the rule of barbarians who had overrun their homeland) grew strong enough to revolt and take over the government, possibly about 442. Arthur, or someone like him, briefly restored British rule. He may even have expelled the Saxon settlers from this area so as to divide their main settlements.[13] But his triumph was short and it was not until the rise of the great kingdom of Mercia that secure and lasting government returned. Legend, rather than reliable account, identifies Arthur with the British victory at the battle of Badon (possibly Bath) in about 500. Gildas says the British were led by Ambrosius Aurelianus. The last links with Roman organisation are apparent and Morris says that it established Britain as the only place in Europe where the barbarian invaders had been held back. It seems that Saxons were deliberately cleared out of some areas and Morris suggests that ours was one of them.[14] He points out that the large cemetery at Kempston has produced more Saxon grave goods than anywhere else in England but, whereas there are plenty from the late fifth and late sixth centuries, there are none from the early sixth century. This final British rule was short-lived but with the return to power of the Anglo-Saxons came a long period of reorganisation and development from about 669-850, dominated by the Christian church.[15] Our pictures in the following centuries are blurred. The Saxons marched this way after their victory at Bedcanford (although this is no longer thought to be Bedford)[16]. It was their people who gave this place its eventual name referring to the loop of the river in which the settlement then lay at a time when one Bruna was the local worthy.[17] It was their successors who founded the great central Kingdom of Mercia and we are standing on what was the boundary between Saxon and Danish England. But this has long ceased to be the centre of settlement on this river bank. That now lies to the east and south. Before 850 Dunstable, Shefford, and Bedford had "minsters". Bedford was in the kingdom of Middle Anglia under Penda (625-51) who began the process of conquest of surrounding kingdoms which, completed by Offa (757-96)[18], formed the great central kingdom of Mercia. Despite its power and organisation; it had ambitions far to the west, as Offa's Dyke witnesses; Mercia gave place to Alfred's Wessex, and to Wessex fell the burden of the long resistance to the Danes. Alfred was forced back on Athelney, but regrouped and defeated the Danes in May 878, sufficiently consolidating his defences to resist a counter offensive in 892. His son and daughter, Edward the Elder and Aethelfled, began the reconquest of England from the Danes. Alfred and Guthrum had agreed a frontier in 880 which, at its southern end, followed the meanders of the Ouse and the Lea. It was to this part of it that Edward directed most of his energies between 917 and 920. It has been suggested[19] that Alfred saw Bedford as a strategic point which he was anxious to retain in Wessex because the boundary with Danelaw was drawn in a straight line due south from that point to meet the River Lea and this is by no means the most natural border. Bedford, which was English, would have faced Danish Northampton, Huntingdon and Cambridge. Bromham, as a second border river ford, might have merited some defensive fortification. As it turned out, however, the boundary set by this Treaty of Wedmore (or Chippenham) did not hold for more than a decade and the Danes appear to have reoccupied both Bedfordshire and Buckinghamshire.

Eventually, however, Edward defeated the Danes at Tempsford (important as a river port on the navigable Ouse and on the main north-south road) in 917. English Mercia was divided into shires in the 10th century and Bedford became a shire town.

But the struggle went against the English later. In 1010 Thorkell the Viking attacked directly from Scandinavia (whereas the English had seen the principal Viking threat as coming from Ireland). He crossed Suffolk burning and plundering as he went and burnt Bedford, Northampton and Oxford on his way even further south. Aethelred (who was not so much unready as ill-advised, or "redeless") had the misfortune to captain England at the time and, like later English sportsmen, had a lot of bad luck both against Thorkell and his successor Swein who came to England in 1013 expecting to win. Aethelred fled to Normandy in that year, had a bit of good luck when Swein died in 1014 but then suffered from a revolting son Edmund. Edmund was a good deal more successful and managed to hold Cnut, Swein's successor, to a draw (usually referred to as a stalemate). Cnut won in the end, though, because Edmund died in 1016 and Cnut, the Dane, became king of all England.

The country was divided into earldoms. A vast area of East Anglia and the South Midlands became the earldom of Central Wessex under Godwine. It was broken up on his disgrace in 1051 but, when he made a comeback, was returned to him and his son Harold. Harold claimed that Edward the Confessor, on his deathbed, had granted him the throne. William, the Norman bastard, claimed that Edward had acknowledged him as rightful successor as early as 1051. Harald of Norway thought it a good time to invade anyway.

Harold's army would have marched both north and south on the old Roman road we call the A1. North to defeat Harald at Stamford Bridge on 25th September 1066 and south to defeat by William at Senlac Hill on 14th October. This was a battle Harold should have won had he taken a few more days before confronting the Normans and had his men not fallen for the oldest trick in the military manual when William faked a withdrawal. We tend today to record the changes in land holding and the legal system without noticing their real effect on the native English, which must have been catastrophic. They had an early taste of the change when William, having waited five days in vain for them to concede defeat, marched in a wide circle around London, through Canterbury, Guildford, Abingdon, Wallingford, Buckingham, Bedford and St Neots, and Hertford burning and pillaging, yet again, until the southern English gave in and he was crowned in London on Christmas Day 1066. William's route passed south east of the town of Bedford and his army laid waste to Kempston but not to Bromham or anywhere north west of it.[20]

We shall, in due course, recount the land changes in Bromham produced by the Norman conquest and recorded in the Domesday Book, and following on in the next 400 years. Since the Normans marched through the south east after their victory the track to the west upon which our earliest settlers relied for trade has been replaced by a new road and a bridge which channel several routes from the west through Bedford. So far as significant effects on this area are concerned we can move on to the death of the last of the Normans, Henry I. England would have been spared another period of unrest if Henry's son and heir had not drowned in the sinking of the White Ship in 1120. Stephen of Blois and Matilda both claimed the throne. Stephen, who largely retained control of the south-east, including Bedford, fought at Bedford in 1138, 1146 and 1149. He ultimately surrendered the succession to Henry II and England settled down to a little internal peace and some good government. Both were again shattered by the arrogance and stupidity of John, who was lucky that the opposition largely lacked a viable alternative ruler. Most of the east of England, north of the Thames, was held by John's opponents, who, in the absence of a good candidate to replace him had extracted his signature to Magna Carta. In 1215 a rebel force marched from Brackley, via Northampton and Bedford (and therefore quite possibly over the new bridge at Bromham) to London which it captured, forcing further concessions from John, who died in 1216 and was succeeded by his son Henry III. William de Beauchamp, who after the battle of Lincoln had ended any support for an alternative to Henry, claimed possession of Bedford Castle.

Falkes de Breaute, however, who had supported John against the barons including Beauchamp, had seized the castle on November 28th 1215. John, indeed, discussed campaign plans with Falkes there in March 1216.[21] Not surprisingly, Falkes had been awarded the castle and celebrated by plundering St Albans on January 22nd 1217.[22] Initially Falkes strongly supported John's son and his support and that of other barons like him largely assured the succession. But Falkes became unruly and Henry III was persuaded, possibly by Hubert de Burgh, the unusually upright justiciar and excellent builder of Welsh castles, who disliked Falkes, to turn against Falkes. Farrar describes what followed as "the deliberate ruin of a brave man". Falkes was charged with murder (he must surely have committed at least one). Falkes' brother William was in charge of Bedford castle and carried off there the king's justices in eyre. The wife of Henry de Braybrook, one of them, complained to the King, who was at Northampton and he set out, to Bedford Castle. Henry's troops would either have splashed through the ford at Clapham or gone dry-shod over the bridge. Stefan Langton, Archbishop of Canterbury (and no friend of John), accompanied by a number of bishops, stood before the gates and excommunicated Falkes and William. On 14th August 1217 fire was set to the props in the mine under the keep. The King's men had already taken the inner bailey. The women and prisoners were sent out and the remaining garrison surrendered. Eighty or so knights and men at arms, including William de Breaute were hanged. Falkes was located and captured and taken to Elstow Abbey where the King was then lodged. He was spared execution, partly from fear of the reaction of the Pope, but banished after he had surrendered all his land and goods. Not unexpectedly he fell into the hands of Louis, King of France and son of the unlikely alternative to John, whom Falkes had defeated. To save himself he swore to go on a crusade. He died in 1226.

Someone of the Breautes survived if the baker at Bromham in the late nineteenth century, who then spelt his name Bruty, was right to claim direct descent. If he was right they live on for that baker's grand-daughter Pauline Poole who was at the Bedford Girls Modern School (as it then was) during the Second World War was aware of the connection. Bedford Castle and the largest part of Bromham was returned to the Beauchamps, although they were to find themselves on the losing side at Evesham in 1265.

The Gallant Horseman

The manors of Bromham, once largely the possession of the Beauchamps, were eventually gathered together by the first Sir Lewis Dyve in the latter part of the sixteenth century . We are back at our usual spot and this is obviously not going to be a peaceful visit. This time we know the year precisely. It is 1642 and we are annoyed because we had heard a rumour that King Charles I was to come from the north to stay at Bromham Hall. He would certainly have crossed our ford for the drive to that house is clearly visible. The rumour is obviously wrong for today there is a noise of musket fire which we would not have expected to mark such a visit. There is a good deal of shouting and we hear the thunder of horses hooves on the path leading from the house towards our ford. A single horseman bursts into view and gallops across the ford.[23] No one seems very keen to pursue him and we are not surprised for we recognise him as the second Sir Lewis Dyve, grandson of the first and, like his father, one for a good fight. We learn later that Sir Samuel Luke has been ordered by Parliament to apprehend him and has, obviously, failed to do so. He has to content himself with seizing Sir Lewis' horses.

A Victorian Lady

It is late in the nineteenth century. Our last snapshot is of a carriage on the more familiar southern road from Bedford. There is, indeed, a very grand avenue of trees running from iron gates near where we saw Sir Lewis. But the lady in the carriage does not care to risk the ford, and her coachman agrees with this decision, now that he can cross the river by the raised stone bridge rather than a cart track too often half washed away by the last winter's flood. Not that it would make much difference if he did not, for Miss Rice- (which should really be Rees-) Trevor would not give much for any opinion other than her own. A group of children are walking from Bromham into Bedford, and they wish they were not doing so at this time. Especially they wish they had not been caught on the bridge where they will have to press themselves against the wall as the coach goes by. They are with their friends from Bedford whom they know will laugh as the carriage passes them and the Bromham girls and boys, with some difficulty, curtsy and bow. Miss Rice-Trevor owns their houses. Their parents work on her farms. She is the sixth largest landowner in Bedford, the daughter of Lord Dynevor, the direct descendant of the princes of Glamorgan, and, worst of all for some of the girls who are members of her Sunday School class, they depend on her for two new outfits of clothes each year. She would demand a personal explanation if they neglected this duty. But things are changing. They go to the school she and her sister have built in the centre of the village. At least the education offered there is more acceptable to them than the training in lace-making which she used to provide for their parents. For all her fine graces she has no direct heir and her successor will sell Bromham Hall and its estate, on which she has lavished so much care. After that sale in 1924 taking snapshots will be a common pastime. There will be much more to photograph. We must wait to see if it will be as interesting.

[1] See, Krystyna Bilikowska: *The Anglo-Saxon Settlement of Bedfordshire* (1980) 14 Beds Arch Journal 25 at 27.
[2] Before the Romans the east of Britain, possibly as far north as Derbyshire, traded with Belgic Gaul in raw materials (and also in slaves and mercenary soldiers). In turn Belgic leaders raided the area and set up resident communities, largely in Kent, Essex, the Thames estuary and north-west Hertfordshire. As the evidence of settlement at Bromham shows, craftsmen settled in a wider area and they would be likely to have traded with the relatively well organised little kingdoms in the South East of Britain.
[3] See, Peter Tilson: *A Belgic and Romano-British Site at Bromham* (1973) 8 Beds Arch. Journal 23 at 64.
[4] *Op.cit.*
[5] *Op.cit.* 27 to 29 and 31
[6] Peter Tilson: *The Excavation of an Iron Age Hut Circle at Bromham* (1975) 10 Beds Arch. Journal 5, 19 to 24.
[7] A full account of excavation of this settlement, much of the evidence of which had been destroyed by gravel working in 1968, is contained in (1977) 18 Beds Archaeological Journal pp.23 et seq.
[8] *The Independent* 4th June 1991. The building was 150 feet long by 60 feet wide with a large courtyard. It was largely destroyed in the fifth century.
[9] Godber at p.5.

[10] VCH ii pp.5-6 In this well was found, among other things a sculptured figure which was taken to the grounds of Bromham Hall. The VCH also notes that a bronze head steelyard weight was ploughed up in a field in Bromham in 1853. If this Roman road existed it led to a crossing point of the river considerably south of the bridge at Bromham.

[11] See, Catherine Johns and Caroline Wingfield: *A Roman Gold Ring from Bromham, Bedfordshire* (1991) 19 Beds Arch. Journal 108 to 111. The authors disagree with the suggestion of a votive offering (p.110) on the ground that there is no evidence of a spring or watercourse in the area. But the excavations described by Peter Tilson revealed twelve inches of silt overlying the gravel, suggesting that our lake was by then, and would long remain, an established feature.

[12] See, generally and in detail, John Morris, *The Age of Arthur* (Weidenfeld 1993).

[13] John Morris: *The Age of Arthur.* (first published by Weidenfeld in 1993) Phoenix 1999 at 136.

[14] Morris, *op.cit.,* at p.136.

[15] Missionaries from England went even to Saxony to convert the still pagan population.

[16] Morris, *op.cit.,* at pp.293 and 515. But see Alan Crawley and Ian Freeman: *Bedford's Oldest Streets* (1998) 18 Beds Arch. Journal 99.

[17] Mawer and Stenson; *The Place Names of Bedfordshire and Huntingdonshire* (1926 Cambridge) p.28.

[18] Who may have been buried at Bedford.

[19] Allen Crawley and Ian Freeman: *Bedford – an Alfredian burh* (2001) 24 Bedfordshire Archeology 40.

[20] See Godber plate 4b.

[21] Farrar, *Old Bedford* (FR Hockliffe 1926) at pp.40 et seq., who appears more reliable than he often is, save in respect of his defence of Falkes' atrocities, suggests that it was on this visit that St Paul's church was destroyed.

[22] Farrar, *op.cit.,* at p.44, suggests this was to teach the Abbot a lesson for disloyalty to John!

[23] Rev. J.T.Marshall in a series of papers entitled <u>The Censor</u> in the Gentleman's Magazine for 1823 seems to be responsible for perpetuating the story that Sir Lewis Dyve escaped by swimming the river. In the hands of Rev.C.F.Farrar: *Ouse's Silent Tide* (Sidney Press, Bedford, 1921) p.60 Sir Lewis is said to have wounded Sir Samuel Luke five times before he fled. In my childhood the story provided for him swimming the river in full armour. I doubt any of this. Bedfordshire was a largely Parliamentarian county and Sir Lewis would not have got far on the Bedford road, soaking wet and without a horse. In any event he had acquired some support in North Bedfordshire (and he was at the siege of Newark in March 1643) so that it seems much more likely he would, more sensibly equipped, have taken what should still have been the more usual route from his house to pick up the road at Clapham towards the north.

Chapter II
EARLY LANDSCAPES

Names

The name of *Bromham* itself seems to have gone astray and, for this reason, it is suggested that the meaning given in Mills Dictionary of English Place Names[24] is the product of reasoning backwards from a false start. This was never, it is submitted, a farmstead where broom grew.[25] That author himself admits that he might be wrong and that "Brom" is a corruption of the Old English "Bruna", which would be the name of a person. It would have been common to name a settlement in this way[26]. The first name is most likely to have been "Brunan-ham", and the Domesday Book lends support to this view by giving the name as "Bruneham" in 1086.[27] Various official documents including the Assize Rolls for 1247, 1276 and 1287 keep within sight of this (Bruham). The Assize Rolls for 1276 have a field day of alternatives such as "Brumbham", "Brynham" and "Brunham". Those for 1287 also alternate with "Brunham". But the Assize Roll of 1227, as well as "Braham", with a blinding foresight produces "Bromham" for the first time. This is repeated in Charter and Close Rolls during the thirteenth and fourteenth centuries.[28] Mawer and Stenton suggest that the derivation was lost by Anglo-Norman pronunciation from a strong centre like Bedford which turned the *n* into *m* and, by losing the source, became confused. It is this confusion that marks out the difference in the names given to Bromham from simple misspelling like the "Brommom" of the Independent congregation at Southill[29]. The confusion does not resolve itself quickly. J Ellis, in his Modern Map of Bedfordshire of 1765 gives the name as Brunham (which is odd because Lord Trevor, who owned it, thought he was "of Bromham").[30]

What then of "ham"? As spelt this would mean a homestead or farmstead. But Margaret Gelling[31] points out that "hamm" means "land in a river bend". This would obviously apply to Bromham, as to a number of other Bedfordshire "hams". We shall never know why Bruna was so notable that the land he owned on the western bank of the great bend of the Ouse should for ever be known as his but a change to *Brunanhamm* would add an air of historic distinction and may well be correct. If so, Bruna is the earliest named inhabitant.

Other, somewhat later, landholders may have left their name. There was a Bowels manor in Bromham until the end of the Dyves' connection with the village and there is still a Bowels wood. Mawer and Stenton[32] say that this name doubtless derives from the Boeles family, one of whom held two virgates of land in 1242-3.

People do not figure in the road names of Bromham before modern times. Even

Mollivers' Lane was, as Grange Lane and Lower Farm Road, that leading to the farm.

In 1956 the Parish Council decided to submerge Bridge End into Stagsden Road and The Hill, The Green and Vicarage Road into Village Road.[33]

The Domesday Survey – 1086

Three feudal overlords are listed as holding land under the King in Bruneham in 1086.[34]

Land of Count Eustace
Count Eustace holds 1½ hides in Bruneha. Arnulf of Ardres holds from him. Land for 1½ ploughs; 1½ ploughs there; 1 plough possible.
Meadow for 1½ ploughs.
Value 10s.; when acquired 20s.; as much before 1066
Alfwold and Leoffric, King Edwards men, held this land; they could grant and sell it when they would.

Land of Hugon de Belchamp[35]
In Brunehaten Sesto de ros [Rots] holds 6 hides from Hugh. Land for 6 ploughs. In lordship 2 ploughs
16 villagers have 4 ploughs. 5 small holders and 6 ferui [slaves][36]
1mill, 20s. and 125 eels; meadow for 6 ploughs; woodland, 40 pigs
In total value £7; when acquired 100s.; before 1066 £4
Alfsi, Queen Edith's man, held this land; he could sell.
[Alfsi had also held one hide in Biddenham]

Land of Countess Judith[37]
In Brunehaten Hugh holds 2 hides for the Countess. Land for 2 ploughs; they are there
5 villagers and 2 smallholders
1 mill at 40s. and 100 eels; it is of the Countess' Holding but it does not lie in this land. Meadow for 2 ploughs
Value 20s, when acquired and before 1066, 10s.
Godwin, Earl Harold's man, held this land; he could sell

Land of the King's Reeves and Almsmen

In Brimehaten Osgeat holds 1 virgate and two parts of 1 virgate
Land for 1 plough; it is there
Meadow for ½ plough

Value 10s.; before 1066 5s.
He held it for himself then; he could grant.

Notes

1 Hide = 4 virgates = 200 acres at most (variable). A Hundred was roughly 100 hides of lands owned by feudal overlords. The total area of Bromham is about 1800 acres. The total landholding recorded is about 1200 acres.

Value is the sum due to the lord for the land. It seems that Bromham did not suffer as much as some of the surrounding villages from the depredations of the Normans. Its total value actually increases from £5.15s.0d before 1066 and £7 in 1066 to £9 at the time of the Survey in 1086. It was also only one plough team short of its land requirement.

Land for ploughs is an estimate of the amount of arable land. It refers, however, to taxable potential rather than to actual acreage. Two fighting men per plough team or the equivalent in money was required if the host was summoned. Bromham had land for ten and a half ploughs. There was woodland for forty swine. Bromham in 1086 had 21 villagers, 7 smallholders (bordars) and 6 slaves (serfs).

Meadow for ploughs is pasture for the oxen (reckoned at 8) which pulled each plough. Bromham could pasture 10 teams

Queen Edith was the wife of Edward the Confessor and daughter of Earl Godwin.

The Feudal Manor

The subsequent succession to the Bromham lands, which became divided into four separate manors before being again united, between 1550 and 1600, under Sir Lewis Dyve, is set out in Appendix I.[38] A little more detail concerning those who held as tenants in chief and, under them, as mesne tenants will be added here.

Manors, of course, did not necessarily follow parish boundaries. Count Eustace was much the most important of those who, in 1086, held land in Bromham. His relatively small holding in this village, however, was on the Stevington boundary and is usually treated (as in the Victoria County History) as part of that village. The tenant in chief of all the lands of Count Eustace in Stevington, Pavenham, Turvey and Odell, was Arnulf of Ardres and, as the Domesday survey records, Arnulf was also tenant of the Count's holding in Bromham. The Countess Judith is also recorded as having land occupied by five villains and 2 bordars in Bromham. By 1087 Hugh de Beauchamp was the tenant in chief of that land and he was, by marriage, the lord of the manor under the king of the rest of Bromham. In effect, therefore, Hugh was the lord of Bromham. His tenant in chief was another Norman, Sesto de Ros. No doubt that meant little in terms of presence. Like most lords under the king Hugh was an absentee. He may well have seen Bromham from time to time as he travelled to and from his castle in Bedford but he would prefer, on such occasions, the comforts of home. He was the largest landowner in Bedfordshire possessing all, or in a few cases a substantial part, of twenty one Bedfordshire villages.

All this he had acquired by the noble art of marriage to an heiress which has served great landowners, including the Dukes of Bedford, well over centuries. Hugh himself does not seem to have been an important enough knight at Hastings to have received a direct grant of any manor. Hugh, however, married Matilda, the only child of Ralph Tallebose.

He kept the manors of Bromham, Cardington, Putnoe, Ravensden, Willington, Stagsden, Haynes, Houghton (Conquest), Salford and Stotfold in his own hands. More important, from the point of view of his king, he maintained a substantial force at Bedford castle. In return for his lands he had to provide, on demand, thirty six fully equipped knights, each with horse and esquire. He was confirmed as baron of Bedford on the accession of William II (Rufus) in 1087 and he acted at his coronation as almoner, distributing alms to paupers and lepers (and coming off best by being able to keep the silver bowl which had contained the money).

On his lands at Bromham Hugh, or the other tenants in chief, had three classes of tenant. The Normans found the rather flexible Saxon classes untidy. In order to produce the systematisation they desired they introduced a new top class called Villein (variously spelt and tending to be misleadingly translated as "villager"). Some of them would have occupied more important roles in Saxon society, in which many of them would have been freemen. Under the Normans they paid "rent" for their land in both goods and service. The manor was required, for example, to provide two fighting men for every plough team. The king was probably more than happy to hire professional soldiers in place of the locals but he would require the villagers to pay for the maintenance of their share of the army. Godber says that a villein might occupy between 20 and 60 acres of land, and sometimes more. The average in Bromham was probably no more than 30 acres. Of this the national average was 35% arable. As everybody knows the arable land was located in two vast open fields which were divided into strips. A villein would probably have a share; perhaps as much as half, in a plough team with which to plough his strips of arable land. The strips were marked out simply by the furrows on each side. The turf would be turned inward by the plough so each strip would be a long mound drained by the side furrows. Much later, when this arable land was enclosed it was simply grassed over for sheep and the shape of the mounds still appears quite widely in England. In Bromham a very small portion continued to exist to the north, and at the east end of, Grange Lane until, in the 1950s, it was levelled to form part of a village playing field. The furrow was a furlong in length. Obviously this varied a little until measurements were standardised but it was what a plough team of six oxen could manage, with a single furrow plough, without a rest. A strip would be about half an acre in extent. The number of arable fields was the product of the agricultural system in force which provided for each field to be fallow in turn. Land brought into cultivation from the waste, therefore, would be added to one of the fields. But later a new, third, field was usually cultivated, thus doubling the amount of land ploughed and sown each year. Each individual's strips would be scattered about the fields so as to share out fairly the good and bad land. Tenants would graze their cattle, if they had them, on the waste, on the stubble after harvest and in the meadows when the hay had been gathered in. Pigs roamed the woodland. Some villages did not have pigs but, as we see, Bromham, in 1087, had enough woodland for forty.

Bordars, who ranked below villains, are often referred to as smallholders. This, again, conveys little since the villain's holding would, today, look more like that of a smallholder. It is suggested that, again, Godber is being rather generous in suggesting that a bordar might have between fifteen and thirty acres of land and, possibly, two oxen. The lowest class were called by the surveyors "ferui", which translates as slave. They were a little better than modern slaves because they might well have a few acres to farm. They had existed under the Saxons. One might lose what little freedom a higher status conferred as a punishment for crime. But one might equally do so because of inability to pay one of the feudal "fines" due to the lord as the price of transfer of land on the death of the former tenant (heriot) and even the marriage of one's daughter. Nationally, about 10% of the population were in this category. The percentage was highest in the South and West and Bromham, with six out of its thirty families, had 17%. Among these tenants, and mostly among the villains, there would be craftsmen. In Bromham, whoever else there may have been, there would have been a miller. He was likely to be the most unpopular character in the village. The tenants were compelled to have their grain ground at the lord's mill, and were fined if caught using their own hand mills. The monopoly thereby created was undoubtedly exploited by the miller who overcharged for poor grinding. Perhaps it is fortunate that millers tended to be muscular enough to defend themselves. In 1272 William Passelowe's carter was flung from his cart by a loose horse.

Just as hired soldiers were likely to be better than those forced from their lands so the lord of the manor discovered that he had a better return from hired labourers than the surly tenant providing his weekly obligation of work on the lord's demesne. It became increasingly common for tenants to commute their service. Either the tenant or the lord might suffer from changing economic circumstances.

An unprecedented growth in population in the twelfth century led to severe land shortage and high rents. The Black Death, in the single year of 1349, however, may have wiped out a third of the population thereby putting labour at a premium and forcing the imposition of the first system of wage fixing. Subservient the Saxon tenantry may have been in 1086 but within 150 years it was in a much better position to make demands.

Hugh's grandson, Miles, would be seeing only the beginnings of some of this change but Godber notes that a lady of the household of his sister Beatrice warned her husband, in English, that one of his opponents in the North was in arms. The assumption that the Norman landowners were isolated by language may be overstated if their household communicated in English as a matter of course. Stephen ordered Miles to surrender Bedford castle to Hugh le Poer, whom Stephen created Earl of Bedford and who seems, like his master, to have lacked the ability to attract support. The king in the feudal system depended on the support of his barons both for finance and military force. They, in turn, preferred the order the system provided to chaos. But incursions on their privileges, especially if imposed by a king whose title was in some doubt, inspired revolt. Miles stripped Bedford of all the food he could find and settled down to resist a siege in 1137. He was, however, forced to surrender before Christmas of that year. He retook the castle in 1141 but his supporters lost it again to Stephen. The future Henry II retook it in 1153 and Miles young nephew, Simon, who succeeded him, owed, in 1166, the service of forty four knights in addition to nine provided in respect of Newnham Priory, which he had founded.

Simon, who was no soldier, was succeeded, in 1206/7, by his son William, who was. William fought under John in Scotland and also at Poitou. But he joined the discontented barons against John and received the northern rebels at Bedford castle in 1215. John had a close and loyal follower in Faukes de Breaute, a professional soldier with whom he planned campaigns. Faukes forced the surrender of the castle on 2nd December 1215 and John gave it to him, whereupon Faukes strengthened it with stone from the neighbouring St Paul's church. John died the next year but Faukes remained loyal to his son Henry III and he took William Beauchamp prisoner at Lincoln in May 1217. Perhaps a little surprisingly, William's lands were restored to him in that year and he accompanied Henry on expeditions in Wales and the Welsh border in 1223, 1233 and 1244. He was thus in the position to be described as "our faithful and beloved servant" when Bedford castle was attacked by Henry III in 1224 and taken and destroyed. All the knights in its defending force, including Faukes' brother were hung and the land was returned to William to enable him to build on it an unfortified residence. Faukes owed his downfall largely to overplaying his hand. Hubert de Burgh certainly would not tolerate a baron arresting the king's justices and imprisoning one of them, and Stefan Langton, Archbishop of Canterbury, would have been incensed by his attacks on the lands of the church. Between them they would have had little difficulty in persuading the young king that Faukes was a threat and they were both present at Bedford to see the surrender of the castle.

William Beauchamp continued to do well. On July 6th 1234 he was appointed a Baron of the newly created Court of Exchequer. In 1235 he was appointed sheriff of Bedfordshire and Buckinghamshire. He married three times and acquired the manor of Bromley by the first, and of Newport (Pagnell) by the second. In 1255 he paid a fine of 100 marks, as a form of commutation of heriot duty, in order to settle his lands on his eldest son William, and he died in 1260. John, his only surviving son was not so lucky. He was one of a large number of barons who supported Simon de Montfort against Henry III. At first this revolt was successful and Simon de Montfort, having surprised everyone by winning the battle of Lewes in 1264, actually ran the country for about a year. Unfortunately the future Edward I escaped from captivity and won the battle of Evesham in May 1265 at which John Beauchamp was killed. As a reward for his victory Edward was granted John's lands, but they were regranted to William Beauchamp's widow and then divided between John's three sisters. Appendix I shows the subsequent descent of these tenancies in chief and we need only note the maintenance of the tradition of revolt by John second baron Mowbray. Edward II, and his favourites, were distinctly unpopular with the barons; so much so that they were even prepared to support the almost as unpopular Thomas eighth Earl of Leicester. Perhaps John had foreseen the risks because, in 1316 he had settled his lands on his father in law William de Braose (or Brewos). This did not prevent them being forfeit to the crown when the rebel barons were defeated at Boroughbridge in Yorkshire in 1321. Edward was in no mood to be lenient to those he blamed for the death of his friend Gaveston and both John and his leader were hanged at York. It comes as something of a surprise, therefore, to find his lands regranted to John's son in recognition of the past services of his family and the hope of future loyal service.

The last holders of the manor of Brayes before Sir Lewis Dyve stem from Sir Reginald Bray who bought it in 1491. He was treasurer to Henry VII. Considering that that king was more interested in filling his treasury than any other English sovereign this must have been an important position. Sir Reginald was a newcomer to Bedfordshire and was granted the manor of Eaton. He also bought a manor in Stotfold. He seems to have been keen to stamp his identity on his position since it is from him that the Bromham and the Stotfold manors are called Brayes and Eaton, of course, is Eaton Bray to this day. For all this the family did not stay long in Bedfordshire. Brayes in Bromham was sold to the first Sir Lewis Dyve in 1565 and Eaton Bray was sold in 1574.

Bowles ?

The descent of Countess Judith's land which came to be called the manor of Bowles is the least certain of the four divisions following the end of the Beauchamp line.

At some time in the early or mid-fourteenth century John Wideville had a warren in Bromham. He had obtained an estate in Bow Brickhill by marriage into a family by the name of Fermband which had itself succeeded the family of Boeles or Bolle. Harvey[39] speculates that Wideville's land at Bromham was part of the manor of Bowles acquired through this connection. If it was then both the Boeles and the Widevilles were mesne tenants because the tenant in chief of the manor of Bowles by about 1272 was a Passelowe. Since the Passelowes were also, around that time, mesne tenants of Wake and Bromham there would not seem to be room for a continuous tenancy from Boeles to Wideville. This does not mean, of course, that the Boeles family could not itself have had either the head, or the mesne, tenancy sometime between 1086 and 1272. The reason this is the subject of separate mention is that Harvey observes that when he was writing, around 1870, there was a wood and a small close called Bowels in Bromham. In fact, in 1844, there were several fields bearing this name. All of them abutted on the wood so one may assume it was this area of land which had formed the manor. It is just possible that the manor house was then on this land but no buildings with that name appear on the map of Bromham of 1780 and the manor house had certainly moved to its present location by the sixteenth century. The wood is that between Grange Lane and Mollivers Lane. Immediately to the east of the northern half of this wood there existed, until 1940, some earthworks of which no record can be found. These were approached from the West, which they faced through what later became a bridle path cutting Bowels wood in half at its narrowest point. That path still has a firm stone base. From the rear a stone based road ran as far as the village green. Traces of it could be seen until the 1950s, when they were obliterated to level the ground for a playing field. The roads approached a group of earth mounds and a very deep, steep sided hollow to the south of Mollivers Lane. The hollow could not have been the warren because it regularly filled with water in winter.[40] There were signs of a ditch on the western side. The mounds indicated the outlines of large rooms and there was a small circular mound which might have been the remains of a small tower. When this site was levelled by bulldozer in 1940[41] there were brought to light a large number of stone roof tiles about six inches square, each with a neat hole in one corner for a peg.[42] There are no surviving houses, save the Hall, from this period with stone roofs in Bromham. There is, of course, no record of what caused the abandonment of this small settlement but it is suggested that it is likely to have existed before the manors were combined by Sir Lewis Dyves. It is worth noting that it would have been close to the probable west to east ridge track from Stevington which crossed the river by the ford at Clapham and was, before the Conquest, the main route through Bromham.

Tenants in chief

The manorial lords mostly let their lands to tenants in chief. As we have seen some of these, like the Count of Guines were themselves significant feudal nobles, with considerable landholding. Hugh de Beauchamp himself held the land of the Countess Judith in Bromham as a tenant. The Malherbes similarly, at a later date were tenants in chief at the beginning of the thirteenth century when one of them gave the church, and other land, to Caldwell Priory. They continued to be so at least until the latter part of that century when Ralph Passelowe was tenant in chief of the part of the original Beauchamp lands which passed to Beatrice. We shall see[43] that John Mallerbe was one of four knights summoned to the general eyre in 1227 to settle a land dispute in which the respondent seems to have been one of his family. Later, this family were also benefactors of Newnham Priory. Their land holding was also the subject of official survey and is described thus:

> William Malherbe has in Bromham 4 hides of land from the barony de Bello Campo of Bedford. He holds in chief from the heirs of the said barony and they themselves from the King, and that holding is assessed at 3 hides for scutage and sheriff's fee, 15s a year for hidage, suit and ward from each hide. He has in demesne 160 acres of land, 18 acres of meadow, 14 acres of enclosed wood, a fishery in the river called Ouse from a place called Holm as far as Brochiseved in common with Ralph Passelowe. In villeinage 3¼ virgates, each of which owes him 20s a year or works to that value at his will. The tenants of these are serfs bound to redeem their tenure at his will, and the tenants are Robert Neuman ½ virgate; Roger de Wylden and William Berngate, 3 quarters; Thomas le Juvene and William Sutor, 3 quarters; Nicholas Frend, John Perenhale, William Sutor and William Osebern, 1 virgate; Henry Kip, Alex & Mary Scot, 3 quarters.
>
> The ancestors of the said William gave the church of that vill to the Prior of Caldewell in the time of King Richard with 30 acres of land from

which the same church is endowed, which the said Prior holds with the said church for his own use.

The said William also has in free tenants for annual service and foreign service: Richard Malherbe with his tenants, who also holds 2½ virgates of it for 2s, suit of court, and foreign service, of whom Thomas de Faccon holds from the same Richard ½ virgate for 2s, William de Bosco, 5 acres for 10½d, and the heirs de Bello Campo 7 acres for one root of ginger. Also from the said William, Roger Grant, ½ virgate for 10s and foreign service; William ad Boscum, ½ quarter for 2s, suit, and foreign service; Henry Godiman, William Ros & William Sweyn, ½ virgate for 2s, suit, and foreign service; Walter le Plumer 1 quarter for the same service.

They did not leave their name on one of the manors but they did on a field that William Boteler, four hundred years later, regarded as particularly fertile[44] and which he appears to suggest was part of the Latimer and Neville manor. Ralph Passelowe was the tenant in chief of other Beauchamp lands in 1272 and he also rented the rights of fishery, in common with the Malherbes, "from his court to Biddenhambridge," from Beatrice Beauchamp's second husband. His successors were tenants of Ida de Steyngreve in the manor later called Wake. Around that time there were eight free tenants on the Steyngreve land (Wake) and four on the Monchensi manor (Bromham). In what was probably the next degree of tenancy, Robert Swinesheved, who, unlike the Passelowes, was not of distinguished Norman descent, then held seven acres in Bromham. We know more about Robert Parentyn who held sixteen acres of arable and one of pasture in Bromham. The land had previously been held by Alfredus atte Marche, followed by John le Marche. Robert's son William, however, left Bromham and moved to Burchester in Oxfordshire where, in 1407, he acquired land opposite the priory gate, which must have been convenient because a Richard Parentyn was prior of Burchester at that time. In 1314 Richard le Rous of Clophill, summoned to Parliament as a knight of the Shire held land in Bromham, presumably as a mesne tenant.[45]

From the point of view of later history the most important tenants in chief stemmed from Thomas Widville whose daughter Elizabeth married Sir Reginald Ragon in 1417. We shall see[46] that by a series of further marriages this brought the Dyves all but one of the four manors. So when Sir Lewis bought the tenancies in chief he was, effectively the sitting tenant. His action probably seemed at the time much the same as we would today see the buying out of a ground rent or rentcharge.

[24] AD Mills, *A Dictionary of English Place Names* (Oxford 1991) at p.54.
[25] That may be more likely in the case of the other Bromham, in Wiltshire, which seems never to have suffered a change of name.
[26] See Godber at p.4.
[27] Harvey, at p.29, adopts this as the original version.
[28] For all this, and more, see A Mawer & FM Stenton, *The Place Names of Bedfordshire and Huntingdonshire* (Cambridge UP 1926) at pp.28-30.
[29] See ch.III – The Chapel.
[30] The second edition of George Rollo's map of the County dated 1769 names the village "Brumham". Cary, however, has "Bromham" in 1787 and sticks with it in his magnificent map of 1801. Cox, *Bedfordshire* gives the two versions as alternatives.
[31] Margaret Gelling, *Signposts to the Past* (JM Dent & Sons 1978)
[32] n.28 above. They are wrong to place this wood on the border between Bromham and Stagsden. It actually runs between Grange Lane and Mollivers (or Stevington) Lane. What they had in mind is Hanger's Wood.
[33] (1956) 5 BM at p.133-137
[34] The text used here is that reproduced in John Morris (Ed), *Domesday Book – Bedfordshire* (Phillimore 1977).
[35] Hugh Beauchamp, baron of Bedford.
[36] The singular is feru. One of the numerous alternative meanings of the word "fero" in Latin is to carry off, or plunder. Hence "slave". Slaves had existed in Anglo-Saxon times and were simply completely unfree people below the cottagers whom the Normans called villains and who were themselves closely tied by feudal duties to the lord's will.
[37] The Countess Judith was the daughter of William the Conqueror. He had given her in marriage to a surviving Saxon Earl, Waltheof. Before the Conquest his earldom had covered Northamptonshire and Huntingdonshire. Unfortunately he did not survive long because William executed him. His lands would normally have been forfeit to the Crown but obviously Judith retained some of them. William also gave her land at Elstow where she founded a nunnery which survived until the Dissolution. The surviving portion of its church, considered, at the Dissolution, as a possible cathedral for Bedfordshire, is now known as Elstow Abbey.
[38] The source of this information is VCH iii. But Harvey has slightly more detailed information.
[39] At p. 38.
[40] As the buildings were of stone this could, perhaps, have been the quarry.
[41] Which I regard as another of the major acts of vandalism to have afflicted Bromham, although in the circumstances of a pressing need to increase national food production this may have seemed to be justified.
[42] The author can confirm this because he gathered some of them, and other pieces of limestone, to make a dry stone wall at 16 Grange Lane.
[43] See ch. IV – The People – Their brushes with the law.
[44] Appendix V, "Field Names".
[45] See (1951) 32 BHRS at p. 28.
[46] See ch. V Portraits – the second Sir Lewis Dyve.

Chapter III
RELIGIOUS WORSHIP

The Anglican Church
The structure

The fullest account of the architecture of the building is that contained in the Victoria County History[47]. This states that the earliest walls are thirteenth century. That of the north aisle of the nave is of rubble, crowned by a fifteenth century embattled parapet. The south arcade is also "plain but good" thirteenth century work. This contains "three bays in two chamfered orders, springing from pillars formed of four slender engaged shafts with moulded capitals and bars." Next in age is a fourteenth century re-used piscine, in the jamb of the south-east window; "a very good example, with a ribbed canopy, an octagonal shaft at the angle with a moulded capital and bar and trefoiled ogee arches springing from it opening north and west." Both the upper and lower doors of the fifteenth century rood loft remain and the stairway between them lies in the thickness of the wall behind the present pulpit. The north doorway is also fifteenth century although the porch leading to it, itself with a fifteenth century wooden door frame, has lost its "lofty chimney" which Harvey saw in 1860. The parvise above that porch served as the schoolroom financed by the first Lord Trevor from at least 1717 and probably used until John Trevor provided a purpose built school in 1811. Pevsner[48] thinks the "dainty minor s. doorway" also likely to be thirteenth century. He says the chancel is Decorated (which would date it to sometime between 1290 and 1350) and that the rest of the church is Perpendicular (which covers the period 1350 to 1530). The nave has a plain fifteenth century roof in four bays and was somewhat damaged by fire in 1906. The chancel roof was presumably put in during Butterfield's restoration in 1868.

The Tower is 70 feet high and is of fifteenth century construction . It is divided into four stages by strings with an embattled parapet having gargoyles (mostly badly weathered) at each corner. Over the west doorway is a window of three cinqfoiled lights. There is a stairway turret at the south-east angle. There are six bells, of which two (made by the Russels of Biddenham and Wooton) are dated 1739. Two earlier ones, naming one "Chandler", bear the date 1686. The remaining two are dated 1826 and 1852 respectively.

Monuments

There are three very fine monuments in the chancel. Two were originally against the north wall which stood next to the altar. That wall was demolished in 1866 to give access to a new mortuary chapel built in 1868 by George 4th Baron Dynevor over the Trevor family vault. The brass to the memory of Thomas Wideville and his two wives dated about 1435 and appropriated by Sir John Dyve, who died in 1535, to commemorate himself, his wife and mother, which originally lay on the floor next to this wall now lies in front of the altar. Conveniently for Sir John it depicts a knight and two ladies. The giveaway, which Dysons[49] originally missed, is that it depicts the Wideville arms twice, impaled with those of each of the ladies. Dysons thought it had been brought from Grafton in Northamptonshire but Harvey[50] doubts this, pointing out that Thomas Wideville owned estates in Bromham. On this same demolished wall was the marble monument paid for in 1730 by John, eventually the third baron Trevor, to the memory of Thomas, first baron Trevor and his wife. [51] A fine marble memorial to the third baron, erected by his widow, is on the wall by the North door

Now at the north-east corner of the aisle, is "a large alabaster monument with a canopy supported by six Ionic columns over the effigy of an old man in full plate armour on a pedestal with shields"[52] Over it are the arms and helmet of Dyve between the letters J and D and the date 1603. The presence of numerous other Dyves armorials on the monument leave little doubt that Harvey is right to conclude that this is the monument to the first Sir Lewis Dyve who died in 1592. The monument was erected by his son John. There is also, on the west wall, a memorial to the third daughter of George Rice Trevor 4th baron Dynevor. She was Eva, who died in 1842 at the age of 12.

History

Bromham was one of four churches given by an ancestor of William Malherbe as endowment of Cauldwell Priory at the beginning of the 13th century. Initially the church seems to have been dedicated to St Andrew since several 16th century wills make bequests to the church at Bromham under that name. Strangely, there seems to be no record of rededication to St Owen. It seems likely that it occurred before the nineteenth century or Harvey, who notes the change, would have been able to ascertain its source. Perhaps the Trevors were misled into the belief that he was Welsh. It seems, however, that he was French and lived in the 7th century.[53] The initial endowments were appropriated to the Priory before 1257 because their value was small. At the taxation of 1291 the church was valued at £4.6s.8d. By the time of the Dissolution, when the Priory ceased to make presentations to the living and the property passed to the Crown, this church was valued at £11 and was granted to Eton College which, with the exception of occasional periods of lease, such as that to Sir Lewis Dyve in 1635, continued to present to the living until late in the 19th century. Eton had some good lawyers and the 1635 lease is hedged around with detailed rents and conditions. The lease was for 21 years at an annual rent of £12.13s.4d; 9 quarters, 4 bushels of best wheat and 13 quarters of good barley malt, or their value in Windsor market. The tenant was to repair and maintain the chancel, to give every year to the parishioners at Rogation the customary "drinking", to find straw (for the floor) at needful times and to provide decent lodging for one day and two nights each year for the Provost, if he should choose to come to survey the property. The Dyves had presented before this in 1597 and 1608. The Earl of Bristol, in 1633, presented in right of his wife (who remained the owner of the Bromham estates). So, presumably, the living was then also let to them. The 1635 lease had not expired when the Dyve property was sequestrated in 1646 and the Provost of Eton then reported that the Bromham Rectory belonged to the College. The 1633 presentation was the last to be made other than by Eton College, although the church lands were normally leased.[54]

The first person recorded as such as vicar of Bromham was Radulph of Bedford appointed by Cauldwell Priory in 1235 and remaining in office until 1257.[55] But a William Saceredos of Bromham witnessed a charter in the reign of either Stephen or Henry II.[56] The Earl of Bristol, in 1633, presented Antony Waters to the living and he remained in office until the living, and that of his curate Oliver Thorowgood,[57] were sequestrated (by the parliamentarians) in 1643. In that year two committees were active; that for Scandalous Ministers and that for Plundered Ministers. Plundered ministers were those who had been removed in the visitations under the authority of Archbishop Laud. They were often returned to their parishes in place of the Scandalous Ministers. If Thorowgood, as curate, was sequestrated it looks as if it was he who replaced a curate of Bromham suspended by Laud's commissioner Walker in 1637.[58] Laud had revived the long disused claim to Metropolitical Visitation and, during a vacancy in the bishopric of Lincoln, had sent Sir Nathaniel Brent to report upon the condition of the entire, vast, diocese which included Bedfordshire. In some instances this action seems to have been overdue. At Knotting, for instance, cockfighting took place in the church. It was not uncommon for pigs to be kept in churchyards and in one place the bailiff to the lord of the manor was found, in the chancel, melting down the lead he had taken from the church roof. Divers ministers in Bedford were suspected of "Noncomformitie". Of the same order was the then curate[59] of Bromham who was censured for being too zealous and "a constant Preacher" who used "words tending to faccion, and the scandal of the Church governors". The vicar, who was presumably of royalist tendencies, must have slipped up in his interviewing technique.[60]

Record keeping, particularly in respect of Parish Registers, lapsed into chaos in the Commonwealth and it is not clear who ministered during that period, except that one of them, Nicholas East, does make an entry in the register. Eton College presented Andrew Cater in 1661. Robert Richards appears to hold the record for length of time in office. He was appointed in 1712 and died at Bromham, where he is buried, in 1758. Although Vicar of Bromham and Curate of Oakley he and his predecessor had lived at Oakley until 1720. In 1717 Rev. Richards reported to the Bishop of Lincoln[61] that "Public Service is read on Wednesdays, Fridays and holy days when the Lord Trevor's family is here: because then a congregation may be had". It is surprising how small were the number of regular communicants in the early eighteenth century. Communion was celebrated three, or at most four, times per year and the Easter communion, which one might expect to have been well attended, was partaken of by no more than twenty.[62] By 1847, however, there was only one service (presumably per Sunday). By then the parishes of Bromham and Oakley had been officially combined (1818)[63] so one may assume the vicar conducted another service at Oakley as he had done in the early years of the previous century[64]. The commentator thought the shortage was due to the narrowness of the stipend which forced incumbents to take other duties. On the other hand the vicars of Bromham and Oakley seem to have been resident in one parish or another rather than supplementing their stipend by pluralism.[65] But there were two Sunday services by the time of the 1851 Ecclesiastical Census despite the age of the vicar. The most popular vicar, in the twentieth century, was Canon Browning,[66] incumbent before the First World War. He was succeeded by Canon Berne and then by Rev. E Denby Gilbert, who was a useful batsman in the village cricket team.

In 1822 it was reported that the vicar appointed one person as both clerk and sexton. He was paid £1.5.0d by the churchwarden, 15/- by the lord of the manor, 2/6d by each farmer and 1/- by each cottager, together with fees for christenings weddings and burials.

Works

The church seems once to have had a turret clock. This was repaired at Shefford in 1701 for the enormous price of £5. It was cleaned there in 1727, repaired again in 1731 and maintained in 1737 by Charles Butcher of Bedford. It seems to have been prone to trouble because William Russell charged £3 to repair it in 1738. He looked after it until 1769. It was cleaned in 1774 and again repaired in 1782 when John Taylor of Wooton provided a new spring for it. It was serviced by the Carits of Harrold and Carlton for ten years from 1787 and yet again repaired in 1815 (£1.1.0d), 1818 (£35.4.2d !), and 1821 (£3.14.7d.). Thomas Clare of Bedford cleaned it in 1824 and 1827.[67] Presumably one of the subsequent nineteenth century renovations removed it, probably as an unjustified drain on resources.

In 1823 singing in the church was accompanied by a Mr Wiles on the clarinet. He was paid £1 per year for this. By 1844 an harmonium had arrived. A singing gallery, built by William Tucker for 12 guineas in 1810, and roundly criticised as unsightly in a visitation of 1847, was removed in 1868.[68]

The critical visitor of 1844 also deplored the existence of designated pews. In 1851 the ecclesiastical census reported 224 free sittings and 106 others. This latter seems rather a lot because the average congregation was said to be 77 (with 70 Sunday School scholars).[69]

The present pipe organ was put in after Butterfield's restoration in 1868. Butterfield, a noted nineteenth century church restorer, was commissioned by Elianore Rice-Trevor to restore what Harvey describes as the dilapidated chancel. Harvey records that this work cost a total of £1400.[70] Eton College and the parishioners contributed, but the bulk of the expense was defrayed by Miss Rice-Trevor, although it was her father who seems to have inspired the work in the last year of his life.

The nineteenth century works on Bromham church are summarised in the fourth part of the Bedfordshire Historical Records Society's *Bedfordshire Churches in the Nineteenth Century.*[71]

Date	Works	Cost	Builder	Others
1810	New west gallery	£12	William Tucker	
1816	Repairs after lightening	£207	Thos Maxey -carpenter	Hinde-plumber William Drew-mason
1825	Repairs-orders of Archdeacon	£145	Thos. Maxey	
1844	Repairs & seating alteration	£100	Thos. Maxey	
1868-9	General restoration&Dynevor chapel [movement of a number of monuments]	£1366	(Wm Butterfield architect) William Osborne of St Neots	Edwin Harrison Rattee&Kett carving Window-Lavers & Barraud

Further extensive renovation of the fabric occurred in 1903 costing £374. Repairs were necessary, particularly within the tower, after the fire of 1906. The belfry windows were replaced after this fire. The organ chamber installed in 1907-8 cost £240.

The Parish Library

The second Lord Trevor established a parish library in the room over the south porch of the church in 1740. A tablet on the wall near the entrance states that it was freely given for the use of the minister and parishioners but that no book should be taken out without the permission of the minister or lord of the manor. Harvey[72] says there were 600 books[73] including Walter's Polyglot Bible. Simon Houfe[74] says that in 1994, there were 860 books, including Bacon's *Wisdome of the Ancients* 1619, *The Clergyman's Companion* 1709 and *The Office and Authority of a Justice of the Peace* 1707 (which might have provided some information useful to the local poachers). Since it is likely that some of the books would have been added by the first Viscount Hampden, who enjoyed working in the library, which does command a good view, it is not surprising to find *A Tour through Holland* 1788 among them. When the present writer last visited the library in the 1950's there was, lying on the writing desk in front of the window, a copy of the Latin poem *Villa Bromhamensis* by this Lord Trevor. Houfe provided a translation of part of this poem which seems to be thanks to his brother for providing him with a place for a rainy day when his beloved fishing was less pleasant.[75] "If perchance the rain lord hanging above watches over fish, making watery the sky which is shortly to be covered, then may the learned contents of these shelves give refreshment. The direction of my brother proclaimed in the past that this should be publicly used by the ministers pledged to the sacred office, lest a good supply of books should be lacking." Eighteenth century ministers often read to their congregations a sermon of some more eminent divine, published partly for that purpose. There were plenty of such volumes on the shelves.

Houfe[76], sadly, records that the library was removed from its original location "for safe keeping" in 1984 after an attempted break in. He tracked it down to a basement of the County Library in Bedford where also was housed the only other remaining parish library for Bedfordshire; the much smaller one from Yelden. There is no public access to it and the atmosphere is too dry for the safe keeping of leather bound books.[77]

The Chantry

The Chantry of St Mary and St Katherine at Biddenham Bridge in the parish of Bromham was founded originally by Matthew of Dunstable in 1295. The practice of founding chantries devoted to the saying of mass in commemoration of the founder, or others, had only begun in the middle of that century. At some time in the next century this chantry fell into disuse and was refounded in 1325, for the express purpose of saying mass for the souls of Geoffrey Smith and others, by Simon de Wolston (or Wulyston) who had been granted an indulgence by Bishop Burghersh to repair the chapel.[78] There is a spring, once regarded as a holy well, at the western end of the bridge near to the site of the chapel.[79] The springs of Bromham have a reputation for healing. It is reasonable to presume that the spring, and its reputation for curing fresh wounds[80] long predates the chantry and its existence (though by no means in its present form) may have influenced the siting of the chapel. The first recorded priest at the chapel was one called Geoffrey and on his resignation John of Oseberton was appointed on November 3rd 1334. On some occasions the priests were also vicars of Bromham.[81] The last priest, at the Dissolution, was the 50 year old Peter Wever (or Weyver), appointed on November 3rd 1539, who is recorded as a naturalised Frenchman, "but meanly learned" and with no other source of income. He left quietly and was granted an annual pension of £5. At that time the chapel was said to be "verye ruinouse and in sore decaye" and there had been no grammar school, preaching nor payment to the poor since Michaelmas (1547), although 125 people were said to be qualified to receive communion there.

The chantry was then sufficiently endowed to have paid the amount of this pension as a stipend leaving some spare for repairs or alms to the poor. It seems, however, a little unfair to expect it to repair the river arches of the bridge.

It was, of course, common to leave bequests to such institutions, as well as to churches, very often to add the testator to the list of those for whom a mass was said. Usually money or a piece of land was left, but cows and sheep might also be bequeathed. At the Dissolution the Crown meticulously valued all the sources of revenue which passed to it. Sir John St John, Sir Thomas Rotherham and William Smith were the commissioners for this purpose in Bedfordshire under Edward VI when the smaller religious foundations were dissolved.[82] The endowments they listed for the chantry, still referred to as of Bydenhambridge in the Parish of Bromham, included a free rent of 6 pence per year, assigned by William Boteler of Biddenham. There were other, much more valuable, assets such as a farm with lands in Bromham and Biddenham of which Robert Dawson was the tenant and which was valued at 50 shillings. Another, in the tenancy of Thomas Warnet, was valued at 53s.4d. The Victoria County History[83] also records that the Grocers Company of London, of which the Botelers were members, granted the incumbent £6 per year.[84] The gross income was subject to various obligations to pay "reprises" to feudal overlords of the lands, and these are also listed. When they were deducted the net value was £7.5s.11d.[85] The site of the chapel was granted to William Place in 1551 and passed from him to Francis Ventris who had sold it, before 1593, to Sir Lewis Dyve. Fragments of the stonework were incorporated in the miller's house, where Harvey says they could be seen in the mid-nineteenth century. It seems unlikely that they survived the rebuilding of that house after 1902.

The Chapel

Whilst Bromham remained an estate village there was no chance that nonconformists would be able to buy land on which to build a church. The lords of the manor dealt equally with saints and sinners. The only public houses were on the extreme southern edge, both actually being in Kempston. Noncomformists living in Bromham did attend their own churches in Bedford and elsewhere. The Declaration of Indulgence of 1671/2 suspended penal sanctions against dissenters on the ground that, while in operation, the sanctions had failed to induce them to conform to the established church. On January 2nd 1694 the Independent church at Southill received Thomas Glover of "Brommom".[86] Thomas Brown of "Brummam" was proposed for fellowship at Bunyan Meeting Bedford on 4th October and received on November 15th 1696.[87] An Independent church had been founded at Stevington as early as 1655. It soon became a Baptist church and flourishes still. No records exist in its books of this period of members specifically said to be from Bromham, although there are a number from Oakley. But although it is at the far end of the village it is not a long walk over the fields from Bromham and it would be surprising if none of the numerous members whose origin is not recorded lived in Bromham. Certainly, in the early eighteenth century, there were two or more families of Independents living in Bromham. It is interesting to contrast the situation with neighbouring Stevington where half the larger population were of "Divers Sects" and "Promiscuous Principles" and the curate (who lived in Bedford and was a curate of St Mary's) estimated that two hundred people attended the registered meeting house on Sundays.[88]

The Methodists claimed to have been the first to hold services in Bromham. A system of voluntary registration of assemblies of dissenters was introduced in 1672 and continued by subsequent, more effectively tolerant, legislation until 1901.[89] This contains only two entries for Bromham. The first is in 1832 and records meetings of an unspecified denomination (almost certainly Wesleyan Methodist, because at that time an evangelical vicar supported the Methodists) at the house of Samuel Hall. The second refers to a Wesleyan meeting, registered in 1889, at a building occupied by someone of the name of Odell. The credit for introducing noncomformity to the community in Bromham is normally given to William Biggs, the miller. He had been converted to Wesleyan Methodism while living in Margate between 1810 and 1814 and attending the newly built Wesleyan church there. He had returned to Bromham in 1814 and sometime after that had heard the vicar, Rev. Mesham, address the Sunday evening meeting he conducted in the schoolroom as to the responsibilities of the better classes. The vicar had probably had Biggs in mind as the most likely volunteer because his subsequent offer of help was not unexpected. Biggs pointed out that he was a Methodist. One may suspect that the schoolroom meeting was designed for those unlikely to attend the church services, for the vicar was what we would now call "broadminded". He asked Biggs to help him with the Sunday evening meeting and the miller later took over the service as the aging vicar found it too much. In 1818 Biggs married a fellow Wesleyan and because of him Bromham was placed on the Wesleyan plan.[90] Biggs died at the age of 92 on December 28th 1870. Present at his death was William Henman, the farmer at the Grange and a fellow Methodist. He seems to have taken over the leadership of the Bromham Methodists and periodic meetings, including meetings of the Methodist Missionary Society, were held in his barns.[91] For eleven years from 1818, however, William Staines, the owner of Berry Farm and a member of Bunyan Meeting Bedford, held meetings in his house. So it may well be that the Independents of a century before were still represented. But Bromham non-conformists for most of the nineteenth century were Methodist and their meetings continued at various farmhouses, and eventually in the buildings of the bakery at the north end of the Green, until 1911.

At the end of 1920 Julius Rideout moved to Moor End, Kempston (which is actually just over the southern boundary of the parish of Bromham).[92] He was a Baptist who had, literally, been cut off without a shilling by his staunchly Anglican mother. While in the trenches in Flanders in the First World War he and his fellow private, Percy Chilvers, had vowed that if they got out alive they would found a Baptist church. He started a meeting for "Free Church" people in his cottage which, in a few months, had overflowed the accommodation. It was resolved to commence saving for a building and the Bedfordshire Baptist Union was asked to support the project. Apparently there was discussion as to the denomination to which the church should adhere, given that the majority of those attending were Methodists. Mr Rideout, carefully concealing his vowed commitment, informed them that they would have considerably more independence as a Baptist church, and this was probably true. The congregation did not express significant opposition; no doubt because they were glad to find someone who looked like producing a church; although some of them imposed the condition that they should not be required to "go in that there tank". It was, however, because of this early mixed membership that the church always described itself as "Bromham Baptist Free Church". At one time its notice board expressly stated that it offered general open membership.

Mr Rideout was lucky. Much of the estate was sold in 1924 and he purchased a prime site just opposite the village school for £250. The Bedfordshire Baptist Union did offer considerable support, and individual members continued to do so until, after 1990, the church needed it no longer. One of the leading lights of the BBU was a Mr Shirley Blott (who went on to own the largest departmental store in Bristol). He donated £50 initially.[93]

This and other donations, together with £70 raised at the laying of foundation stones and £40 raised on a special offering day, enabled the members to purchase, from Hobsons of Bedford the top of their range of celebrated wooden farm buildings. This came in bays and the five which constituted the church produced a lofty structure easily seating 150. Its cost was paid off within two years, whereupon the church, which had always intended this structure, which was guaranteed for fifteen years, to be temporary, began saving for a permanent building. The present writer had been told that Rev. Gilbert, who was the vicar before, during and after the Second World War, when conducting the scripture lessons in the school opposite, referred to the edifice as "the hut across the way". He waited patiently to confirm this and was not disappointed. Mr Rideout acquired the most magnificent, solid mahogany, Victorian bed-head to form the face of the pulpit. It was replaced in the 1950s by a less dominating, but much more pleasant, oak structure built by Mr Mark Hillyard of Grange Lane. The original oil lamps, which no modern regulations would sanction, were replaced by electric lights before 1930. With great delight the author's father purchased a "Broadwood" grand piano (in very good condition) for £25 to supplement the American organ. This was widely considered sinful, but it stayed.

The last service was held at Moor End on August 31st 1924. The new church was formally dedicated by Rev. Marshall of Cotton End on September 27th 1924. There seems to have been a great deal of enthusiasm in those days (as there is again at the start of the 21st century). What others would call a recruiting drive, but the Baptists call a mission, was conducted in 1925 by Rev. Hugh McCullough of Clacton. He records that he was met at Bedford railway station by Mr Rideout and walked to Bromham on a wild wet night, passing several posters for the mission torn down by the wind and rain, only to be faced with an all night prayer meeting. The mission was an enormous success and much of the core of membership in the 30s and 40s derived from it. Methodists and Congregationalists continued to attend and, indeed, because it largely depended on lay preachers, they frequently conducted the services.

The church was largely dependent for leadership in its early days, after Mr Shirley Blott left the district, on the resident Baptist minister at Stevington. It was so served by Revs. Stanley Reed, JA Brooksbanks, Frank Hurford and George Griffiths. In 1941 Mr HN Hall from Bedford took over. He was followed, on his retirement as minister of Mill Street Baptist Church in Bedford, by Rev. Wassell. He was succeed by the greatest of all the lay leaders, Mr John Sinden, a deputy editor of the Bedfordshire Times who, it is not too much to say, was primarily responsible for the upsurge of enthusiasm and effort that led to the building of a permanent church (at a cost of slightly more than £8000 of which, it is believed, £4000 was paid by a legacy left by Mr Garlic of Bedford) which was dedicated on October 1st 1966 by a former president of the Baptist Union of Great Britain and

Ireland. That, which turned out to be an interim church, was designed by Deacon and Laing of Bedford and built by L & B Saunderson. In fact, it probably cost more than the builder charged. The owner of the company said that he had always wanted to build a church and he included a number of items extra to the specification (like hard wood window sills and a roof so full of timber supports that it was difficult for the builders to insert themselves in the gaps). In the programme of the dedication the old wooden church is referred to as the church hall and so it remained, in regular use for almost 70 years.

In 1991 the old wooden church was dismantled, sold and re-erected elsewhere to make room for the present vast new church which has simply swallowed Mr Sinden's first permanent building. The new church was dedicated on November 14th 1992. After the death of John Sinden a permanent resident Baptist Minister had been provided with a manse.

During the Second World War the Baptist church filled a considerable social need in a village not then endowed with a village hall or any significant social gathering points apart from the Boy Scouts (two rival packs at one time), the Cubs and its own, and the Anglican, Sunday Schools, and the Mothers' Union. There was no Women's Institute until the late '40s. Every Wednesday it had a flourishing Women's Meeting, but its main contribution was to provide some sort of evening assembly for the large number of evacuees from Willesden who arrived in 1939 (as well, of course, as the locals). This took the form of what was then called the Band of Hope, sponsored by the Temperance League, which would have been very surprised by the apparently massive support for total abstinence. Very wisely, the present writer's father, who was then church secretary and ran this organisation, was somewhat pragmatic in his approach to rules. But some of its members certainly signed the pledge although the writer is unaware of any campaign to induce evacuees to do so. The writer's father was a firm teetotaller who fiercely opposed a proposal, in about 1947, to establish a public house in the old bakery on the Green. He won, and a number of the deacons of the church had to continue to walk down the Hill to "The Swan" after the Sunday evening service.

The overcrowded day school also overflowed into the chapel in 1940, as it did again in the early 1960s. The teachers from Willesden found a Bedfordshire winter unbelievably cold. The present writer can remember lessons in the chapel when the coke fired "Tortoise" stove glowed red until within a foot before its chimney disappeared through the wooden roof. There would have been no way out had the roof ignited, as it should have done on any reasonable expectation.

The adjutant of an armoured battalion, which had brought its tanks to the Park for an exercise in training for D-day, requested that his men might sleep in the chapel. Not surprisingly he had not realised that that is what it was and although the author's father indicated that this could be done if nothing else could be arranged he withdrew his request and my father took him to see the outbuildings of the bakehouse, which proved satisfactory.

After the War attendance at chapel services declined considerably for no apparent reason save, as its leaders said, that those living in the dormitory village of Bromham were not greatly attracted to a wooden building. It has to be said that it survived whilst many non-conformist churches in permanent buildings around it closed. The Anglican church had no larger congregation and a smaller Sunday School and blamed the walk across the Park. The Baptist church, however, acquired a new spirit under the leadership of John Sinden. Since then it has adopted a more evangelical approach, popular among young people. The congregation, which at its worst one wet Sunday in 1952 had been three, has risen to undreamt of levels, providing a level of income which would have seemed to the founders on a par with any Old Testament miracle. At a time when all round it village churches had closed Bromham Baptist has flourished.

---

[47] VCH iii at p.47.
[48] Pevsner, *The Buildings of England – Bedfordshire and the County of Huntingdon and Peterborough* (Penguin 1968).
[49] *Magna Britannia* Bedfordshire p.33.
[50] At p.66.
[51] Harvey describes it at great length at p.68. He records that some of the marble cost 26 shillings per foot by the time it was dressed and brought to London.
[52] This account in VCH iii at p.48.
[53] Aedoenus or Ouen (or even Dadin) – 600 to 684. Chancellor of King Dagobert I. Usually described as a little known saint. He seems to have been characterised by extreme loyalty to his friends. He founded a monastery in the Forest of Brie. Elected Bishop of Rouen, which see he occupied for forty years. Saints day, August 24th. Only six churches seem ever to have been dedicated to him. The former St Peter and St Paul in Rouen is the only one with an apparent connection. One in Newgate Market in London was pulled down in 1546 and the same fate fell one in Bristol in 1820. There is still a parish bearing his name in Gloucester, although the church no longer exists. The only survivors are Bromham and a church in Hereford.
[54] As to Lord Hampden in 1817. Harvey at p.55 when the total paid for the year was £62.13s.1d.
[55] Harvey lists them until 1866.
[56] The same person was often vicar and priest of the Chantry of Biddenham Bridge.
[57] It was quite common for relatively small communities to have more than one priest. In the late 14th century twenty Bedfordshire parishes had only one priest but Roxton, with half the number of Bromham's 68 taxpayers had ten. – Godber at p.111.
[58] (1986) 65 BHRS at p.28.
[59] One, Grobie. (1986) 65 BHRS 28.
[60] Not surprisingly, the rector of Odell resigned because of the conditions he was required to observe. His sister was the wife of Sir Oliver St John of Keysoe who became Cromwell's Chief Justice. The rector joined the Pilgrim Fathers in 1635.
[61] See, Bell (Ed.) *Episcopal Visitations in Bedfordshire 1706-1720,* 81 BHRS (2002) p.118.

[62] Bell, above, at pp.20, 118 and 196.
[63] Robert Mesham was the first vicar of the combined parish.
[64] See, Bell, above, at pp.118 and 196.
[65] Rev. Rogers, for instance, lived in Bedford and served Goldington, Stagsden and, later Carlton.
[66] See Margery Roberts, *Bromham* (1960) 7 BM pp.132-137 at 135.
[67] Chris Pickford, *Bedfordshire Clock and Watchmakers 1352-1880*. (1991) 70 BHRS.
[68] Chris Pickford, *Bedfordshire Churches in the Nineteenth Century – Parishes A-G* (1991) 73 BHRS pp 144-149. The reference to the clarinet and the harmonium is in 3 BM at p.101. This account states that the gallery was removed in 1844. Although £100 was spent on repairs in that year the gallery seating and stairs were altered in 1864.
[69] The population at that time was 343.
[70] See, for a full account of Butterfield's work – Paul Thompson, *William Butterfield* (1971 Routledge and Kegan Paul). There is a short review of this book by Richard Wildman in (1972) 13 BM at p.235. Among Butterfields many achievements was his habit of removing thick layers of whitewash.
[71] Chris Pickford (Ed.), Bedfordshire Churches in the Nineteenth Century Part IV (2001) BHRS Vol.80.
[72] At p.59n.
[73] See (1991) BHRS at p.145.
[74] Simon Houfe, *Bedfordshire* (1995 Pimlico County History Guides) at pp.136-7. This count is derived from a catalogue prepared by EC Cooper and published in 1959.
[75] Although, in my experience of fishing this stretch of the Ouse, more profitable.
[76] (1993) 24 BM at pp.81-2.
[77] The present writer contacted the Charity Commissioners, arguing that this removal was clearly a breach of trust. The Commissioners had no record of this trust (which is, of course, charitable) but doubted whether they could take any effective action since the trustees (presumably the vicar and lord of the manor) would contend that removal was necessary for its safety.
[78] JE Brown, *Chantry Certificates for Bedfordhsire* (Bedford Arts Club) at p.14n gives the date as 1472 and cites a licence of the 12th year of the reign of Edward IV. This must be a mistake although Edward IV was reigning from 1461 to 1483.
[79] Godber at p5n notes three such wells in Bedfordshire, at Bromham, Odell and Stevington.
[80] VCH iii 44.
[81] There is a complete list in Harvey at p.54.
[82] Similar inventories were taken of the churches in 1552 and on that occasion the first Sir Lewis Dyve was a commissioner. The church inventory for Bromham is lost. Brown (ed. Eeles), *Edwardian Inventories for Bedfordshire* (1905 Longmans Green).
[83] VCH iii at p.49.
[84] This, of course, would not be an asset of the chantry to be seized.
[85] JE Brown, n.78 above. Harvey, at p.55 puts the figure at £6.16s.1¼d
[86] Good Bedfordshire phonetic. The same scribe refers to reception of visitors from Bidnom and Stagdon. HG Tibbutt (Ed) *Some Early Noncomformist Church Books* (1972) 51 BHRS at p.67.
[87] HG Tibbutt (Ed) *The Minutes of the First Independent Church (now Bunyan Meeting) at Bedford 1656-1766* (1976) 55 BHRS at pp.114-5.
[88] Bell, n.61 above, at p.237.
[89] Edwin Welch (Ed) *Bedfordshire Chapels and Meeting Houses 1672-1901* (1996) 75 BHRS.
[90] That is to say that it would have been supplied with regular, probably lay, visiting preachers.
[91] See e.g., The Bedford Mercury 21st June 1878, 7th August 1880. There were also meetings of the Band of Hope, a temperance organisation with noncomformist origins – see e.g., The Bedford Mercury 2nd August 1884, 31st January 1885, 26th February 1887.

[92] The author begs leave to deal in more detail than normal with the early history of this church because, so far as he is aware, most of it is not recorded elsewhere.

[93] He had a brother, Reginald, who for many years had a flourishing drapers shop in Bedford High Street. Reginald holds the record, kept between 1940 and 1953, of 12 minutes for the longest uninterrupted prayer. Unfortunately the record for length of sermon was captured by an American, the then chaplain (Presbyterian) of the US base at Chicksands, who preached for 36 minutes.

Chapter IV
THE PEOPLE

The Population
There were 68 taxpayers in Bromham before the Black Death.[94] In 1671 the population was 153.[95] Between 1706 and 1720 the Episcopal visitations[96] report between 24 and 30 families and one can therefore guess the average family to consist of six people. The population had risen to 297 in 1801. Throughout the nineteenth century it remained around 350 reaching a peak of 373 in 1871.[97] This is about the same as Biddenham at that time but significantly less than Stevington (735 in 1871) or Stagsden (727 in 1851). Oakley rose from 265 in 1801 to 516 in 1831 but declined by 1901 to 299. In 1901 the population of Bromham was 321 and it was still only 328 in 1921.[98] The reason is, of course, that Bromham was one of about twenty "closed" villages in Bedfordshire; that is to say, most of the property was rented from a single landowner. There was unlikely to be land available for new building. Poor people did sometimes build a cottage on waste land by the roadside which, not uncommonly, they cultivated. It is not difficult to imagine, however, that the local organisation by the lord of the manor would ensure that this did not often happen in such a village.[99]

Up to the Second World War a similar population total was generally quoted, but by 1951 the population was 1,220 and by 1961 2,722. Nowhere else in North Bedfordshire increased at anything approaching that rate. Clapham (2,203 increasing to 3,284) and Kempston remained larger but otherwise Bromham vastly outgrew its neighbours.[100] The reason, of course, following the removal of the protective effect of the estate, is the growth of the Bedford-Kempston conurbation which, in 1961 had a combined population of 75,000, and the ready availability of Bromham as a dormitory. The long term effect is that we may no longer expect the existence of long established family names. Individually owned properties are likely to change hands within a generation and pass out of a family on the death of a particular resident.

Family names
The richest source of names of later inhabitants is, of course, the parish registers. There are many other sources such as the Probate Registers of the Archdeaconery of Bedford 1484 -1858[101] and the Muster Lists.[102] Names of Vicars, chantry priests and landowners will be noted in appropriate sections of this history. Of most interest, in respect of mere lists, is those names that tend to recur over a lengthy period indicating an established family. Margery Roberts[103] remarks on the

survival of names in Bromham and this may be true as from the nineteenth to the twentieth century. It is suggested, however, that it is surprising, in a village almost totally within a single estate, that most names in earlier periods do not survive for much more than 150 years at the most. Emmison, in his introduction to the parish registers of Bromham in the series of Bedfordshire parish registers published by private subscription by the County Record Office in 1937, remarks that there is little continuity of surname. The only name that comes to modern times from the earliest available registers is that of King. It is in the earliest of Emmisson's registers, appearing as a birth in 1571. It continues to appear regularly in the register of baptisms until 1706. But John King continues the story in the register of Marriages when he marries Anne Biggs[104] on October 15th 1792. Samuel King married Martha Richards on August 15th 1807. The author recollects that the widowed mother of Derek King regarded her family as of old Bromham. She and her son lived in the village in the late 1940s when he left for national service as a "Bevan boy".[105]

Those who carried on a particular trade at fixed premises such as the smithy and the mill are also inclined to pass on the business from father to son and appear in the register for some length of time. Biggs, the miller is one example. The blacksmiths of the family of Prudden[106] were well established in 1786 and the last of whom living in the village died in the 1950s. It is proposed, therefore, to identify some of the longer surviving names from the Parish Register.

Harry Franklyn, son of William Franklyn was buried in April 1582. Henry is, presumably the one in the militia Muster List for 1539.[107] His son William, a carpenter, who died in 1625, had six children in as many years, and a further three by 1585. Edward Franklin had the misfortune to be conscripted (or impressed) for service in Ireland, along with Robert Savadge and Richard Cannon, between 1591 and 1602. They had calivers, a firearm which preceded the musket. Another Franklyn is recorded as a builder in 1613. A near record was set by four Franklyn girls all of whom married in 1629. In 1671 widow Franklyn was assessed for tax on two hearths and in 1678 Henry Franklin married Margaret Alsop. The name is common around Bedford to this day. (One built, and briefly lived in, the house at 16 Grange Lane between 1932 and 1936, but he did not originate in Bromham.) But the Franklins seem to have left the village by the end of the seventeenth century.

Emmison draws attention to the fact that between March 9th and April 20th 1604/5 the families of Simpsonne, Leader and Lewins lost eleven members (none of whom were newly born children) and suggests an attack of the plague. There is, however, no other record indicative of such an outbreak. Negus is a surname common in the area, including Stevington. It appears first in the Bromham registers in 1686 and the family is still there in 1809. Two brothers Negus took the lease of Grange Farm from Sir Thomas Trevor in 1707. By far the largest family group in the seventeenth century registers is that of Rachell. The will of John Pertnall of Bromham who died on September 19th 1505 is witnessed by William Rochell[108] and the will of Thomas Rachell of Bromham was registered on November 13th 1525. The last record of the family in the Parish Registers is the death of both Mary and Humphrey Rachel in 1696-7.

The Hearth Tax return for 1671 contains several surnames then, and later, well established:[109]

1 William Coleman	3 Stephen Earle	1 Mathew Fortune
1 William Ellwood	2 Lewis Haines	3 Andrew Cater
4 Robert Man	3 John Hooton	2 Widow Franklin
2 Henry Nottingham	1 Henry Peacocke	2 Widow Horne
1 Widow Ganford	1 Henry Cox	2 John Godfry
1 John Nottingham	2 Thomas Christmas	5 Henry Lewins
1 Francis Ellson	1 Thomas Savadge	
1 Edward Steffe	1 Symon Bunny	[Sum of hearths] 64
1 Robert Nottingham	2 William Yett	
15 Francis Dives Esq.	3 Ralph Pawlin	
	1 Lewis Rachell (and a forge)	
	Discharged by Certificate	
Richard Bull	Widow Haines	Widow Simpson
Widow Wynemill	Widow Cox	Widow Pixley
William Benson	Widow English	Henry Rachell

In addition the name Ravensden appears frequently from the mid-eighteenth century. Odell is at least as widespread as Negus. A Richard Odell lived in Stevington in 1737 but the name appeared in the Bromham registers when William Odell married Agnes Franklyn (one of the record breaking four) in 1629. Presumably they lived in Stevington for the name does not reappear in Bromham until 1735 when a Thomas Odell came from Bedford to marry Mary Richards. They do seem to have stayed in the village because another Thomas Odell married Alice Pell on September 19th 1775 and, secondly, Martha Church on July 16th 1780. It was probably his son who married Mary Dainty (another fairly long lasting name) on May 15th 1793. In the early days of the Baptist Church[110] a Mrs Odell[111] was a member and her daughter married a Mr Purser who was the first organist at that church. A number of other names still present in the mid-twentieth century first appear in the registers in the eighteenth century. Church appears very frequently from the mid-eighteenth century and a Church, living in the mill house, was a director of the company running the mill when it finally closed in the 1970s. Peacocke and Waller had actually appeared as early as 1603 and 1663 respectively. A Mr Waller was the last butler at Bromham Hall and lived half way up the Hill in the 1940s. Wallinger appears in 1790. Thomas Wallinger, a labourer aged 37 volunteers for the defence muster in 1803, and a husband and wife of that name were among the first members of the Baptist church in 1924. Inskip was regarded as a well established Bromham family at that time.[112] The name had appeared in the registers in 1786.

Harvey[113] found many of these names on gravestones in Bromham churchyard. He records, among others, those of Waller, Gurney, King, Biggs, Reynolds, Odell, Hart, Osborne, Islip, Rogers, Ward, Millard, Church, Henman, Preden (?), Mayhew and Chambers.

The Pruddens (or Prudens) provide an example of survival until recent times. Thomas Benson (another name still in Bromham in the mid-twentieth century) had married Sarah Prudden on October 15th 1783. Probably it was Sarah's father John the blacksmith who beat his wife in 1786. It seems that Sarah had a brother William because a son of his and his wife Judith was baptised James on October 15th 1798. This William was 34 in 1803 when he appears, not as a volunteer, in the defence Muster List[114]. William and Susan Pruden buried a son John on February 18th 1805 and another on February 24th 1810. He had been born a twin on February 11th and baptised William on February 15th 1810. The second twin was baptised on Christmas day 1810. Susan herself died aged 35 and was buried on February 26th 1812. William Pruden was the tenant of the smithy at the eastern end of the bridge in 1924 when it was sold, as part of the general sale of the estate. It seems that he bought it because he appears as the ratepayer for the property in 1928 and the present author's brother remembers him there as smith in the 1930s.[115]

Their brushes with the law

Less serious crimes were dealt with after the Norman conquest by the manor courts. Various inhabitants owed suit of court and were obliged to attend. Their duty was to bring before the lord of the manor outstanding disputes which had arisen since the last sitting. They had virtually ceased to function by 1500 but in 1466 Robert Lumbley, William Stowe and Richard Russel were accused of cutting wood in "the lord's wood known as Malavres".[116] They were fined 2d., 6d. and 4d. respectively. Stowe was fined most because he had taken an oak tree. More serious matters awaited the king's justices in Eyre. Cases before the general eyre, like cases before the manor courts, most frequently concerned land. In 1227 "Matthew de Layham, Thomas de Chalverstone, John Malherbe, William de Faldo four knights; summoned between Simon son of Richard, claimant, and Geoffrey Malherbe tenent, concerning six acres of land in Braham". The Botelers took a long running dispute with the Dyves over land in Biddenham and Bromham to the Star Chamber.[117] They also issued the writ *Quo Warranto* asking by what right Sir John Dyve held a court leet in Biddenham. They supposed it was because he had somehow assumed the wardship of the Botelers' heir (who did not have that right) but Sir John replied that the right had belonged to Queen Elizabeth I ("the late queen") in right of the honour of Gloucester, that she had granted it to others who had, in turn, assigned it to him.

In 1247 "Avicia, wife of Thomas de Cramfeud drowned by a mill-wheel at Bruham; no one suspected. Judgement: accidental death. The sheriff will answer for 2 shillings the price of the wheel the village of Bruham amerced for not having the price before the justices."[118] Maurice (Knot) of Bromham was acquitted by a jury of a charge of attacking William de Pynkeny of Biddenham in 1314. On the contrary William is found guilty of attacking, beating and ill-treating Maurice.[119] Among the more notable criminals Cornelius Coleman was hanged at Bedford in July 1612 for killing his wife or, as the register puts it, "Suspensus apud Bedford pro occid' uxor". Trials seem to have moved more quickly then. She was buried at Bromham on June 4th and he on July 18th. Rev. Benjamin Rogers records in his diary for October 5th 1731[120] that "one Islip" of Bromham was charged with the manslaughter of John Stokes, a farmer from Oakley. Stokes was having a drink at the door of the Green Dragon when William Goodhall, his wife and Islip passed on their way home and Goodhall paused to light his pipe in the doorway. Stokes, as was his custom, roundly abused William, persistently calling him a rogue and his wife a whore. So William took his horse-whip to him. At this point Islip got down from his horse and kicked Stokes "about his privities". Three days later Stokes seemed well enough when he went to Bedford and he did not complain of the kick. He did not tell Mr Fleming, the doctor, either "and so he lost his Life thro' negligence." Rogers does not say whose was the negligence but in those days one would probably not have suggested it was the doctor. John Prudden, the blacksmith, was convicted, in 1786, of kicking his wife about the room.[121] By far the worst criminal case to involve the inhabitants of Bromham occurred in 1829 as a result of which the brothers Lilley, one aged 21 and the other 29, were hanged at Gallows Corner on the highway outside Bedford for the attempted murder of a gamekeeper in Bromham. They said they had warned him that they would shoot him if he moved and fired when he did move. He denied the warning and insisted it was attempted murder. The hanging produced a public outcry, but the gamekeeper lived a long life in the village.

The affairs of the mill were before the courts much later at the beginning of the nineteenth century when John Biggs (the second of that name as miller) was indicted before quarter sessions for what we might now call "noise pollution" when his extended activities frightened horses on the nearby road so that "the liege subjects of our Lord the King could not pass with their horses, coaches, carts and carriages". Traffic congestion approaching the bridge must have been almost as bad as it became 150 years later. He was only fined 1s. but, presumably, had to undertake to abate the nuisance.

Bedford Petty Sessions dealt with a number of relatively minor criminal charges against the inhabitants of the village through the nineteenth century, some of them involving poaching. William Perkins, for instance, was fined in 1847 £1 with 18s.6d. costs for this offence.[122] Earlier that year, however,[123] Richard Stafferton was let off with a warning. William Odell, who was employed by Mr King the farmer, had set a snare in a hedge and settled down to see who would take it up. Richard emerged from the hedge holding a hare. He said he had been tending his employer's sheep and, observing the hare in the trap, had gone to release it before it strangled itself. This noble example of care for wild life probably did not entirely convince the justices, but they were not particularly sympathetic to the practice of creating criminals by subterfuge.

The justices seem to have been stronger on justice than legal procedure when James Church accused the young Charles Wake of pelting him with stones whilst he was tending his garden. It emerged that Charles was with other boys at the time and Mr Church could not prove that Charles had thrown the stones. The charge, of course, should have been dismissed, but the justices adjourned the case for a fortnight to permit Mr Church to produce the evidence, and they summoned the other boys to appear. There is no record of what happened subsequently. Perhaps Mr Church was unable accurately to name the other boys, or perhaps Church concluded that they would deny being present.

The year 1847 was a busy one for crime in Bromham. Samuel Clough of Liverpool, so the Bedford Times reports on March 20th, had been lying drunk, and no doubt minding his own business, outside "The Swan". Harry Yates, who was a miller, sought to assist him – over the parish boundary for preference. Hopefully, Clough asked Yates if he knew a man called Bennett in Bedford. Yates offered to take Clough to Bedford. It seems to have taken Clough a little time to develop a suspicion about this degree of kindness, or perhaps the fresh air he encountered on his way over the bridge cleared his head. For whatever reason he broke into a run and Yates said that he could not catch him up. The picture of the miller failing to catch up with a drunk may suggest that since the latter had crossed the parish boundary the miller did not try very hard. Yates was early about his business the next day for, at 5 a.m., in early March, in the dark, he saw Clough on his way into Bedford evincing signs of having spent the night in a ditch. Like any good Samaritan Yates avoided the sensible course of passing by as quickly as possible and a scuffle ensued when he approached Clough. Clough stabbed Yates in the wrist, cutting through the sleeve of his jacket. A knife was found in the pocket of Clough's coat. Clough was charged in the Crown Court but avoided a conviction for felony. He was convicted of the misdemeanour of assault and sentenced to three months' hard labour.

In this same momentous legal year the Trevors themselves were in a more exalted court.[124] No less distinguished members of the House of Lords than Lyndhurst, Brougham and Campbell decided that the words "issue male" in the strict settlement created by the will of Viscount Hampden dated September 1824 did not exclude females. They relied on use of the word "person" elsewhere in the will and also referring to those who were to inherit the estate as indicating an intention not to confine the succession to the male line. In those days this litigation would have been protracted and the relief felt by their tenants was probably matched by that of their landlord.

If such is the tally for a single year it is obvious that many other small brushes with the law will have occurred in the subsequent history of Bromham.[125] One other nineteenth century example is worth a mention, not least because it concerned the Wesleyan tenant of the Grange, Mr Henman. The case was heard in the County Court in Bedford on May 19th 1854[126] after being adjourned from Saturday (!) April 30th . The defendant was at the time the tenant of Bromham Hall and had the right to shoot on the estate lands, including those rented by Mr Henman at Grange Farm. Mr Henman was particularly troubled by the large number of rabbits living in Salem Thrift and emerging to eat his crops. He was in the habit of shooting them but Mr Cochrane told him he wished he would not. Henman ceased shooting rabbits in reliance on a promise by Cochrane to pay for the damage they did. Inevitably the amount Cochrane had promised to pay,set against the amount of damage Henman alleged, became a matter of dispute, the rabbits continued to feed and multiply and Henman's son shot one of them. Cochrane's claim before the Court must have been based on a right of property and it must be deduced that, when the judge, after a good deal of indecision, dismissed the case for want of jurisdiction, he had concluded that the issue was one of interpretation of a contract.

Notables

It has to be said that Bromham has not, to date, given birth to many notable people, with the exception of some of its lords of the manor. A few of local note have been, or will be, mentioned, elsewhere. Harvey[127] notes one Henry Humphrey Goodhall whom he describes as "the geologist and antiquary" and whose obituary appeared in The Gentleman's Magazine for March 1836. Elizabeth, widow of Thomas Goodhall, gent. Died on November 2nd 1792, aged 57, and is buried in the churchyard. Her son Thomas is recorded on the same gravestone. He died on October 20th 1794 aged 35. He is, presumably, Henry's father. In turn, his grandfather would remember the "Green Dragon" at Oakley.

Lord Trevor caused a stone to be erected on the grave of Joan Birt. She was born in Biddenham in 1665 and died in Bromham on April 2nd 1770.

It will be observed that Miss Rice-Trevor created a champion of trade unionism. In 1834 the population of Bromham had included 53 farm labourers and there would have been about the same number in 1873 when Miss Rice-Trevor caused notice to quit to be served on the mother of one of them, named Mayhew, who lived with his wife at that house. This is another well established Bromham name and we may assume the family had inhabited the cottage for some time. Young Arthur Mayhew had become the branch secretary of the Agricultural Labourers Union. Her ladyship was probably unmoved by the meeting reported in the Bedfordshire Times for June 24th 1873 which took place on the village green. Various union officials who addressed the crowd, however, were inclined to think it all the fault of her agent, Golding, and to be sure that if only she knew of the conditions in which the three were living she would actually rehouse them. The one upstairs room was said only to be fit for a storeroom and the downstairs bedroom had a brick floor. One speaker remarked upon the number of farm workers with rheumatism.

Frank Bransome was born in Bromham. In 2002 he became the first directly elected Mayor of Bedford.

Jeff Millman was not born in Bromham[128] but he played for its cricket team after the Second World War. He missed, therefore, the singular pleasure of playing on the old cricket ground which lay between the vicarage and the church and was approached by two footpaths just past the northern end of the Green and the vicarage. Fringed with elms next to the church wall it was a very pleasant place on a Saturday afternoon although a ball hit towards the vicarage would disappear very rapidly down to a small stream. The ground was ploughed in the war and cricket moved into the main park behind the Baptist Church after the war.[129] Millman achieved great distinction as a cricketer. He was primarily a wicket keeper, but no mean batsman. He twice scored more than 1000 first class runs in a season and he scored three first class centuries in his career. He went on from Bromham to play for Bedfordshire (1954-56 and 1966-68) and for Nottinghamshire (1957-65), which he captained between 1963 and 1965. He played six test matches for

England, two of them in England, and was regarded as being unlucky not to be selected to tour Australia. His highest test score was 32 against India in Madras.

Occupations and Possessions
Trades

Most of the inhabitants of Bromham were either tenant farmers, agricultural workers (labourers) or servants of the lord of the manor. Bromham had a free fishery in 1278 which is last mentioned in 1700[130] and a fisherman (Henry Kemeshedd) was among the Tudor inhabitants.[131] Bromham had two mills at the Domesday survey. This probably means that it had two sets of millstones in the same building. It is understandable, therefore, why it should be mentioned that that belonging to the Countess Judith, which was valued at 40s. and 100 eels, was not on her land. The other belonged to Hugh de Beauchamp and was valued at 20s. There were still two in 1276. In 1700 there were three, and later four, sets of stones. The earliest miller we know by name was George Casse in 1622.[132] John Biggs succeeded his father as miller in 1798.[133] Quarries were worked in the sixteenth century and one, belonging to the chantry, was valued at 6s.8d.[134] The registers also record shepherds, glovers, shoemakers, a bone-lacemaker, falconers, a shereman and, of course, yeomen and gentlemen.

There was still, in the 1950s a plantation of osiers on the south western edge of the Park and on the banks of the Brook, just before it joined the river. One assumes, therefore, that there must have been some local basket making. Osiers are also used in thatching but in Bromham it would have been more likely that split hazel would serve this purpose. Mollivers Wood still had a number of recognisable hazel coppices in the 1950s and it is again reasonable to suppose that these were deliberately cultivated for the thatchers. Spindle was also quite common in all the woods. It could have been used for the tools of cottage industries, such as spindles for weaving. It makes good spade and axe handles and it is quite possible that local craftsmen made their own. The author remembers one very late example of cottage toolmaking by Frederick Blythe, who had, in 1924, bought the smallholding at the top of the Hill. He made all the wooden hay rakes used on that farm. Children, who, like the author "helped" with haymaking, from time to time broke the polished wooden tines. Mr Blythe would sigh resignedly but the rake would be repaired by the morning.

Possessions

Even at the end of the eighteenth century the goods most of the agricultural workers had to pass on death were relatively few.[135] They commonly provided a bequest to the church, often as conscience money for unpaid tithes or other tax. So

John Pertnall of Bromham[136] who died, as we have seen above, on September 19th 1505 left the following will:

> *For his principal as is customary: to the high altar for tithes forgotten 3s.; to the fabrice of the mother church of Lincoln 2d.; to the upkeep of the bells 20d.*
>
> *To Alice, the daughter of his wife, a cow with a calf; to testator's d. Joan a cow; to d. Joan Hammerton, a cow a sheep; residue to exors.*
>
> *His son is to keep w. Agnes during her lifetime, as he would keep his own mother. If Agnes marries or moves with the good will of those mentioned above, she is to have a half part of the movable goods.*
>
> *Exors. S.John, w.Agnes. Witn. Henry Bain, Wm. Rochell, Rich. Francis, Wm Aby chaplain. The vicar to be overseer.*

Thomas Brownfeld, dying in 1511:

> *To be buried in the church yard of St. Andrew of Bromham. To the High altar for tithes forgot 6d., to the church of Lincoln 2d., to the Rode Lyght in Bromham 2d.; some loose ston to mende the way from my house to the p'sonnage; to my wife my house with the appurtenances, and one acre and a half of land with half an acre of mede".*

John Warnet in 1532 made similar bequests to the church and left to his wife the residue of a lease from Cauldwell Priory.

Thomas Rachell, whose name we have already noticed, died on November 13th 1525. He too remembered the tithes he had forgotten and, with some precision, left his house and lands to his wife for life, reversion to his son Thomas and his issue and in default of issue the property to be sold and half the proceeds to be given to the church at Bromham where most need is in the opinion of his executors. A modern trusts lawyer would have no difficulty with this but it is indicative of the extent of relatively early development of the equitable device of the trust that such a succession of interests should be possible at this time.

Gregory Compton, dying in 1530, also desired to be buried in the churchyard at Bromham. He left Nicholas Morgan the quarter of malt that the latter owed him.

Commonly, the vicar oversaw the drafting of these wills and Rev John Patynson, who did so in the case of Richard Maud of Bromham who died on May 2nd 1533, was plainly no lawyer. Richard left his farm to John Harper if John Harper "will help Jane my wife".

William Dixe of Bromham left the following will on March 20th 1599:

> *To be buried in the Parish Church of Bromham; to the poor of Bromham xxs. To be distributed by the Minister and Church wardens; to the church of Lincoln iiijd.; to Robert Careless (son-in-law) and to Jane (daughter) his wife xx li.; to John Barton (son-in-law) and to Dowglase (daughter)*

his wife xx li.; also a like sum to their children;……..to repairs of the Parish Church of Bromham ij s. vi d; "Item to ffranc's Snt John Gent. My good freend one silur spoone, to my freend John Davies Gent. One spoone, the rest of my plate to Jane Careless and Dowglase Barton, the residue to my wife Dorothie executrix, hoping and desiring her to be good to my daughters and their children.

This is rather strange. William Dixe is obviously a man of some substance with influential friends elsewhere in the County. He was not married in Bromham and none of his children were baptised there. The burial of his wife there the month after his own death is the only other record of their name in the parish registers near that time. So the Dorothie Dixe whose will, like his, was proved on June 5th 1600 must have been his widow. Yet her will names two different daughters and a son. The explanation must be that she had these by a former marriage. By ignoring her later offspring was she complying with her husband's wish?

A substantial landowner, Humphrey Worth, had succeeded to the manor of Great Offley in Hertfordshire at the age of 16 in 1502. when he died at the age of 51 he left his farm in Bromham and half his 300 sheep, his oxen and beasts to one of his brother's sons. This son does not seem to have settled in Bromham.[137]

Several inventories of the property of those dying in Bromham in the seventeenth century exist. If we are correct in considering the Kings to be the longest surviving of Bromham families it may be of interest to note that of Dorothy Kyng, widow, who died on 26th November 1619. She had substantial possessions such as one would expect of a yeoman small-holder:

Her apparel 40s.
In the hall: one long table, 1 little table iij joined stooles j buffet stoole ij chairs iij glass cases iij little joined stooles 30s.
Parlour: one standing bedstead with a joined tester j half headed bedstead ij joined chests j court cubberd j presse and j box 46s.viijd; j featherbed ij bolsters ij pillows j coverlitt ij blankets j matresse 18s.
Lynnen: iij payres of flexen sheets iij sheets of tayre hemp and iij sheets of harden 20s. ij short table cloths iij pillowcases j towel v table napkins and one warming panne 11s.

This house had a chamber over the hall. It also had what would later be called a dairy:

In the milk house: one cheese presse j salting trough iij shelves j drink stalle, certaine treene ware ij little barrels…...xj pewter dishes…..iij salt sellers iij porringers 11s.

She also kept three cows, valued at £5, two hoggs (10s.) one cock, fifteen hens and three chickyns (2s).

All these possessions came to £25.0s.6d.

Compare these possession with those of a Maulden farm labourer in 1838.[138]

" . . . John Cooper, who worked for Mr Overman, at Maulden, and has done for 20 years . . . The outside of the cottage, that is the outer wall, if it is to be so called, is nearly down; the floor is a mud floor, with no tiles upon it; the window – there should be 32 diamond squares of glass but there is only half that number. – Furniture – there is a table of two boards and a piece, put together on four hedge stakes; one chair, three stools and a coffer which is an old chest; the bed is a fair one, laid upon straw, without a blanket, without a pillow, without a bolster; that is in the first bedroom: the second bed is a straw bed, part of it covered and part of it not; no blanket, no pillow, no bolster, no covering."

Nine people shared these two beds which were actually straw laid on a farm hurdle supported by two posts driven into the ground.

It is reasonable to assume that labourers in Bromham would not be so badly off and this is obviously quoted as an exceptionally bad case.

Taxation and the poor

Provision for the poor might be made, of course, by private charity and it will be seen that the eighteenth and nineteenth century lords of the manor, and particularly Miss Rice-Trevor, made such provision. We shall see, when we consider education, financial provision made by various of the Trevors for the education of the poor. The reason formal poor relief is here linked with taxation is that local taxation was either directly for that purpose or, in the case of repair of the highways, might be used to provide work for the poor.

There were usually, for most of the period covered by this history, four separate local taxes, all of which were based on property. The surveyor of highways was a parish official and the parish was responsible for maintaining all roads in its area, save those assigned to turnpike trusts after the mid-eighteenth century. The surveyor not only had to collect the rate for the roads but ensure that the inhabitants turned out to do the work. The overseer of the poor was also a parish official. He was charged with collecting the poor rate and laying it out in relief to individuals who qualified for it. We will turn to this shortly.

A rate was also levied by the churchwardens on freeholders and tenants and used as a form of emergency charitable relief. In 1680 the lord of the manor paid 10s.6d, Sir Richard Alston 8s., John Jarrow 3s.4d, and even widow Coleman 6d. The total for that year was £1.15s.0d. In 1680 the accounts contain the item, "Paid to a stranger that lost all he had by a flood 3s." Special collections appear to have been made in 1690 when the accounts record,

"Collected for Eastmill flood in Middlesex £1.9s.0d
Collected for Stafford fire £1.6s.0d"

The fourth form of taxation was the ancient obligation to pay tithes. In Bromham they were due both to the vicar and to Eton College as the holder of the advowson. Until the early nineteenth century they were payable in kind. The religious houses which had been entitled to them before the Dissolution, as is well known, often built large tithe barns to hold the produce. What Eton College did with them is not clear. The commutation of Tithes Act, early in the nineteenth century, provided for the replacement of goods with a monetary rentcharge.[139] A number of the properties in Bromham, including all the major farms, were subject to one or other of these charges until they were abolished shortly before the second World War. In the catalogue of the estate sale of 1924 £69.7s.0d per year was payable on Park Farm and almost the same amount on Mollivers. Berry and Grange farms got away with £2.18s.4d and £3.8s.5d respectively. The tithe on Bowels wood was £2.6s.8d. Cottagers, if they were liable, paid less than 10s.

The Poor Law

The following account of the poor law is designed to give a picture of how it worked generally in a rural community. Such a picture would not be gained from mere records of payment and, consequently, only examples of these relating to Bromham are included.

The "old poor law" was introduced in 1552 and operated until 1834. It is generally assumed that it was intended at first to replace help given to the poor by the monasteries, although it is clear that a number of them, and as we shall see, chantries like that at Byddenhambridge, did so only intermittently, if at all. In 1597 and 1601 reforms were made to render collection of the poor rate more efficient. The Justices of the Peace were given a general supervisory power but, essentially, the system was operated by each parish which annually appointed an Overseer to collect and distribute the money. The system took over two basic concepts from an even earlier provision of the Statute of Cambridge in 1388. The first was that of the "sturdy" beggar, who was capable of work and so was expected to work in return for relief. He was distinguished from the "impotent", unable to work by reason of age or disability. The second was that of residence which was designed to settle the poor in a fixed place. A parish became responsible for a pauper if he had settled in it for forty days. In practice this meant that parishes were keen to remove the wandering poor. Some, however, seem to have been tolerated in Bromham. "Old

Ned" had obviously been a local character when his burial is recorded in the parish register under the title "Homo Pauper vocatus Old Ned". There was a more subtle drawback. If someone moved to another parish and worked without becoming chargeable on the poor rate the forty days did not begin to run. Such a person might work and support himself and his family for twenty years or more in a parish to which he had moved, and in which he would have paid the poor rate, only to be returned to his original parish within forty days of becoming a liability through age, infirmity or, as we would put it today, redundancy.

By the beginning of the nineteenth century demands upon the system threatened it with collapse. Enclosure (though not in Bromham) and a serious agricultural recession had significantly increased the number of those claiming relief. In some parishes in North Bedfordshire it was reckoned that up to half the agricultural labourers were on relief.[140] Paradoxically, at that time the old poor law had developed a high degree of organisation and, indeed, of caring. Some parishes estimated need case by case but others, including Bromham, did so by a mathematical assessment of need which was not uncommonly based on the price of bread. So Rev. Wade-Gery said that whereas a good labourer, in 1818, could expect to earn between ten and twelve shillings per week, often, but not always, rising in the harvest month, he calculated the subsistence level (not including rent) at 3d. per person per day. So, he said, magistrates allowed a poor rate of 2s.6d. per person to a family[141] of 5 or 6, and more per person if the family was smaller. This provision of subsistence, which may well be exaggerated, begins to appear less adequate when it is borne in mind that rent might well be 50s. per year, fuel might cost as much and clothing, particularly shoes, somewhat more.[142] Relief in kind would be ordered if it was thought that the recipient would misuse money. What the pauper and his family earned would be discounted against this provision. Before 1800 an agricultural worker would probably have earned 10s. a week. A wife and three working children might, in good times have almost doubled that. But wages were cut in the agricultural depression at the beginning of the nineteenth century, often to 8s. per week, and children might be unable to obtain paid work at all. At times a labourer with a large family might be better off on poor relief than endeavouring to earn his own living.

The "sturdy" pauper was expected to work and so, according to Rev. Wade-Gery, from about 1804 in North Bedfordshire he was sent as a "roundsman" to the local farmers. This date may be too late for the beginning of the roundsmen system. The overseers accounts for Bromham in 1789 and 1790 indicate that local farmers were paying into the poor rate their portion of the wage due to paupers. It appears to have been fairly standard practice to require the farmer to pay a roundsman half the nominal rate set by the parish poor law, the remainder being made up from the poor rate. Boys in a pauper's family might be put out to work at 1s.6d to 2s.6d per week and this would often be paid wholly from the poor rate. So organised had the system become that farmers might, by agreement, take a quota of those on the parish in accordance with the acreage they farmed. At the time of the 1818 enquiry by a committee of the House of Lords the system of roundsmen had developed a number of disadvantages. On the one hand it was reckoned that the worker often arrived late and left early; nor did he have any sense of loyalty likely to bring from him a high level of effort. On the other hand, farmers realised that they could secure workers at half cost if they turned off their own farm workers and took on the roundsmen. So the poor law system itself tended to increase the very problem it was designed to alleviate. Bedford magistrates sought, at this time, to suppress the system of roundsmen and this did result in some lessening use of it. The House of Lords committee of 1818 pointed out that if a farmer acted in this way in respect of workers living in his own parish he would increase the amount demanded of him by way of contribution to the poor rate. Rev. Wade-Gery replied that farmers saw an advantage in transferring the cost of labour to a general fund to which everyone contributed. He suggested that some of the problem could be solved by employing the poor on road maintenance. The parish surveyor could not be compelled to do this. But Rev. Wade-Gery pointed out that the surveyor tended, for obvious reasons, only to repair the surface. In his view, much wanted widening and repair of banks could be done with assistance from the poor. There, of course, was the rub. The money had to come from somewhere. The suggestion concealed the seeds of a point of view that was to characterise the reformed poor law. Parish work-houses did exist under the old poor law and a significant shortage of available cottages forced people to resort to them. Those in such workhouses were often put to work on the roads. Work on the roads was more likely to deter people from seeking poor relief than the farm work to which they were well used. The lesson of the marked unpopularity of the work-house was not missed. No doubt good Christian principles prompted his further suggestion that the children of the poor should be sent to the workhouse at the age of three or four so that their mothers were free to do lace making, weeding or stone gathering.

    The lot of those contributing to the poor rate might not be much better. The labourer would be required to pay the rate on rented property valued at more than £5 per year. Rev. Wade-Gery was sure that some could not pay. Farm labourers often lived very close to financial disaster. Agar records the account of one of them from Eversholt who gave evidence to the parliamentary committee of 1824. He had never sought poor relief, except for the funerals of six of his thirteen children, and had been in steady employment for many years with the same master. He had earned either 8s. or 10s. a week and this was never supplemented with gifts of food. He looked forward to the chance of piece work at 2s per day. His family, he said, lived on bread and cheese, potatoes (which he grew in his garden), gruel and water. If they ever got meat it was likely to be bacon on a Sunday.[143] The inhabitants of Bromham seem likely to have had a reasonable chance to supplement their diet from their gardens. The sale catalogue of 1924 contains nine separate plots of allotment with a total of just over nine acres. It seems most likely that the vast majority of this would have existed from the eighteenth century, since it would have been unlikely that it was carved out of farm land at a later time.

A sympathetic overseer might not enforce the payment of the poor rate against a farm labourer, but he had to find money to make the payments and those paying would undoubtedly complain if they had to pay more because others were being let off. The overseer was entitled to distrain. It was possible to have a situation in which someone receiving poor relief was assessed for contribution on the value of their property and had what miserable furniture they possessed seized because they could not pay. A pauper in the Hitchin area, on the other hand, who was not liable to pay the rate, was, in practice, granted relief without being required to sell his furniture and might, therefore, be in a better position than the labourer who was just managing to make ends meet but could not find the rate.

The earliest overseer's accounts for Bromham are dated 1788, although it is obvious that the system had been in operation long before that and the earlier records have been lost. It is almost certain, however, that the situation of the agricultural worker during the Napoleonic Wars significantly worsened so that the records we see would not have been as bad at an earlier date. Even in 1788 relief was only paid in Bromham to seven paupers. It should be borne in mind that Bromham was a "closed" village in the sense that the lord of the manor controlled entry because he controlled housing. The relatively small population would not have had to carry outsiders to the extent likely in villages where the property market was more open. The amounts paid weekly in 1788 varied between 1s.6d. and 3s.6d.

Bromham had three overseers of the poor between 1788 and 1805. They undertook a number of other duties such as swearing in the militia for which, in 1789, for example, they claimed 6s. expenses. The contributions they raised in 1789 reveal a rate of 1s. in the £ on the value of chargeable property, producing a total annual income of £50.11s.6d. In 1790 the rate was 6d. But by 1802 it had risen to 8s. in the £ on the value (annual rent) of property and in Bromham in that year the total received was £455.16s. The increase is not surprising. In 1795 no less than 16 labourers received poor relief and this rose in 1800 to 26. The Bromham overseers seem to have been more generous than in some places. Some labourers in that year received 12s. per week. Presumably they had large families.

The worsening situation in rural areas could not continue and a Royal Commission on the Poor Law reported in 1834. The vicar, rather than the overseer, made Bromham's return to its questionnaire. He reported that the expense of the poor law, per head of a population of 324, was £1.0s.5d. There were then 53 agricultural labourers in the parish and the vicar reckoned that was the number needed. Five (men) were not inhabitants and so would not be entitled to poor relief. The relief given at that time was much lower than Rev. Wade-Gery had estimated 16 years earlier. Rev. JJ Goodall of Bromham said that poor relief for family members began with three children and would be at the rate of 1s. per week per child over 2 and under 10 years of age. He avoids answering the question on how many employed labourers received relief but the inference from his answer to the remainder of that question is that some did.

The Poor Law Amendment Act of 1834, which introduced what is generally called the new poor law, which was to remain in existence for more than a century, was primarily the work of Sir Edwin Chadwick who had been largely responsible for the Report of the Royal Commission. He became secretary of the national Poor Law Commissioners created by that Act, and head of the Board of Health, which succeeded them in 1848. He was a notable social reformer, particularly in the field of public health, and it is perhaps unfortunate for his reputation that his reform of the poor law was driven by the belief that the old poor law made too generous provision, encouraging idleness and large families and sapping initiative. His policy was not only to reduce the amount of individual relief, but to discourage application for it. The 1834 Act combined parishes into Poor Law Unions administered by a local board of guardians under the overall supervision of the Commissioners. The parish overseer, however, continued to be responsible for administration and payment of those sent to work in the parish. Bromham was in the Bedford Union. The unions were required to set up work houses and in theory the only recipients of relief were to be the inhabitants thereof. In practice some outdoor relief continued because industrial area work-houses could not cope in time of depression, but we may assume that in rural areas such as Bromham it largely ceased. Work-houses were designed to be uninviting.[144] Charles Dickens and others have ensured that we are all well aware of the ignominy and fear of the work-house. In the Bedford Union it was located next to what was then St Peter's Hospital. This hospital served Bromham and the author himself experienced cases of the elderly who required hospitalisation declaring that they would not go to the work-house. Not surprisingly the new system provoked widespread unrest, some of it in Bedfordshire. None is reported in Bromham.

One of the functions of the guardians was to reduce claims on the system by paying the cost of passage of emigrants and at least one family from Bromham emigrated to Australia with this assistance.

Education

At the time of the dissolution of the monasteries the priest of the chantry of Biddenhambridge in the Parish of Bromham was supposed to run a grammar school. The title is, no doubt, a little grandiose. The last priest was not particularly well educated and probably knew little of Latin grammar himself, it is not entirely clear who among the youth of Bromham would have needed it and, finally, there is no evidence of it being provided at any time. On the other hand, one might have expected the commissioners to be more critical than their comment that it had not been provided for the past year if, indeed, no one could remember it ever functioning.

One can be certain that there was some organised education in Bromham between the mid-sixteenth and the mid-nineteenth centuries. Harvey says that the room above the north porch of the church was once used as a school room. The first Lord Trevor contributed £5 per year for education of the poor before 1717[145] and raised the amount to £10 in that year. It seems reasonable to suppose that, before this date, some of the clergy would have supplemented their income by passing on some of the learning they had acquired although the normal content of such education consisted of teaching the catechism.[146] Before and after Lord Trevor's provision it is likely that teaching was done in the room over the north porch of the church. In 1811, however, the vicar reported that John Trevor, brother of Viscount Hampden, had built a school where between 16 and 20 children were taught by a master paid for by public subscription. The vicar was satisfied that the poor of the village had sufficient means of education,[147] although the schoolroom itself was said to be ill-ventilated. In 1833 the then Home Secretary, Lord Melbourne, sent out a questionnaire to the parish overseers of the poor seeking information on the existence of both day and Sunday schools. He was told, in respect of Bromham that in a parish of 324 people 28 males and 26 females attended a day school with a further 6 males and 12 females attending on Sundays. In 1825 George Rice Trevor undertook, to continue to contribute £20 per year to the cost of the school, the parish added £10 and the minister £1.[148] In 1833 there were 28 boys and 28 girls registered as pupils. Those who regularly attended were mainly between the ages of 5 and 6. This probably exaggerates the youth of those children expected to work on the land, if boys, and at straw plaiting, lace making or embroidery, if girls, but that factor would certainly reduce attendance of children over the age of 9. An Anglican Church School enquiry of 1846/7 revealed a slight fall in numbers to 21 boys and 16 girls attending the day school and 31 boys and 32 girls attending the Sunday School. Of course, if one's parents happened to be non-conformist, and there were Methodists in Bromham, no education would be available in the village.[149] In 1851 there were 102 non-conformist Sunday Schools in Bedfordshire but only 14 non-conformist or non-denominational day schools.

Many poorer children were employed in lace making or straw plaiting in Bedfordshire. Lace making was the more skilled of the two and tended to inspire the establishment of lace making schools, as at Bromham. Wages were bad and hours long so it may well be unwise to join in the criticism of those who, like Eleanore Rice-Trevor, organised these schools that they did so largely to exploit cheap labour. It may well have been one of the more desirable ways of adding to the family income. There were a number of these village lace schools in North Bedfordshire and they appear to have taught some of the three Rs. The building where the Bromham lace school was conducted still stands in the grounds of Bromham Hall. Miss Rice-Trevor continued to run it as an "industrial" school for older girls after the foundation of her own village school. The building is now a dwelling house but it is apparent that the school-room was lofty and airy, so she appears to have taken note of the earlier criticism of John Trevor's school.

In 1861 Eleanore Rice-Trevor and her sister, the future Countess of Longford paid for a new building. Its teaching area consisted of a single, lofty, L shaped room one arm of which was 43ft by 18ft 6ins and the other 22ft by 18ft. The roof with dormer windows rose from 12ft to 18ft in the centre. There was a small adjoining room 11ft 6ins by 18ft. It is not clear what this was intended for; perhaps the teacher's office. But under pressure of numbers in 1940 the present writer received his first lessons there, sitting on the window sill. Above this small room was a charming gallery, roughly the same size and lit by a large dormer window. Its balustraded balcony overlooked both arms of the classroom and Miss Rice-Trevor would sit there when she visited, which must have frightened the master as much as the pupils. A new class room was built in the same style in 1896 measuring 18ft 6ins by 18ft and with the same lofty ceiling configuration. It served as a refuge room from 1940 to 1944 but was otherwise an excellent classroom, partly because its large open fireplace heated it rather better than the "Manchester" stove in the centre of the main room or the later "unsatisfactory" hot water radiators. The children entered through a large enclosed porch at the junction of the arms of the main classroom which served as a cloakroom. Double doors at each end would have taken them at a rush had they ever been allowed to mount one.

In the late nineteenth century no one had any doubt that one, and perhaps the primary, object of education was the inculcation of religious knowledge. The early school reports provide as much for religious as for secular instruction. The Misses Rice-Trevor made sure there was no doubt about this by placing over the outside gable end of the main room the text:

Those That Seek Me Early Shall Find Me[150]

What early pupils, who had difficulty reading in any event, made of the roman script is of less importance than the pride instilled in all who learned beneath this bold declaration.

Just in case there was still room for doubt the then vicar, Rev. Goodall, set about removing it in his address at the stone laying in February 1861. (The Rice-Trevors did not stay in Bromham in the winter.) The Bedford Times reported that , "He dwelt upon the importance of instructing the young, but always bearing in mind the paramount duty of blending with useful knowledge sound precepts of Christianity, as inculcated by the Church of England".[151] The reporter, who obviously knew the proper order of things, continued, "By way of making an agreeable impression on the minds of the children the kind hearted vicar distributed a quantity of pence."

The school did not get off to as good a start as these preparations might have indicated. Rev. Goodall did not send the inspector's report of his visit in November 1864[152] to the Dynevor family, who were in Cannes, claiming that it was unfair. It recorded the impression that "reading was indifferent, wanting in expression and [in] enunciation defective." Writing was said to be moderate but the children were adjudged backward in mathematics. Books were deficient and discipline only moderate. The only good point was that the children were clean and had good manners. Rev. Goodall was particularly incensed by the inspector picking as an example a child in the infants who the vicar considered "not very bright". The inspector thought the infants were "left to forge for themselves." Damage limitation was immediately undertaken and the older girls were required to write to Miss Rice-Trevor. One may reasonably suppose that more than one draft was prepared. No doubt Miss Rice-Trevor did see the report because the next time the inspector came, on March 24th 1865 (with the vicar) he noted that the deficiency in books had been remedied and reported a considerable improvement in the standards of education. Thereafter she frequently paid for equipment. In 1892 she provided, among other things, 65 "readers" in four grades, two dozen drawing manuals and two dozen drawing books and 60 poetry cards as produced by Arnolds of Leeds.

The Education Act 1870 required regular returns of the provision of education in every parish. Bromham, not surprisingly, was regarded as adequately provided.[153] Statutory provision was also made for the establishment of parish School Management Boards. Among other things noncomformists saw this as a way of achieving some influence over "church" schools and the scene was set for a good deal of acrimonious disagreement among board members. Not in Bromham. Rev. CF Johnstone was appointed HM Inspector for Bedfordshire and Huntingdonshire. It will come as no surprise that in 1881 he reported that Bromham was one of only nine parishes in these counties without a school board. He had doubts about the suitability of this institution to the needs of small villages but he suggested that these exceptions should not be allowed to continue.[154] The regulation of education through parish boards was, inevitably, regarded as unsatisfactory and the Education Act 1902 transferred the task to local authorities.

In 1882 the Rice-Trevors appointed Joseph Carrier as headmaster.[155] He had been born in Biddenham to a farm labourer[156] and had lost an arm as a result of being hit by shot fired by a careless sportsman, for whom he was acting as beater. Nevertheless he became a prolific artist producing pictures of many local worthies, among whom, in 1892, was Miss Rice-Trevor.[157] Appropriately, that large canvas has hung in the main class room of the school ever since. Mr Carrier records it as his initial impression that the children were particularly clean, their writing was good but their arithmetic and spelling were especially backward. He makes a note on 22 December of his first year that there must be more attention to learning tables. He seems to have maintained discipline with an air of authority. One of his monitresses was "set at defiance" by a boy who refused to clean his slate and copy down his home lesson. Homework, no less! The boy continued to refuse even though encouraged to change his mind by two strokes of the cane. So he was sent home and a note written to his parents saying, "when he comes again, if he refuses to obey I shall at once send him home and you must find another school for him. I certainly shall not have him here to give the trouble he does unless the Hon. Miss Rice-Trevor wishes me to do so." That is a nice touch by way of apparently casual reminder of the ultimate sanction. She certainly would not have required readmission.[158] Would she have approved the action of Mr Carrier's successor in October 1897[159] in giving the children two days off for the annual "feast" (which was kept rather quietly that year)? Mr Carrier had not allowed time off and had complained of the resultant high level of absence. Miss Rice-Trevor had drawn up a set of Rules and Mr Carrier enforced them . On March 16th 1883, for instance, he spoke to several girls about the state of their hair which offended against Rule 3. Carrier's term of office was not without its external troubles. He writes a graphic account of the effect of the building being struck by lightening on July 5th 1884. On April 20th 1885 the school was closed by an epidemic of typhoid fever. It did not reopen till July 2nd. In 1893 more than 30 children were away with whooping cough, although, even in the 1940s that was regarded as a fairly normal characteristic of the winter. Mr Carrier frequently complained about attendance levels and in 1887 he reckoned that of 104 pupils only 66 attended regularly.

Subsequent inspector's reports generally reflected the improvement of 1865. Only the boys' lavatories consistently drew adverse comment, and in one report they were described as very offensive. The report for 1885 regards the teaching of elementary subjects as satisfactory. In January 1892 the inspector was almost fulsome. "The discipline and tone [in the Middle School] are admirable," he wrote, "and the school generally is in a most creditable state of efficiency. The written work is marked by neatness accuracy and intelligence, and the Reading, though somewhat wanting in expression, is fluent and intelligent.......The infants who are in excellent order sing sweetly and recite with good expression. The drill is smart and the elementary subjects, with the exception of Handwriting of the first class and Arithmetic of the second class, show careful and creditably successful teaching". Even this inspector criticised the boys' lavatories. He said they needed repairs and partitions between the seats.[160] The 1899 report is almost as satisfactory; the standard being said to show "the higher grant" to be well deserved. The new classroom was noted. On this occasion heating of the main classroom, another perennial problem, was considered insufficient. Hot water radiators were installed in 1908. At such an early date in the history of central heating it would be uncharitable to remark that five old style cast iron radiators were likely to prove unsatisfactory, and so they were adjudged. The heart of the problem, of course, lay in the upper reaches where the heat accumulated and disappeared out of the single glazed windows.

Joseph Carrier was replaced by John Thomas Grandy in 1896. He only had to move from the next school to the south, that at Church End Kempston. He left, after 33 years, in 1928. Truancy became the subject of official attack as early as the Education Act 1876 which required the appointment of an attendance committee and an attendance officer. It is possible, however, that the eighty two pupils present in December 1902 out of 90 on the register were, in part, encouraged by the fact that in January 1903 Mr H Gillibrand, the tenant at the Hall, was to distribute attendance prizes. Mr Grandy introduced a wide range of new activities, beginning with gardening which, rather inauspiciously, commenced on November 21st 1906.[161] In 1910 he began "rustic" woodwork. From January 1913 he organised games on Fridays if the weather permitted. He must have felt a sense of great achievement when, on September 22nd 1910 his two top girls took up junior county scholarships at what was then called the Bedford Girls' Modern School and he was further rewarded in 1913 when his own son was one of two boys taking scholarships to the Boys' Modern School.[162] The final HMI report on Mr Grandy's long term of office in 1929 said, "The school is one in which work on old-fashioned lines is conscientiously carried on, examined and criticised. There is little which cannot be praised given these conditions: the weaker children are known and considered: the better children get on well."

Mr Grandy's successor, Miss Prickett, (who lived in Stagsden and had the great privilege of a petrol ration during the second world war) had the task of coping with the influx of evacuees from Willesden in 1939. She also admirably filled the role of social arbiter in inter-parental disputes over such matters as the coating with tar of one set of offspring by another[163]. She was a stern, and effective, disciplinarian. On one occasion an outbreak of stealing was dealt with by requiring the whole school to spend an entire morning repeatedly writing the text, "my house shall be called a house of prayer but ye have made it a den of thieves". Religious education continued to have an important place. The day began and ended with hymn and prayer (Miss Walton could play the piano and the vicar came at least once a week to take an hour's teaching session). Not surprisingly the pupils of 1940, like their grandparents of the 1860s, learnt the Catechism.[164]

In both morning and afternoon playtimes before and during the second world war the schoolchildren organised themselves into the singing games so fully researched by Iona and Peter Opie.[165] The author remembers "I sent a letter to my love", "Poor Jenny", "The farmer's in his den", "Oranges and Lemons", "In and out the windows", and a late addition, "The Big Ship Sails on the alley alley oh" (except that we said "ooh").[166] These were a sort of social event and were very popular. One only had to start one to have everyone join in.

Miss Markham replaced Miss Prickett on the latter's retirement in 1943. It was then that we stopped using slates[167] (and started reading Enid Blyton and singing Cecil Sharp's English folk songs). A number of Bedfordshire villages such as Elstow had very long traditions of observance of May Day with dancing on the Green. There was a tradition of it at Bromham which had been revived before the second World War. It lapsed under pressure of war but Miss Markham organised it very successfully for a number of years from 1943.[168] A parents association (later to be called a Parent-Teacher Association) was formed in 1945 and formal Parents' days were held, originally usually at the end of the Christmas term. In 1945, as a result of the "Butler" Education Act of 1944, pupils over the age of 11, who had previously remained at Bromham until they completed their schooling at the age of 14, were bussed to a newly established secondary modern school in Kempston, unless they were selected, as a result of an "intelligence test", for one of the Bedford "grammar" schools. The exodus must have come as an enormous relief to the teaching staff who had coped with what today would have been regarded as impossible age ranges. Two, or at best three, teachers had taught pupils ranging over an age difference of ten years.

On March 26th 1957 the school, which then had 88 pupils, was renamed as a "Controlled Voluntary Primary School". Links with the Church of England, which had served it well, were weakened, as demonstrated by the absence in 1959 of an

Ascension Day holiday. The population of Bromham was growing rapidly and accommodation was becoming a problem. Eight children from the Brookside caravan site had been refused a place in November 1956 (although ten were re-admitted in January 1958). The lower arm of the main room was curtained off for the first time in 1956 to avoid one class distracting another. It seems incredible that this had not been thought necessary before but so good was the original design that the present writer has no recollection of such distraction. By January 1960 there were 107 pupils in four classes. This had increased to 142 in 1961 when Mr Ellison became headmaster. There was then a kitchen providing lunches for 120, although it had only been designed for 75.[169] Both the village hall and the Baptist chapel were used at this time for overflow classes. Another classroom had been added and in 1962 talk began of the provision of a new school. In 1963 numbers had risen to 174, there were six classes and the building was being used also for further education. Portacabins were in use by January 1964. The new school, to be known appropriately by Miss Rice-Trevor's name, was built in Grange Lane in that year and Mr Ellison moved to it as headmaster. His first major action after his appointment in 1961 had been to introduce a school uniform. Miss Rice-Trevor would have approved. On May 3rd 1965 Frances Elizabeth Wise became headmistress of the re-named St Owens Infants School. She had in her charge 106 children in three classes with two other teachers. Roughly 100 years after Miss Rice-Trevor took the initiative we will leave the history of her school at this point. Much was still to develop. It acquired a swimming pool which caused constant problems and eventually burst, flooding the playground. In due course further reorganisation of the educational structure brought about merger with its offshoot.

The Oakley Hunt

Bromham's sport has always been of the inter-village variety of cricket and football. If it has a sporting reputation it has to be (with apologies to those who would question the name "sport") the annual meet of the Oakley Hunt. Oakley House was built at the very end of the eighteenth century by the then Duke of Bedford. In 1788 his pack was described as "the most numerous of any in England" and he is recorded as having new kennels at Woburn and at Eaton Socon. On March 20th 1798 he wrote to Samuel Whitbread saying that he would subscribe £500 per year so long as hounds were kept at Oakley. It is clear that he was referring to his existing private pack which he proposed to transfer in that year to a group of subscribers, and this became the Oakley Hunt.[170]

The Oakley Hunt, which is the only one located in Bedfordshire, usually met at Bromham[171] on each Boxing Day. In the years after the second World War it attracted many sightseers from Bedford with the end result that it moved its meet from the "Swan Green" (a minute triangle on the main Bedford-Northampton road) to the Village Green. No doubt in past days the Swan did a good trade in stirrup cups. One of the hunt members notes in his diary for October 3rd 1888 the result of such a meet:

> Bromham Swan 6.30. Trotted on to Hangers [Wood], found a leash of foxes, had several rings in cover, foxes all slipped away without being seen. Drew Astey Wood, Whites Wood and Becks Ash blank, found at Salem Thrift, went away to Bowels Spinney, rattled him well and went to ground, bolted and killed. Trotted on to Biddenham, found on the island by the river, away over the Biddenham road . . .

It is just as well that the best reason for meeting at the Swan seems, in the author's recollection, no longer to have been apparent after the second World War since there was not a pub in sight in the village centre.

Second World War evacuees and other wartime events

Before the second world war Bromham was almost as isolated from towns as villages such as Stagsden and Stevington. Buses came on only two days a week and women walked into Bedford to do the shopping that the village shop did not provide for. In such an atmosphere something of the nineteenth century community spirit survived and it was reinvigorated by the War. The principal annual event in the 1940s was the Sheep Dog Trials in the park, instigated by Mr Ayres who leased the park for his sheep (which he drove from and to his farm by the Stevington turn on the Northampton Road). The gymkhana, which was originally intended as a popular extra, became the principal attraction. Sunday school treats were held in the park (for want of the means to travel further) and despite rationing everyone seemed to have birthday parties and Christmas parties. The men left in the village had their own entertainment because they joined either the ARP or the Home Guard. The ARP only had three incendiary attacks to deal with but was, apparently, regarded as a model of efficient organisation. The farm buildings at Grange Farm were the only buildings in Bromham to be bombed in the Second World War. A single enemy plane, whether at random or because it was mistakenly supposed that Bowles wood was being used to store ammunition, dropped a stick of incendiary bombs across the southern end of those woods, the main road and the farm buildings. It had been raining heavily and the woods failed to burn. The fires in the buildings were easily extinguished by the farmer and the local ARP.[172]

The evacuees came to Bromham, mothers and children, in 1939 from Willesden. They felt the cold and one could hardly blame the mothers, sitting on the Green in the gathering gloom of a winter afternoon, largely unwanted in the homes on which they had been compulsorily billeted, from preferring to brave the bombing and return to London. Of the adults only a few teachers remained. My first was an evacuee teacher called Miss Elvey. She taught 30 children in the small middle room of the school before a blazing fire, wearing a thick woollen suit and a hat. I can see the hat now. It was Cambridge blue, round and typically "thirties". Ron and Derek Williams had boarded the wrong train. Someone with a sense of what was proper had intended them to go to South Wales. They sat all the day of arrival in the school playground whilst, one by one, the natives selected the number of children which was their quota (if I remember rightly they had only been told their quota that morning). No one could select the Williams, because they were not officially there. Eventually, since there was no mechanism for returning them, Mrs Pailes, the local WVS organiser, took them. They moved from the village school at the age of eleven to their own school, Dame Alice Owens, itself evacuated to share the buildings of Bedford Modern School. Horrendous stories are told of child abuse of young evacuees but there is certainly no record of it in Bromham where they all gave the impression, after a while, of being happy. It is to be doubted whether the same can be said for all their hosts. Those caring for the evacuee children received five shillings per week. Far from home and parents, in what must have been the strangest land they had ever imagined, there was a considerable amount of bed wetting. Mattresses drying in the gardens were, initially, a frequent sight. But the local children welcomed the influx. Many of the evacuees readily joined one of the two "gangs", the Thistley Green mob and the Village boys. An entire nursery school moved into the Hall where it appears to have been relatively self sufficient. Its members certainly did not get drawn into the gang warfare.

The two Swain boys were luckier than evacuees. Their whole family came from the United States, apparently as a gesture of solidarity, and arrived in Bromham in 1940. They bought "the Chalet", opposite the school which they attended all through the war. Later, of course, vast numbers of American airmen came with the Eighth Airforce to Twinwoods and Thurleigh aerodromes but they preferred the rather dim lights of Bedford. We watched their bombers return from daylight raids. They always fired red and green flares. Red, we told ourselves, were for dead or injured crew. The news of their heavy losses in the early days of daylight raids they conducted over Germany was among that which it was deemed better not to make public.

Bedford also benefited from the evacuation of the BBC Symphony Orchestra. Its leader, Paul Beard, lived on Stagsden Road. His daughter was a bit out of our league and went to Bedford High School. Its Librarian, Arthur Reeves, became a stalwart of the Baptist church and was able to produce there, from time to time, concerts the quality of which Bromham will not hear again.

The second invasion was by prisoners of war. The surrender of Italy meant that Italian prisoners, who had been taken in large numbers in North Africa, were, more or less, at liberty, but had to be occupied. They straightened the Brook and dug spectacularly deep ditches round Bowles Wood. They were very friendly. For some reason they all seemed good at making aluminium rings set with celluloid "stones". They never tried to sell these to us; they were always gifts. We did not see German prisoners of war, who occupied a camp near Clapham, until the surrender of Germany, but they too could then wander and a group of three walked over to Bromham every Sunday for tea, for which the price was attending the evening service at the Chapel. One of them had been a member of the Hitler Youth movement and was repatriated last. Surprisingly, none of the writer's family can remember any antagonism being shown to them, although it is just possible it was concealed from us, who provided the Sunday tea. They burned down our elm hedge. "What has happened, Franz, to the hedge?" we asked. Franz came from a rural part of South Germany and never managed much English. *Caput*, he said. It was his standard answer for everything that went wrong.

---

[94] Godber at p.111.
[95] 16 BHRS 89.
[96] See, Bell (Ed.) *Episcopal Visitations in Bedfordshire 1706-1720*, 81 BHRS (2002).
[97] VCH ii 115.
[98] See Appendix IX.
[99] But see Appendix V for a suggestion that a plot off Lower Farm Road may have been so occupied.
[100] (1964) 9 BM at p.152.
[101] Indexed in two volumes by Alan F Cirket. (British Record Society 1994).
[102] Nigel Lutt (Ed) *Bedfordshire Muster Lists 1539-1831* (1991) 71 BHRS.
[103] *Bromham* (1960) 7 BM 133-137.
[104] The author was at school with Roy Biggs until 1946. He may have been a descendant of these millers, arriving in the second half of the eighteenth century and flourishing for most of the nineteenth century.
[105] Bevan boys were those who, after the second World War, exercised the option to work in coal mines instead of serving in the armed forces.
[106] See page 32 below.
[107] Nigel Lutt (Ed) *Bedfordshire Muster Lists 1539-1831* (1992) 71 BHRS at p.14.
[108] (1966) 45 BHRS at p.55.
[109] See Lydia M. Marshall (Ed) *The Bedfordshire Hearth Tax Return for 1671* (1934) 16 BHRS reprinted 1990 at p.89.
[110] See, ch III Religious Worship – The Chapel.
[111] She was the post-mistress in the first quarter of the twentieth century.
[112] An Inskip held the office of Piller (the official designated to take charge of stray animals) in the mid-nineteeth century.
[113] At p.71.
[114] Nigel Lutt (Ed) *Bedfordshire Muster Lists 1539-1831* (1992) 71 BHRS 216.

[115] He had two sons. The youngest (Ted) emigrated to New Zealand. Tom, whom it is believed did not marry, remained in England. Ted was, of course, not the first Bromham resident to emigrate to New Zealand – see, (1986) 20 BM 201.

[116] Mollivers' wood is the smallest of the three in Bromham and lies between Mollivers' Lane and Oakley Road.

[117] See, ch V Portraits – The second Sir Lewis Dyve.

[118] Reference to the price is a reference to an early form of compensation payable to the next of kin of a person killed by some object, which might include an animal, and which was deemed forfeit to God. The owner would, in effect, redeem it by paying the price. An early rhyme runs; "Whatever moved to do the deed is *deodand* and forfeited".

[119] (1951) 32 BHRS pp.52 and 53.

[120] CD Linnell (Ed) *The Diary of Benjamin Rogers* (1949) 30 BHRS at p.31.

[121] Godber at p.425.

[122] The Bedford Times 9th December 1847.

[123] Ibid 1st May 1847.

[124] See The Bedford Times 15th May 1847 under the heading "Rejoicings at Bromham".

[125] The author recollects that two boys were convicted, in the 1950s, of stealing eggs from chicken huts behind the mill which were the property of yet another Mr Church of the Mill House.

[126] The Bedford Times 27th May 1854.

[127] Harvey at p.50n.

[128] He was born in Bedford on October 2nd 1934 and educated at Bedford Modern School

[129] Although the old cricket ground is still not built on.

[130] VCH iii 47.

[131] Godber at p.208.

[132] Godber, at p.361, records a woadman. Harvey at p.29 records that woad *(Isatis tinctoria)* was cultivated in the parish in the eighteenth century and that there was still a piece of land called the cabin-ground where the huts of the labourers who cultivated it had stood. He says that this area extended over 40 acres. The leaves of the plant are dried, powdered and fermented with ammonia to produce a blue pigment. This was the principal source of blue dye until superseded by indigo. Raw cloth was often woaded before other colour dyes were applied because they were then more durable; hence the expression "double dyed". A picture of the plant appears in the pictures section.

[133] He appears in the Muster Lists for 1803 (1992) 71 BHRS 215. See further Later Landscapes – The Mill below.

[134] VCH iii 47. The quarries were of limestone, mainly south of the Brook and just West of the Hill. Very rich deposits of gravel exist, mostly in the bend of the river against Clapham. These were not extensively worked until the twentieth century. An old quarry was traceable to the north of Grange Lane immediately east of Bowles wood. If it was of limestone its western edge could have been exposed by the small stream that ran beside the wood. Its eastern bank was an excellent site for defensive emplacements that we built as children in the second World War but it is now a housing estate. There are the remains of another quarry still with signs of limestone outcrop just inside the park and half way up the Hill.

[135] See, Nigel E Agar, *The Bedfordshire Farm Worker in the Nineteenth Century* (1981) 60 BHRS at pp.90-91.

[136] And whose forbears, presumably, had moved to Bromham from Pertenhall.

[137] A number of these wills, together with some others, were collected by Harvey (see pp.73-4). Others appear in Patricia Bell, *Bedfordshire Wills 1484-1533* (1997) 76 BHRS and Margaret McGregor, *Bedfordshire Wills proved in the Prerogative Court at Canterbury 1383-1548* (1979) 58 BHRS. For other wills see Patricia Bell's earlier collection in (1966) 45 BHRS.

[138] Nigel E Agar, n. 135 above.

[139] See Appendix VI.

[140] See the evidence of Rev. Wade-Gery of St Neots (presumably Bushmead Priory in that parish as he was very clear that he was not the rector of St Neots) in Nigel E Agar, *The Bedfordshire Farm Worker in the Nineteenth Century* (1981) 60 BHRS at p.41 et seq. Wade-Gery was a JP administering the poor law for the Hundred of Stodden.

[141] In North Bedfordshire girls (and sometimes boys) from the age of nine were expected to earn by lace-making. They might earn as much as 3s per week in such work if all went well. Unfortunately the market for this suffered a glut at this time. It was, moreover, common for the entrepreneurs in this, as in other, industries to operate the "truck" system, paying in kind rather than cash. It was rarely possible to sell the goods thus received as payment at anything like the valuation placed upon them as wages.

[142] Agar, n. 135 above, at p.65.

[143] He might not have wished to admit to some supplementation by poaching.

[144] Godber, at p.529 gives an account of Christmas Dinner at Bedford in 1859 but this was obviously a high spot designed to impress the attendant Borough councillors. In previous years food provision had been reduced on the ground that it was too generous.

[145] See, Bell (Ed.) *Episcopal Visitations in Bedfordshire 1706-1720,* 81 BHRS (2002).

[146] Bell, *op cit.,* at p.xiv notes that the first school master of the newly endowed school at Hockliffe in 1717 was an Anabaptist. He taught the catechism.

[147] David Bushby, *The Bedfordshire Schoolchild* (1988) 67 BHRS at p.40.

[148] Ibid at p.65.

[149] Ibid at p.116.

[150] This is the nearest typeface available. See the picture of the School for the actual lettering.

[151] The primacy of Anglican doctrine does not seem to have been challenged until, for the first time in 1959 there was no Ascension Day half day holiday (the morning was previously occupied by a walk over the park to a service in the church). Only in 1963 does there appear to have been any public objection to the vicar taking morning assembly, but in fact the Rev. Evans made clear his continuing authority by declaring that *he* had ensured that the proceedings would be suitable for all protestants.

[152] See the pictures section for the first page of this report.

[153] Bushby, Ibid. at p.205.

[154] Ibid. at p.227. This means that we lack the useful records of the proceedings of such boards existing in most other villages.

[155] 1850-1935. He died in Saanid near Victoria, British Columbia, to which he and most of his family had emigrated early in the twentieth century.

[156] Who, perhaps surprisingly in view of his son's then position, died in what would have been regarded as the workhouse at St Peters, Bedford.

[157] It is said that he painted a portrait of Lord Halsbury LC.

[158] Mr Carrier did send poor Caroline Fox, from Box End in Kempston, home on 2nd August 1895 on the ground that she was an imbecile.

[159] She died on 13th of that month.

[160] The architect, one W Tucker of London, had followed the historic practice of placing the lavatories at the bottom of the garden. The girls had a straight run of about 40 yards to their's through a small lobby with washbasin off the main classroom. After the building of the new classroom the boys path wound round it. I never knew anyone to use the seated accommodation (which was of the bucket variety) but the urinals were self flushing, in the sense that they were open to the elements. They had their own problem with the leaves of a large overhanging chestnut tree and despite the devoted work of a series of long serving caretakers they provided some useful study of the habits of the cockroach when it anticipated danger.

[161] It lapsed between the wars but Miss Markham restarted it in 1944, coincidentally in the first private garden next to the School. It was probably in this house that John Trevor's school had been conducted.

[162] Jim Burley (technically from Stagsden) may have been the next "scholarship boy". He was closely followed by Bill Fowler. Thereafter Bromham School established a reputation for such successes. Jim Burley, incidentally, had time to reflect on the days learning. He lived in the last house on the road to Stagsden, well over the parish boundary, and must have walked at least eight miles a day, morning, noon and afternoon.

[163] Every year, even through the second world war, the almost unused roads received a coating of tar covered with gravel and rolled in by the County Council's steam roller. The tar the author has in mind came from the barrels left over the weekend and was actually applied by and to children attending the Baptist Sunday School. Nonetheless Miss Prickett dealt with the complaint.

[164] One could object and the author's father did, in respect of his older children. Perhaps it was the effect of becoming the first non-conformist governor of the school that caused him to drop the objection in the author's case.

[165] Iona and Peter Opie: *The Singing Game* (Oxford University Press 1985).

[166] See Opie at pp.50 to 54. They publish a photograph of this game at p.35.

[167] We did use paper. I suspect slates were an economy measure. Whether they were the originals I do not know but they were wearing out. Two pupils who mixed up the ink powder (of whom I became one) had the weekly task of painting the slates with that ink to render the writing on them more visible. One quickly adapted to the need to keep one's hand off the slate when writing.

[168] The Bromham May song of the nineteenth century is set out at Appendix IV.

[169] Earlier children from Thistley Green, at its furthest point two miles away, had walked home and back in the one and a half hours of the lunch break.

[170] In 1834 new kennels were bought at Milton Ernest. For further information on the Oakley see, Joyce Godber (ed) *The Oakley Hunt* (1965) 44 BHRS.

[171] Bromham is mentioned, on J and C Walker's map of 1850, as one of its meeting places.

[172] The leader of the Bromham ARP, Mr Lovell Lee, underrates this episode, at which he was not present, in the account he deposited with the County Record Office.

An Armorial

The earliest coats of arms tend to be simple, no doubt because they were genuinely for recognition on a battlefield, rather than for ornament. Among the earliest associated with Bromham is that of the major landowner **Beauchamp of Bedford**.

Quarterly or and gules: a bend sable

Beauchamp of Bedford

Similarly, the very distinguished house of **de Moubray** whose arms reveal its close association with the Crown.

Gules: a lion argent

It will be noted that lions are always standing, sideways on. If the owner wanted the beast facing, Passant, or in any other form, it should be called a leopard.

de Moubray

The manor of **Wake** appeared some two centuries later but the family name is old and the arms equally straightforward.

Or: two bars gules: three roundels gules in the chief

(In fact this description taken from the VCH seems to be incorrect because it should not contain repetition.)

Wake

At one period **Neville Lord Latimer** held lands in Bromham

Gules: a saltire argent with a ring sable for difference upon the saltire

The ring for difference usually depicts use of the family arms by a fifth son.

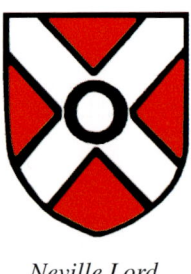

Neville Lord Latimer

Some of the families with early direct associations have equally simple arms. Of these the **Widevilles** are among the earliest and they seem to have collected them. Two appear in the brass in Bromham church subsequently appropriated by the Dyves. One of them, belonging to Thomas Wideville's second wife, uses, in very singular splendour, the well known heraldic symbol of a fleur de lys. The other is definitely not ornamental.

Argent: on a chief d'or a fleur de lis gules

Argent: a fesse and a quarter gules

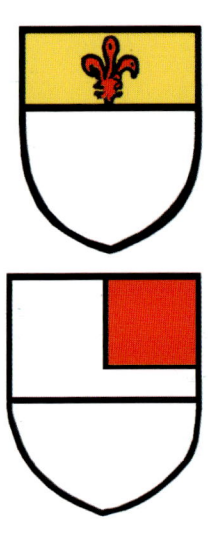

Wideville

Elizabeth Wideville, the sister and heir of Thomas Wideville married Sir Reginald Ragon and was the great great grandmother of Sir John Dyve (hence the borrowed brass). The **Ragons** are primarily associated with other parts of the County, which explains arms unlikely to have been inspired by Bromham but which are more ornamental than those seen so far and worth depiction.

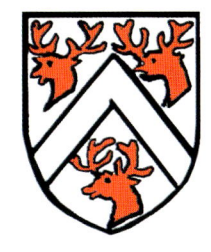

Argent: a chevron between three harts heads gules cut off at the neck

Ragon

The arms of the Dyves *of Bromham*

Gules: a fesse dancety or between three scallops ermine was ultimately borne on a coat including sixteen quarterings of which they figured as the first and last. They also aspired to two alternative crests.

A wyvern with wings endorsed gules and

A horse's leg embowed or (the foot shod azure) between two wings gules

Dyve of Bromham

The close association of the fortunes of the most famous of the Dyves with the Earls of Bristol might seem to justify inclusion of the ***Bristol*** arms in this list.

Argent: a chevron ermine between three chessrooks sable

Earl of Bristol

The **Trevors** bought the estate from the Dyves in 1707 and, considering the political motive of their original ennoblement, have a rather grand coat of arms.

Party bend sinister ermine and erminee: a lion or

Possibly coincidentally they have a variation of the Dyve crest.

Two wyverns regardant sable

One would expect a time-serving lawyer to have the motto

Stat Lege Corona

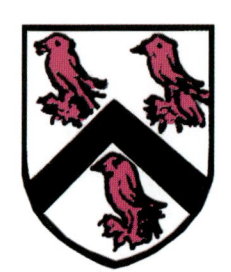

Trevor

The fourth Baron Trevor became the first Viscount Hampden and he and his heirs quartered the **Hampden** arms with those of Trevor. The arms of John Hampden were *Argent: a saltire gules between four eagles displ.argent.* Neither the Trevors nor the Hampdens seem to have had much luck with direct heirs and another line of the Welsh house of Trevor married into the **Rices** who themselves acquired by marriage the title of **Baron Dynevor.** The second Baron Dynevor had been made first Earl Talbot . It was not uncommon, where a senior peerage was bestowed on a man unlikely to have male heirs, for the letters patent to confer on his daughter in her own right that nobleman's more junior title (though she could only pass on that title in the male line). So the third baron Dynevor, (who is actually the fourth person to hold that title) who assumed the name **Rice**, quartered his mother's arms with those of **Talbot** and Rice.

Rice

Talbot

de Cardonnel

St Owen's Church, Bromham, from the East. *(Originally dedicated to St Andrew.) This North facing addition in the foreground is the mortuary chapel built in 1868 by George 4th Baron Trevor. The tower is fifteenth century, as is the battlemented parapet to the north wall. Behind the yew tree can be seen the porch in the room above which the first school was conducted.*

***Harvey's lovely etching of the church at Bromham in the mid-nineteenth century.** It is drawn from what became the old cricket field. The pine tree stood until 1960s. The footpath is there still.*

The South Porch of St Owen's Church. *The room above the porch contained the library established by the second Lord Trevor. The tablet on the wall bears the inscription "this small library was founded and freely given for the use of the Minister and Parish of Bromham by Thomas Lord Trevor in the year 1740. No book to be taken out without the leave of the Minister or Lord of the Manor." The library, one of only two parish libraries remaining in Bedfordshire, was removed to Bedford in 1984.*

Memorial to the third Baron Trevor beside the north door of St Owen's Church. *The black veined marble appears to be similar to that which this Lord Trevor bought for the monument erected to the memory of the first Lord Trevor in 1732.*

The North Porch of St Owen's Church. *The room above was used as a schoolroom in the eighteenth century.*

The Dyve brass Bromham Church.

This fifteenth century brass was originally a memorial to the Widevilles and was probably at Grafton in Northamptonshire. It was adapted to the memory of Sir John Dyve and installed in Bromham Church.

This engraving is copied from Lysons 'Magna Britannia' of 1813.

The Water Mill at Bromham. *The nineteenth century replacement of the former mill house is on the far left. The spring which Farrar thought to be Roman is just off the picture to the left beyond the upper wall. Copyright: Bedfordshire County Council.*

Restored machinery in the Mill. The Mill and its machinery have been restored as a tourist attraction. The machinery is operational.

Fisher's drawing of Bromham Bridge in 1812. *Drawn from the old Mill House just before the bridge was widened. Fisher clearly did not want the Mill to draw one's attention away from the subject since he has omitted the timbered walls.*

The Chantry Spring. *Perhaps one can see why Farrar thought its steps so worn with time.*

The old bridge. *A photograph taken from the new bridge.*

The Mill Stream. *This picture is taken towards the mill from the confluence of the Brook and the River. The new picnic ground is on the right. The nature reserve on the island is on the left.*

Bromham School c.1942. The famous text surmounts a full muster; apart from the two in the bicycle shed, who may have good reason not to appear on film. Miss Pricket's car is in its usual winter place (in summer it was parked in the shade of the elm tree). The seven boys on the right include Ted Prudden (the former blacksmith's younger son), Lawrence (Tich) Green, Len Walker and Fred Pearson. Len's brothers Bob and Albert, and their neighbours from the cottages at the top of the Hill, Derek and Peter Wornast are also in the picture. The smallest child with the slip on straps is Derek Harland. His brother, Roy, is tenth from the left. The author was present but cannot identify himself.

No. _____   Date of Inspection 15th & 16th Nov 1864

Inspector's Report of Bromham   School Mixed
Diocese of Ely   Deanery of Clapham   Parish of Bromham
Number of Children on Books 70   Number present at Inspection 44

I. CHARACTER OF THE RELIGIOUS KNOWLEDGE

(1.) Of the First and Second Classes as to
- Knowledge of the Old Testament — Moderate
- New Testament — Moderate
- Catechism — Fair
- Prayer-Book — —

(2.) Of the Lower Classes generally — Not Satisfactory

II. CHARACTER OF THE SECULAR KNOWLEDGE

(3.) Of the First and Second Classes as to
- Reading — Indifferent. Wanting in expression. Enunciation defective.
- Learning by heart — Hymns, Collects &c. for repetition on Sundays
- Writing — Moderate — Style not good
- Writing from Dictation — Insufficient
- Composition — —
- Arithmetic — 3 pupils fair — the remainder backward
- Grammar — —
- Geography — 1 extra pupil taught. Moderate
- History — —
- Singing from Notes — —
- Needlework — Taught
- Drawing — —

(4.) Of the Lower Classes as to Reading (1), Writing (2), and Arithmetic (3) — (1) Very Moderate (2) Fair (3) Not taught

III.

The Registers	The Time-Table	(1) The Discipline, (2) Manners, and (3) Cleanliness of the Children
Fairly kept	None	1. Moderate 2. & 3. Good

IV.

The Buildings: (1) Schoolroom, (2) Classroom	(1) The Playground, and (2) Yards	The School-fittings	(1) The Books, and (2) Apparatus
1. Excellent 2. —	1. All very good 2. —	Good, but not well arranged	1. Deficient 2. Do.

Information from the Master, Mistress, or Managers.
Whether forms of private prayer are carefully taught to the children, of what kind, and in what way. — M

(Signed) E. Brown Jones, Diocesan Inspector

Points deserving of special notice, such as the relative condition of the School as compared with previous year, &c., to be entered on the other side.

* Describe School, whether Boys', Girls', Mixed, or Infants'.

NOTE. The information required in the above Form may be conveniently noted in Form B, or in a corresponding Note-Book adapted for the purpose, and supplied by the National Society.

A School Report. *Could do better.* The Inspector's report of 1864 which Rev. Goodall decided not to send to Miss Rice-Trevor.

Harvey's views of Bromham Hall in the mid-nineteenth century.

Miss Rice-Trevor with her Sunday School class. *They are in summer uniform. Her steward is in attendance.*

Copyright: Richard Wildman, Bedford.

Harvey's etching of the Vicarage in the mid-nineteenth century. *The building was demolished a little more than one hundred years later.*

The Greenwood Cottages as they were in 1930. *The central hall revealed by Miss Thorne's restoration in c.1937 is said to contain thirteenth century work. If that is so this is the oldest house in Bromham. There was a legend that the great roof timbers, which now appear at knee height in the bedroom to the side of the hall, came from Viking long ships.*

The Smithy in the early twentieth century.

The Crown Inn c.1895 demolished in 1905 when the bridge was widened. James Rust the last licensee and his wife stand at the door. Copyright: Bedfordshire County Council.

Major Hill's Garage in the 1920s. The original tin shed was replaced in the 1930s. Copyright: Bedfordshire County Council.

The village store in 1906. The Websters built a detached house in place of this temporary building. The Staffertons lived in the thatched house behind. Copyright: Bedford Museum.

The Stagsden Gate on the Newport Pagnell turnpike. *The toll keeper's house was almost on the Bromham boundary at Thistley Green.*

Bromham House. *Later Bromham Hospital's administrative building. This picture shows W.H. Allen JP and his chaplain Rev. C.W. Browning, vicar of Bromham, about to enter the High Sheriff's coach during Mr Allen's tenure of that office in 1904-5.*

One third of the population in about 1932. *They are the congregation (and, one suspects, friends thereof) on the annual Baptist Church Women's Meeting day outing to Clacton. Percy Green is hiding on the back on the left. His neighbour, Mrs Pearson is above her daughter in the front row. The author's father, eldest brother, mother and aunt are immediately right of the Minister of Stevington Baptist Church.*

The first Baptist Church with its Sunday School in the early 1940s.

The third Baptist Church building opened in 1991. *It incorporated the second building. The original wooden church was dismantled and re-erected elsewhere.*

The second village hall. *On former allotment land between the sports field and the southern tip of the Green.*

The Jubilee of King George V. *The fancy dress parade. Mr Jesse Gardner, last coachman at Bromham Hall is on the left in uniform.*

The End of the Rainbow. *Performed at Bromham House (later Bromham Hospital) in the early 1940s.*

Erich, Carl and Franz. *German prisoners of war, 1945.*

Woad. *Isatis tinctoria. Harvey, writing just before 1860, says that 40 acres known as "the cabin ground" in Bromham had been occupied by the cabins of the woad workers. Clearly a substantial amount of land in the parish had been devoted to this plant until it was supplanted by indigo as the principal source of blue dye in the nineteenth century. The blue pigment is produced by boiling the leaves or fermenting them with ammonia. This, presumably, is what the workers did.*

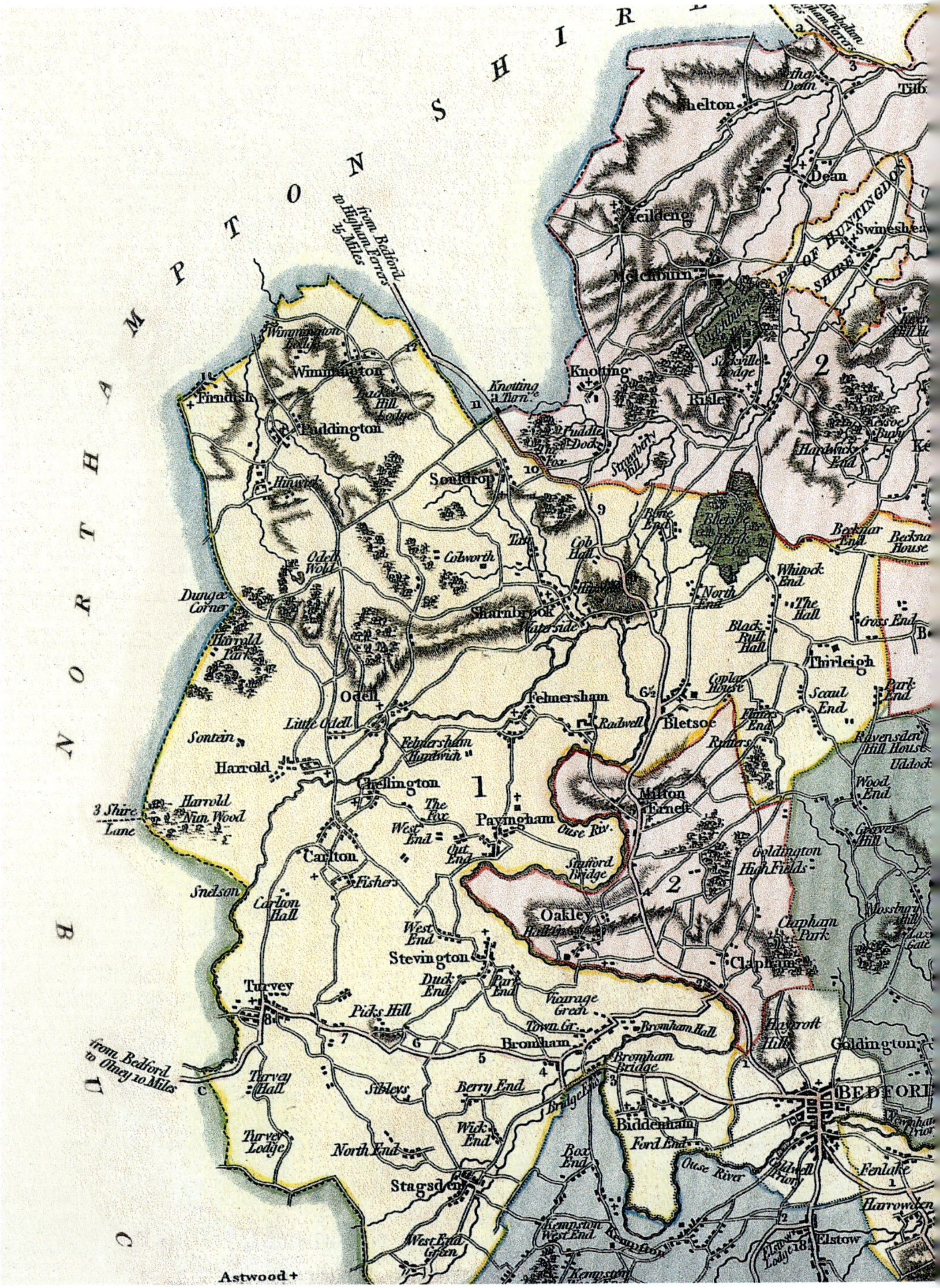
NORTHAMPTON SHIRE
BUC
from Bedford to Higham Ferrers 14 Miles
from Bedford to Olney 10 Miles
Shelton
Dean
Swineshead
Keilden
Melchburn
Knotting
Knotting Turn
Risley
Puddle Dock
The Fox
Strawberry Hill
Sackville Lodge
Hardwick End
Wimmington Lodge
Wimmington
Farndish
Podington
Souldrop
Hinwick
Odell Wold
Colworth
Dungee Corner
Harrold Park
Sharnbrook
Waterside
Cob Hall
Blue End
Bletsoe Park
Bletsoe
Beckmar End
Whitock End
The Hall
North End
Black Bull Hall
Thirleigh
Gross End
Poplar House
Scaul End
Park End
Felmersham
Radwell
Odell
Little Odell
Sontein
Harrold
Felmersham Hardwick
Chellington
Ravensden Hill House
Uddock
Wood End
Milton Ernest
Harrold Nun Wood
3 Shire Lane
The Fox
Pavingham
West End
Out End
Ouse Riv.
Stafford Bridge
Goldington High Fields
Carlton
Fishers
Snelson
Carlton Hall
Oakley
Clapham Park
Clapham
West End
Stevington
Duck End
Park End
Turvey
Vicarage Green
Picks Hill
Town Gr.
Bromham Hall
Bromham
Bromham Bridge
Goldington
Turvey Hall
Sibleys
Berry End
BEDFORD
Biddenham
Ford End
Turvey Lodge
Wick End
North End
Box End
Ouse River
Fenlake
Stagsden
Harrowden
Kempston West End
Kempston
West End Green
Elstow
Astwood
1
2

A

NEW MAP

of the COUNTY of

BEDFORD

Divided into Hundreds.

LONDON:

Printed for C. SMITH, N.º 172, Strand.

January 6.ᵗʰ 1801.

KEY

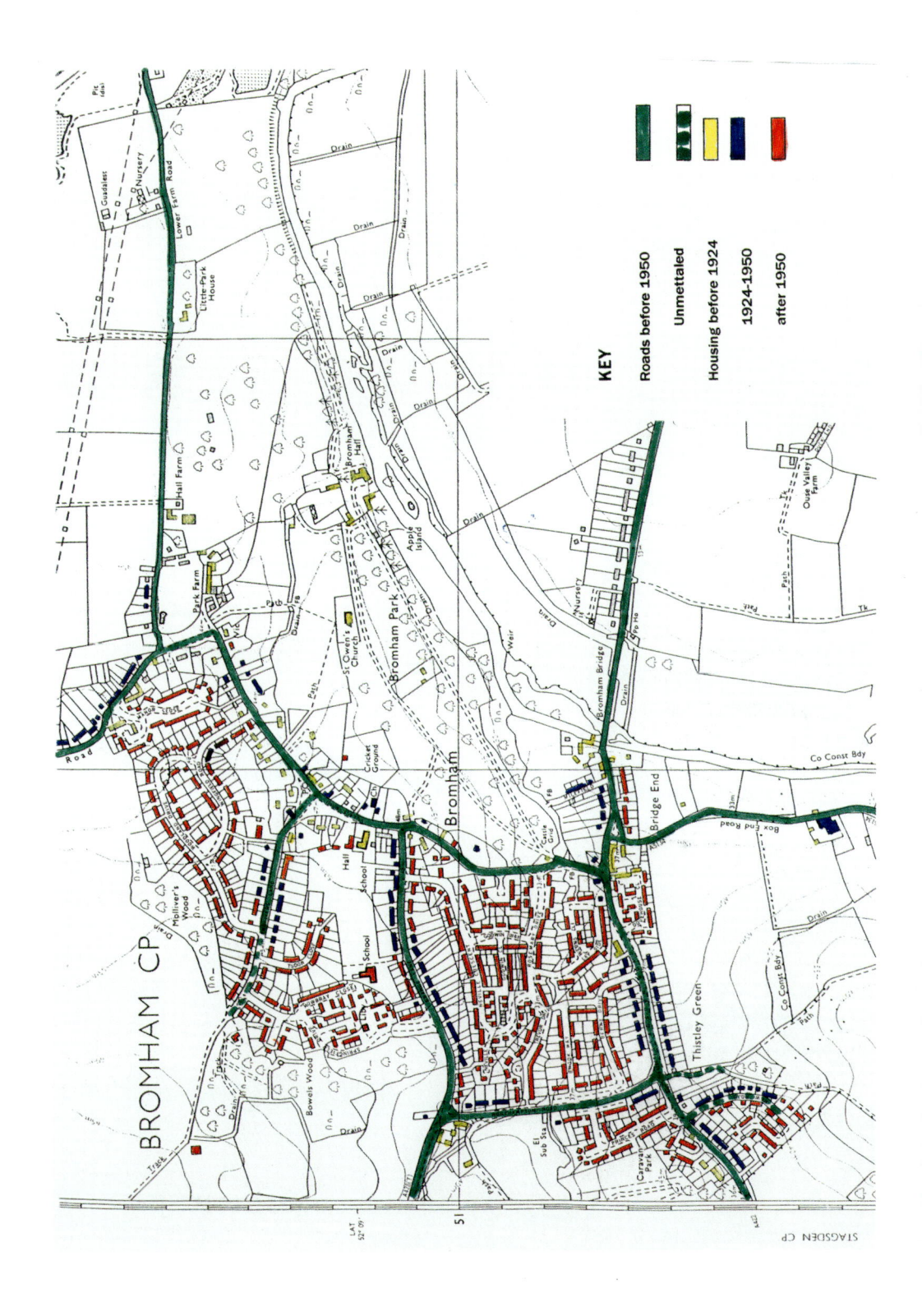

Roads before 1950
Unmettaled
Housing before 1924
1924-1950
after 1950

Chapter V
PORTRAITS

The second Sir Lewis Dyve – his ancestors and family

Reginald Ragon, sheriff of Beds and Bucks in 1396 and 1402, and who was living in 1417, married Elizabeth, sister and heir of Thomas Wideville and so acquired, through her, the mesne tenancy of all the manors of Bromham. Their son, John, had one daughter, his heir, Agnes who married Thomas Wilde of Bursham in Denbighshire. Their daughter, and coheir, Elizabeth married Henry, the eldest son of John Dyve of Quinton and conveyed Bromham to that family. Harvey says that the Dyve family moved their principal residence to Bromham. He notes that the Dyves were of Norman descent. Not only did the Dyves thus acquire Bromham but they also acquired the memorial brass to Thomas Wideville made in about 1435, which may well have always been in the church at Bromham. Henry's son John adapted this brass to commemorate himself and his mother.[173] John was sheriff of Bedfordshire in 1510. His son William had seven sons and seven daughters. The eldest of these sons was he whom Harvey calls Sir Lewis Dyve the elder. He completed the purchase of the whole Bromham estate by adding lands which Reginald Bray had purchased in 1488 and which his grandson Edmund sold to Sir Lewis in 1565.[174] The elder Sir Lewis was himself a colourful character. He was taken prisoner on the fall of Calais and forced, after a year, to ransom himself with a payment of 600 marks. He too was sheriff of Bedfordshire after the county ceased to share a sheriff with Buckinghamshire in 1574.[175]

Not surprisingly the land policy of the elder Sir Lewis included enclosure. There are references to enclosure of arable land in the East and North fields in 1595.[176] His son John says that his father "used persuasion" to enclose a meadow. We may assume Sir Lewis made a thorough job of it. Godber says that the enclosure at Bromham may have been more extensive than elsewhere in the County at this time and there is no other record of enclosure at Bromham, which, in 1807, was described simply as "old".[177]

Sir John Dyve was the only surviving son of the elder Sir Lewis and succeeded him on his death in 1592. He was sheriff of Bedfordshire in 1593 and 1603 and was knighted in the latter year when James I visited Salden House in Buckinghamshire. The media, in those days, were rather less adept at bringing to light the shortcomings of public figures, which may have been fortunate for this aspect of the career of John Dyve. In 1589 William Boteler, who was a wool merchant of the Calais staple,[178] had made his fortune in London and purchased an estate in Biddenham, and, in the English tradition was, therefore, regarded by the old landed gentry as a tradesman. Sir Lewis Dyve, in pursuance of a policy of outbidding the Botelers, bought a piece of land in Biddenham known as Dyves Downs farm which William Boteler had intended to purchase and for which he had already paid £100. In retaliation William bought the reversion of parts of the Latimer and Neville estates in Bromham. This was doubly unfortunate for Lewis seems to have incorporated these lands in others including the parkland. Sir Lewis is normally blamed for what followed, but legal documents filed by Williams' grandson in connection with later attempts to resolve the title to the disputed lands state that in a bill filed in the Court of Star Chamber by the grandfather against Sir Lewis it was said that it was John Dyve, who, as heir had "conceived against your sayde subiect most grievous displesure and deadlye hatred". Forgetting "both his dutye towards God and obedience towards your maiestes lawes" he sought to bring William (the grandfather) "to finall perdition and destruction" Presumably therefore it was John who challenged the London merchant to a duel, which the latter must surely have lost. William demonstrated that he was, as the Dyves had long maintained, no gentleman by wisely refusing to fight. Mindful of the law or not, the Dyves were wise enough not to attack William while he was sheriff of Bedford but he ceased to hold that office on December 23rd 1588 and had thus lost his special protection from attack as a servant of the Crown. He must have been aware that John and retainers had lain in wait for him the very next day in the expectation that he would go to Bedford to hear the sermon on Christmas Eve. Probably that is why he did not go. John issued his challenge on Boxing Day and the following Sunday he, with nine[179] retainers and friends armed with swords, daggers and staves, ambushed William on his way home from church. William was knocked to the ground and bled and his servant Peter Sampson was run through the throat. Robert Sampson was wounded in the right arm and Andrew Wright lost two fingers from his left hand. Well satisfied with this enlivening of the Sabbath John Dyve and his merry men departed "in great braverye and jolitye reoiycinge greatlye of that whiche they had done."[180] The land dispute was ultimately settled by an exchange of lands in Bromham and Biddenham. There is, alas, no record of whether the Star Chamber ever heard the case.

    John first married Douglas[181] who was the daughter of Sir Anthony Denny. Shortly after her death he married, in 1598, Beatrice, daughter of Charles Walcot of Walcot in Staffordshire. The second Sir Lewis was their eldest son and he was baptised at Bromham on November 25th 1599. John had obviously made up the quarrel with the Botelers[182] because Mrs Boteler deputised as godparent for the Countess of Warwick.[183] It was John who erected the most magnificent of the memorials in Bromham church; the canopied marble memorial to his father, mother and first wife. He died in 1607 and was buried "with great solemnity" in

Bromham church on January 16th 1608. His widow later married Sir John Digby who was created the first Earl of Bristol in September 1622. She remained the owner of the lands at Bromham, Sir Lewis being technically the tenant.[184] Thereafter the fortunes of Sir Lewis and the Digbys were closely bound together.

No history of Bromham would be complete without an account of the experiences of the second Sir Lewis Dyve (1599-1669) during the Civil War. He is undoubtedly the most notorious and most extensively chronicled of its inhabitants. Harvey includes a lengthy appendix containing an account of his life. This is scarcely less detailed and authoritative than that in Tibbutt's *Life and Letters*.[185]

George Digby, who became the second Earl on his father's death in exile after the Civil War, was born in 1612, but despite the age difference he and Lewis, his half-brother, maintained a close association before, during and after the War. Lewis matriculated at Oxford on February 21st 1613/14, position probably counting more than academic achievement, and joined his mother and step-father in Spain. The latter was English ambassador to Spain from 1611 to 1624 and was closely involved in the protracted negotiations by the Duke of Buckingham for the marriage of the Prince of Wales to the Infanta. On March 7th 1622 Beatrice wrote a long account to her sister of the arrival in Spain of the Prince who, with Buckingham, had travelled in disguise through France, but risked a day in Paris, notwithstanding.[186] Lewis, who had been knighted at Whitehall on April 19th 1620, had recently been paying a lot of attention to the wife of a Spanish nobleman who had forced her to play and sing on her balcony as Lewis passed by at night on his way home with Sir Kenelm Digby. Sir Lewis fell for the trap and was set upon by fifteen armed men as he walked forward to speak to her. He broke his sword on the helmet of one of his assailants and decided that the better part of valour was to seek help from home. Sir Kenelm, who had also broken his sword, continued to defend himself, but perhaps, with their quarry gone, he found it easier to shake off the attack. He strolled leisurely homewards and met the relief force on the way. The Spanish government had no wish to compromise negotiations respecting the Prince, who arrived next day, and the matter was allowed to drop. Sir Lewis was lucky. The mood did not last. Buckingham and the Prince returned home alleging offence at the manner of their reception in Spain. It seems more likely that they, like the London mob, followed the rapidly changed mood which demanded war with Spain.[187]

The Earl of Bristol and Sir Lewis returned to England in 1624 and in that year Lewis married Howanda Rogers (daughter of Sir John Strangeways) whose first husband had died after only a year of marriage. Their first child, Beatrice, was born in 1625 and died in Bromham, where she is buried, on February 24th 1645/6 when her father was holding Sherborne castle as the only remaining Royalist stronghold in Dorset. Lewis' first son, John, was born in London and baptised at St Clement Danes on May 13th 1627. Francis was born at Melbury in Dorset, as was another Lewis in 1633.[188] Jane, their last child, was born at Bromham in 1639 and died on 9th January 1641.

The second Lewis was returned as member of Parliament for Bridport in 1625[189] and 1626, which is not entirely unexpected since the Earl of Bristol's family seat was at Sherborne . He usefully occupied himself stirring up (for private ends) disaffection among MPs and was detained by Royal warrant on June 28th 1626. But he was later returned as the member for Weymouth. He was a member of the Long Parliament but was disqualified in 1643 as a serving officer in the King's army. Already, in 1641, he had made clear with whom his sympathies lay by publishing, apparently without the author's permission, an objection Lord George Digby had made against the condemnation of Strafford by Bill of Attainder. He was adjudged by parliament a delinquent on February 14th because he received a letter from George. George had wisely departed to the Netherlands from which he wrote under the not very opaque pseudonym of "Baron of Sherborne" to various friends and relations commenting, inter alia, that Parliamentarians were traitors. Perhaps the post was delivered by parliament's supporters, but anyway John Pym intercepted the second of these letters, addressed to Lewis, and reported three others dated the same day. Despite this George had the cheek to nominate Lewis for the post of Governor of the Tower of London. He was, of course, anxious to get that stronghold in Royalist hands. It is scarcely surprising that Sir Thomas Linsford was regarded as "more trustworthy".

Both sides knew that they were manoeuvring towards war and on St George's Day 1642 the King, not very ably assisted by Sir Lewis and others, botched an attempt to seize Hull. The North was primarily Royalist but Hull, which would have been invaluable as a supply port, was not. The governor was suspicious of the reasons for the unexpected arrival of the Duke of York and Prince Rupert. He became more suspicious when informed that the King was in the vicinity, accompanied by 300 horse. He became positively certain when he learned that another 400 royalist horse were also in the vicinity. So when Lewis arrived with a letter stating that the King would come to dinner in two hours he shut the gates and stood the garrison to arms. Sir Lewis may have had the right idea, which was to dispose of the governor, who was, after all, the King's official, and order the gates to be opened. He climbed out of a window in order to pursue the governor with the intention of throwing him off the walls, but the governor saw him coming and could rely on the garrison to arrest him. The governor released him when the danger was passed, but Sir Samuel Luke, whom we shall continue to encounter as a source of trouble for Lewis, moved the Commons to order the Sergeant at Arms to arrest him.

Arrest, or the threat of it, at a time when it was not entirely clear who was the rightful authority, seems often to have been designed more as an indication of where the opposition came from than as a serious attempt to incarcerate it, and Lewis had little difficulty joining George Digby in Holland and assisting him in securing aid for the King.

But Parliament was about to decide to take the arrest of Sir Lewis seriously. It regularly intercepted letters implicating him in fund raising for the King and it probably could deduce that he had returned to England in mid-July 1642. On July 25th he received £1000 from Digby to buy horses and he went to Bedford and had 500 bullets cast. Parliament acted with a speed unusual in modern government. On its instructions, on July 27th the House of Lords' messenger accompanied Sir Samuel Luke of Cople and Sir Thomas Alston of Odell to Bromham to affect an arrest.[190] One wonders whether they can have been serious, or whether they too doubted the advisability of the move for they came with very few men and did not surround Bromham Hall. They sent poor old Lawrence, the Lords' messenger, to enquire politely whether Sir Lewis was at home and, if so, whether he would be so good as to come out as they had some Parliamentary business to discuss with him. The truth of Lady Dyve's answer that he was not at home was somewhat shaken when Lawrence, checking it by entering by another door, had a pistol put to his head. This failed to fire and he scuttled back to report and was despatched to Bedford for reinforcements. Sir Lewis, of course, did not hang about. He came out shooting. He fired at Sir Samuel, who seems to have attracted most attention for he also had his wrist and thigh cut with sword strokes. It turned out that there were fifteen retainers supporting Sir Lewis. They made no attempt to escape with him and it must be that the plan was that they should cover his escape.

This adds to doubts as to the truth of the best known of all the stories of Sir Lewis in which he is said to have escaped by swimming the river.[191] Sir Samuel Luke so reported to Parliament, but he, after all, had to provide some excuse for muffing the job. The local justices, who examined the retainers, state that they did so after Sir Lewis had ridden away. In truth Sir Lewis would have been a fool to swim the river (whether or not in full amour as later glosses added) to emerge, dripping wet, in the marshy land on the other bank, without a horse. From there he would have either to cross the bridge where he would meet Sir Samuel, who did have a horse, or make for the Bedford road where even Sir Samuel could have intercepted him. Since the posse had approached his front door it seems likely that Sir Lewis galloped down the drive from the garden front to the ford at Clapham and thence, by the future A6, north.[192]

Parliament did not know what it possibly missed. Tibbutt says that the King may have intended to move south from Leicester, through Huntingdon, to stay at

Bromham on that very day when Sir Lewis was rapidly leaving. It is a fact that Charles left Leicester on July 26th, but he went to Beverley. It seems unlikely that he would so completely have reversed his progress and one wonders what he would have expected to achieve in parliamentarian Bedfordshire.

Sir Lewis joined the King and, in August, was appointed Colonel of a regiment of foot to be assembled at Nottingham. It did so, for it was at Shrewsbury on 16th September, in which month Sir Lewis also found time to command a detachment of horse in a skirmish at Worcester. Both he and Samuel Luke, on opposite sides, were at Edghill where the over enthusiastic Royalist cavalry charged off across the country, missing the Parliamentary cavalry on the right wing. The latter severely mauled Sir Lewis' regiment.

Sir Lewis and Prince Rupert got on well. They were together on November 1st 1642 near Aylesbury when Rupert charged through two lines of parliamentary infantry and found himself surrounded by their cavalry. A parliamentary account[193] describes Sir Lewis, who saved the day, as "a man of as much acrimony and spleen as any of the malignants". He advanced his own company of horse, each rider having behind him a musketeer who, at a suitable distance, dismounted and fired. Much later, during the first world war, cavalry were again to dismount in the same fashion, although the latter day horses would not have taken two men as did the heavier Civil War mounts. Sir Lewis was reported "absolutely to be dead" after the battle of Turnham Green later in November when Parliament decisively repulsed a Royalist advance on London. He was not. He and Prince Rupert had retreated in the manner best liked by both by charging through the parliamentary foot soldiers.

Armies, in those days, lived off the country (that is to say, the people) and when this jockeying for position changed to garrisoning fortified towns Sir Lewis was to discover that organised supply was not a royalist strongpoint. At the end of 1642 he was appointed governor of Abingdon and complained to Prince Rupert that his men lacked clothes to cover their nakedness and boots to put on their feet. Nevertheless, he was able to take some musketeers to help relieve the siege of Reading on April 18th 1643. It was here that his servant Flower swum the Thames to inform the garrison of approaching supplies of ammunition. For some reason he swam back again and was captured. Parliament intercepted the ammunition. On April 27th the Royalist commander marched out with the honours of war. The King was unaware of the negotiations which led to this and he, Rupert and Lewis attacked a parliamentary force guarding the bridge at Caversham on April 24th. Sir Samuel Luke was with this force and reports that Sir Lewis led the van. In the end, though, disease drove the parliamentary forces out of Reading and Sir Lewis returned to Abingdon.

Luke had not been idle in the affairs of Sir Lewis. He reported to Parliament that Bromham Hall had been sacked. Those involved seem likely to have anticipated the order that they should be recompensed out of the goods seized. All that was reported to be there was some grain which netted £31.1s.3d.[194] The official record states that the residue of Sir Lewis' goods were "caryed away" by soldiers before the sequestration.[195]

Sir Lewis must have enjoyed his next recorded excursion after the battle of Newbury in September 1643. He and Sir John Digby of Gayhurst[196] suddenly appeared, with 400 horsemen, in Ampthill where the somewhat surprised Bedfordshire Parliamentary Committee was meeting. The royalists had moved through Bedfordshire undetected by the simple device of disguising themselves as parliamentarians. To lend authenticity to the deception they had captured a few Londoners and others on the way and let them go when they declared themselves for Parliament. Tibbutt assumes that Sir Lewis went on with the royalists to Bedford[197] because it plundered Sir Samuel Luke's house at Cople on the way.

The parliamentary commander called out the militia but the good people of Bedford, despite a distinct leaning to parliament, apparently saw no point in endangering themselves and only 18 responded, whereupon Sir John Hurry occupied the town on October 16th and 17th 1643. There is evidence that the King expected his forces to remain in Bedfordshire for some time.[198] Parliamentary news sheets reported that the primary royalist purpose was to occupy Newport Pagnell and Bedford. This would have cut Parliament's lines of supply to London. The royalists did intend to garrison Newport Pagnell to this end. Their foray to Ampthill and Bedford may have been intended as a diversion while Newport was fortified by Sir Lewis, who issued warrants demanding money and goods from the surrounding district with threats of plunder and pillage if they were not obeyed. Parliament heard at this time that Sir Lewis was to be made a Lord and the Commons voted his actions to be high treason and appointed a committee to draw up Articles of Impeachment for that purpose. He was described as the "chiefe ringleader of that rebellious crue." No less than the Earl of Essex was instructed to assemble a large force at St Albans, but he admitted that the royalist forces at Newport were greater than anything he could send against them. Wisely, therefore, he sent Sergeant Major General Shippen to attack Newport. Shippen must have been surprised when the royalists abandoned Newport Pagnell without a fight. He can hardly have believed his own explanation that they did so out of "panick fear". Sir Samuel Luke gave the correct reason to John Pym. The truth was that Lewis had neither ammunition nor powder. The King was relatively near, in Oxford, and Prince Rupert and Lewis had been pressing him to send supplies. Not for the first, nor the last, time they were sent too late. They were on their way, but Sir Frederick Cornwallis, who had been sent to tell him this, gave the wrong message. Rupert threw up his hands in despair, writing, "the mistake about Newport Paganel spoyled all", and is told that the King will in future be more careful by whom he conveys his orders. Sir Lewis retired to Towcester, which he had no intention of attempting to garrison, and then returned to Abingdon. To add insult to injury Sir Samuel was appointed to command Newport and did so for the next, crucial, eighteen months. It was a strategic point for the royalists. Holding it would not have won the war but losing it allowed London to be supplied and must count among the military blunders of history.

Abingdon was never particularly important because the royalists, who had lost Reading, had a garrison at Wallingford. Abingdon was abandoned on 25th May after Rupert had relieved Newark. Lewis did not stay long as assistant to the governor of Oxford after the King left on June 3rd. Essex had managed to get himself cut off in Cornwall and Lewis was with the royalist army when it left Exeter in pursuit of him. Essex and the cavalry escaped. The parliamentary infantry surrendered on September 1st. It was the last Royalist success in the West.

Lewis was made Serjeant Major General of Dorset and left to garrison Sherborne Castle with 200 horse and 200 foot. Sherborne was the seat of the Earl of Bristol so Lewis knew it well. There were great plans to increase his force by the addition of 500 horse, 100 dragoons and 1500 foot, supplied by the local gentry. If this force had materialised and Weymouth been held as a supply port the royalists could have held the West. But Taunton was abandoned in December (for which Sir Lewis was blamed) and Colonel Ashburnham was court-martialled in Oxford for losing Weymouth. Lewis retook Weymouth on February 9th 1645. The parliamentarians under Waller counter-attacked. Cromwell was sent to join Waller. Unfortunately Lord Goring was sent to help Sir Lewis. Clarendon had no hesitation in blaming Goring's "natural invigilance" for the eventual loss of Weymouth after 18 days of fighting. Weymouth was a good deal more important than Newport Pagnell. Its loss reversed the advantage in the West. Cromwell brought in by sea to it 1500 horse and 1500 foot to add to the existing parliamentary army of 2000 at Taunton. The King was defeated at Naseby and the New Model Army was marching west. Fairfax defeated Goring at Langport and took Bridgewater. Sherborne, which was to have been the centre of royalist strength in the West, was now virtually the only royalist stronghold there; and Fairfax sent Colonel Pickering, on July 27th 1645, to assess its strength.

On August 1st 1645 Fairfax laid siege to Sherborne and Lewis set about reinforcing it. Lewis gained a considerable advantage by stationing two of his crackshot gamekeepers, with fowling pieces, as snipers, to pick off those setting up the heavy siege guns that Fairfax had sent in by sea. Meanwhile Fairfax had busied himself mining under the walls and had almost been shot by his own men. The guns opened fire on 14th August and made a breach through which ten men could march abreast. Lewis refused to surrender but by the 15th most of the castle and all its walls were in Fairfax's hands. Sir Lewis offered to surrender with honour. Not surprisingly, in view of the language Sir Lewis had used the day before, Fairfax offered the defenders only their lives. Sir Lewis and Lady Dyve were taken prisoner along with 400 others including 32 officers, 18 guns, 600 muskets and 39 barrels of powder. The parliamentary troops plundered the castle and the next day held a great market of their booty for the locals. Fairfax decided to demolish the castle rather than garrisoning it.

The prisoners were taken to London and Sir Lewis was brought before the Commons where he impudently knelt on one knee until ordered by the Speaker to kneel on both. He was committed, for high treason, to the Tower during the pleasure of the House. The House refused his request, in October 1645, that he be granted an allowance from his estates but, on March 27th 1646, allowed him £4 for the maintenance of himself and his children. His wife had died in childbirth at Bromham and was buried there on February 24th 1645. Sir Lewis remained in the Tower for more than two years. He was clearly kept well informed of rumour and intrigue and was keen to persuade the King to work on what he believed to be a growing disunity between the parliamentary leaders and between them and the rank and file of the army. He was sure that it would be a good move for Charles to come to London from where he would be best placed to foster, and benefit from, this situation. Of the mixed bunch of enemies of the Commons in the Tower at the time Sir Lewis found John Lilburne, the Leveller – and the period Trotskyite – particularly interesting. Lilburne told him at length of his conversation with Cromwell when the latter visited him in the Tower on September 5th 1647.[199] The information was passed on to the King who would have been interested in Lilburne's suspicions that Cromwell and Ireton had done a deal with Charles. Lilburne must have struck Sir Lewis as a complex character. He informs the King, on September 13th 1647 that while Lilburne dined with Cromwell and the Governor of the Tower following Cromwell's conversation with him he,

> "... tooke occasion to speake of the hard usage of the rest of the prisoners in the Tower, representing the great injustice and inhumanity was exercised towards them in keeping them so long in prison, takeing all their estates from them and allowing them nothing for subsistence, and not calling them to a legall triall, which hee said gave the world to speake hardly of the Parliament and army, and to believe that their crimes were not such as the law could take hold of wherby to punish them, so as he conceived it would be an action much to [Cromwell's] owne honour and the army's advantage either to procure their liberty or at least for the time past, as well as for the time present, a competent allowance of

maintainance for an honourable subsistence according to their severall quallitys until they were absolutely freed"

On July 31st 1647 Lewis had added a postscript to his letter to the King saying, ". . . it is thought that tomorrow [the House of Commons] will vote your Majestie's return to London with honour and safety to sit in parliament without imposeing any conditions upon your majestie, which is the only thing to be desired if armes were laid downe on both sides, which I hope will be effected by your Majestie's mediation."

    He continued to press the point. In his last two letters to the King from the Tower he suggested that Rainsborough's hatred of Cromwell had led him to stir up a faction intent on avoiding any harm to the King. He was convinced that the majority of the army held this opinion and would join the five regiments that Lilburne told him had promised to adhere to them. It seems that the King cautioned him about trusting Rainsborough for at some time later in November he wrote assuring the King that Rainsborough had, indeed, said what he had reported. This letter seems never to have been sent.

    If he was right then the degree to which Charles mishandled his dealings with the victorious parliamentarians is apparent.

    So Sir Lewis was still in the Tower when the royalist prisoners met for dinner on August 19th 1647. The King having sent them four fat bucks. But shortly after this the Lieutenant Governor of the Tower sued Sir Lewis for debt and he was moved, presumably in November, to the King's Bench Prison where he settled down comfortably enough, despite considering the move unlawful. Sir John Lenthall, the governor of that prison, may well have been regarded as trustworthy, since his brother was Speaker of the Commons, but he accepted Sir Lewis' parole and allowed him to move around outside the walls freely. Presumably, like the inhabitants of Brixton Prison in the 1980s, he was expected to return in the evening, but then he often dined with the governor. When the Speaker heard of this he instructed his brother to have a special care of Sir Lewis, as a most dangerous person. The governor mildly suggested to Sir Lewis that he stay inside for a few days but, as things so often are, once a weakness has been noted, Sir Lewis learned that it was intended to issue a warrant for his close commitment to the common gaol. His informants went further, advising that "there were desperate intentions against me and, . . . as I tendered my life to make an Escape." So he did.

    He told the governor that as he had stayed inside for several days he intended to go into the Town the following evening. The governor then told him about the warrant, saying that he would have to obey it when it came. Sir Lewis simulated rage, banging a candlestick on the table with such force as to damage it, and declaring that he was no longer bound by his parole. Lady Lenthall got involved and accused Sir Lewis of striking her. Sir Lewis reckoned she would have struck him had her husband and daughters not intervened. The next morning (January 15th 1648) Sir Lewis gave instruction for the cleaning up of his new prison cell, which he had been told was "a most nastie and filthie roome not fit for a Dogge to be in." A heap of coals was removed[200] and a fire lit. Any right-thinking person acquainted with Sir Lewis would, upon these signs of apparent resignation, have had him clapped in irons, and even the governor should have become suspicious when he ordered supper and invited his fellow prisoners to join him in a farewell meal. The supper was brought in from outside the prison with much coming and going, and perhaps a little friendly sharing of the wine, and Sir Lewis, on a dark, cold winter's night, simply walked out "into a place where I knew I should be welcome." He did so none too soon for on the previous day the Commons had instructed the Solicitor General to commence proceedings to try him for treason.

Sir Lewis joined the Duke of Hamilton who was preparing in Scotland to invade England on behalf of the King. They marched towards Preston where they met Cromwell who, with a smaller force, annihilated them. Sir Lewis was captured on the battlefield and was awaiting trial in Whitehall on the day Charles I was executed. Yet again his friends had kept an eye on the situation, and, this time, a boat on the Thames. No doubt they stood well back when he arrived. In those days you could guarantee that the lavatories discharged straight into some watercourse or other. The Thames was long regarded as particularly useful for this purpose. So Sir Lewis excused himself and while his guards politely stood outside the door, relying on the fact that U bends had yet to be invented, he discharged himself down the "jakes".[201] Fairfax issued a description of the man he wanted as "of middle size, and hath a flaxen hair, in sad coloured apparel". You would have thought it would have occurred to someone that Sir Lewis would have changed his sad apparel. He was safely in The Hague in June 1649.

He went from there to the Isle of Man, which the Earl of Derby was holding for those who some thought of as the new King, and then crossed to Ulster to deliver to Viscount Montgomery of Ards the King's commission as General of the royal forces there. He wrote a long report on the conduct of the King's affairs in Ireland, including an account of some of Cromwell's early victories.[202] Lord Inchiquin was furious and Lewis later had to admit to Charles that the report contained a number of mistakes. Sir Lewis had not waited around at The Hague for this to surface. He could never resist a good fight. The Thirty Years War had theoretically been ended by the Treaty of Westphalia in 1648 but CV Wedgwood says,[203] "Mazarin's policy of seizing good strategic points on the frontier vitiated the settlement. The Peace of

Westphalia was, like most peace treaties, a rearrangement of the European map ready for the next war". Lewis and George Digby were in the service of Mazarin at the capture of Rethel in December 1650.[204] Lewis continued to have responsibilities in France and Italy, mainly on behalf of the new Earl of Bristol, but the glory had departed. He dined with the diarist Evelyn in The Hague in December 1651 and recounted the fun he had had, including the detail of his escapes. Evelyn clearly found him interesting company but remarks, in his diary, "This knight was indeed a valiant gentleman; but a little given to romance." One might be forgiven for a little embellishment when reminiscing on one's slide down a sewer into the scarcely more salubrious Thames.

George Digby was made governor of the French town of Mantes, which covered the approaches to Paris. He appointed Lewis Deputy Governor of Lile Adam (north of Paris on the Oisse) but he did not appoint him his deputy, as Lewis wished, when he, as second Earl of Bristol, was made ambassador to Spain. Lewis was stuck in Italy with a bad leg when Charles returned as King in 1660.

It is well known that Charles II was neither very anxious to punish those who had rebelled against his father nor compensate, let alone reward, those who had incurred great personal loss in supporting him. Under an Act of Parliament of July 1651 for the sale of lands forfeited to Parliament for treason, trustees, in March 1652, sold the Dyve lands in Bromham, Biddenham, Kempston and Steventon to Sir John Strangeways for £4967.13s.5d. The rents received from the Bromham estates were assessed by the sequestrators in September 1648 at a total of £481.8s.6d together with unlet land valued at £139 and the parsonage at £30.[205] Clearly all the government wanted, as usual, was money. Sir John was Sir Lewis' father-in-law and a royalist who had been with him in the Tower, from which he had been released in April 1648. The lands were returned to Sir Lewis but it is clear that he never made up the financial losses he had suffered. Looking over Pepys shoulder, we catch last glimpses of Sir Lewis Dyve in London on December 6th 1667 and January 1st 1668. Pepys writes, "…. To see how some old gamesters, that have no money now to spend as formerly, do come and look on as among others Sir Lewis Dyves, who was here, and hath been a great gamester in his time." It was estimated, according to Pepys, that he has lost £164,000 in the King's service.

Lewis conveyed the Bromham property to his son Francis before he died at a small estate he then regarded as home at Comberhay in Somerset in April 1669. He is buried there.

Francis Dyve, the heir of Sir Lewis, became a gentleman of the King's Privy Chamber but was never knighted. He died in 1685 without male issue.[206] His younger brother Lewis spent many years with the army in Ireland but never rose above the rank of captain. He succeeded to the Bromham estates and died there the next year (1686). His son Lewis, who the vicar reported, in 1706, sometimes to live there,[207] sold the Bromham estates, in 1708, to Sir Thomas Trevor, Chief Justice of the Common Pleas.[208] The Victoria County History gives the price as £21,394. This is presumably a combination of a number of items of cost including the mortgages since the conveyance itself does not reveal this figure.[209]

Thomas, Lord Trevor and sons

Sir Thomas Trevor, who purchased the Bromham estate in 1708, was just the man to follow the common practice of aspiring men in the eighteenth century to rebuild his mansion as a great country house. He undoubtedly had ambition, which he did not allow principle to interfere with, and he was said to have acquired great wealth in the practice of the law. Neither he nor any of his succeeding sons did so. The reason may be, as the Victoria County History says, that "the Trevors never took any prominent part in local affairs. The first Viscount Hampden was indeed the only one of them who made Bromham Hall his home".[210]

The first Baron Trevor of Bromham came of a distinguished Welsh line.[211] His great uncle Thomas was solicitor to Charles I when Prince of Wales and on May 12th 1625 he was made a baron of the Court of Exchequer. In 1636 he took part in the joint judicial opinion that ship-money was legal and in the trial of Hampden.[212] He was impeached for this by the Long Parliament in 1640 and imprisoned. He paid the massive fine of £6000, whereupon he was allowed to resume his judicial duties. He seems to have learned from this experience to be careful for when Charles I asked the three judges then sitting in London to read in court the writs moving parliament from Westminster to Oxford Trevor B and Reeve J ordered the arrest of the messengers. It seems that the execution of the King was too much for great-uncle Thomas, however, because he, with five other judges, refused reappointment on February 8th 1649. He died on December 21st 1656. His son was created a baronet but that title died with him in 1676.

This Thomas' brother, and our Thomas' grandfather, John, was knighted in 1619 and was MP for Flint in 1620, 1624 and 1625. He remained in the Long Parliament as a moderate parliamentarian and favoured the restoration. He married Margaret Trevanion and died in 1673 the year after his eldest son, also John and the father of our Thomas. This son also sat as member of parliament for Flint. He was a member of General Monk's council which recalled Charles II in 1660. Although he too had been a moderate parliamentarian Charles II knighted him and, in 1668, sent him as ambassador to France. On his return he was appointed to the Privy Council and purchased, for £8000, one of the offices of principal secretary of state. He married Ruth, fourth daughter of John Hampden, whom his uncle had tried. They had four sons, John, Thomas, Richard and Edward, and a daughter Susannah.[213]

Before we consider the career of Thomas we should note his elder brother who stayed at the family estate at Trevallyn but whose grand-daughter, Lucy, (born 1706) married Edward Rice. Their son George married Cecil, Baroness Dynevor. She was the only surviving child of William, first Earl Talbot whose inherited barony of Dynevor was, by letters patent, permitted to pass to her in her own right and thence to her heirs male.[214] Her grandson, the fourth Baron Dynevor died in 1868 without male heir and his cousin became the 5th baron.[215] The fourth Lord Dynevor frequently lived at Bromham and was responsible for several projects, including the restoration of the church, for which his daughter subsequently received most of the credit. He, who had added Trevor to his name, so becoming George Rice Rice-Trevor,[216] had five daughters. The youngest was Elianore Mary, the celebrated "Miss Rice-Trevor" who dominated Victorian Bromham.[217] Her eldest sister married Edmund Ffolliot Wingfield and it was he who ultimately inherited, and sold, the Bromham estate.

Let us return to Thomas, first Lord Trevor of Bromham. It is unlikely that the judges of the reign of Queen Anne were a jolly lot so it says something of Thomas that Mr Speaker Onslow said of him that he was "the most reserved, grave and austere judge I ever saw in Westminster Hall".[218] In pursuit of his career he changed sides from Jacobite to Hanoverian and from Tory to Whig, and back, with a facility which caused some to suggest that he lacked any principle. Yet Onslow said of him, "he was the only man almost that I ever knew that changed his party as he had done, that preserved so general an esteem with all parties as he did."[219]

Thomas entered the Inner Temple in 1672 (the year of his father's death) and was called to the bar on November 28th 1680. He rose at a spectacular rate, becoming a bencher of his Inn in 1689 and solicitor general on May 3rd 1692 under William III. He was automatically knighted as holder of that office. He first declined the offer to be attorney general, but was so appointed on June 8th 1695. He was responsible for conducting trials for treason of those who had plotted the assassination of the King and was said to have been noted for his patience, ability and learning. The Tories forced William III to dismiss Lord Somers as Lord Chancellor on April 17th 1700. Thomas, being then a Tory, was offered appointment as Lord Keeper,[220] but he declined. Perhaps that was one of his many carefully judged moves. He would hardly have been popular if forced upon the King but his refusal was followed by his appointment, on June 25th 1701, to the more permanent post of Chief Justice of the Common Pleas. Queen Anne reappointed him on her accession and he held the office for the whole of her reign. By 1712 he had wisely switched from Tory to Whig, no doubt noting that the Whigs did better under Anne. The government needed the approval of the House of Lords for the Treaty of Utrecht and Thomas was created Baron Trevor of

Bromham on January 1st 1712.[221] He was the first judge since Judge Jeffreys to sit in the Lords and some doubted the constitutionality of this. It was said that some also disliked the difference in his behaviour after his elevation.

George I succeeded Anne in 1714. It should be remembered that, had Anne not taken everyone by surprise by dying, the Stuart faction might have been sufficiently organised to have had their candidate appointed King in preference to the Hanoverians. Thomas had not changed sides quickly enough and so the King was likely to be, and was,[222] advised to remove him from office by the triumphant side, anxious to promote its own supporters.

He was deprived of his office as Chief Justice of the Common Pleas on October 14th 1714. He said he would have tried the question of the power of the King to remove him had it not appeared from the fact that Holt CJ had issued a new commission when Queen Anne came to the throne that his previous appointment ended on the demise of the Crown. These days, of course, the suggestion that an English judge needs reappointment on the accession of a new sovereign would receive no support and the removal of Lord Trevor would seem to have been unconstitutional.

Undeterred, Lord Trevor again changed his party back to the Whigs. He liked being at court and perhaps he had kept his contacts for he was well enough remembered to be made lord privy seal in 1726 and a lord justice when George I went to Hanover in 1727. He retained the office of lord privy seal when George II came to the throne and he was appointed Lord President of the Council on May 8th 1730. Onslow says that he had much joy in both offices, but that in the second was short lived for he died, aged 74, at Bromham on June 19th 1730. Benjamin Rogers heard a rumour of this on 22nd which was confirmed on 25th. He records that the funeral took place at Bromham at 8 pm on July 1st attended by Lord Trevor's three sons, and a number of local land owners who acted as pall bearers.

Thomas Trevor had first married Elizabeth Searle of Finchley, by whom he had two sons, Thomas and John, and three daughters. After her death he married Anne Weldon, widow of Sir Robert Bernard, bart. of Brampton, by whom he had three sons, Robert, Richard and Edward. The three eldest sons each succeeded to the title in turn. Of all his sons only Robert, the fourth baron, had any children. Kuhlicke[223] says that Thomas, second baron, was a quiet pious man of no outstanding qualification. He did have one outstanding achievement. His daughter Elizabeth married the future Duke of Marlborough in 1732 and this seems to have inspired the annual celebration at Bromham of her birthday (December 19th).[224] His brother John paid the £250 which the memorial to their father in Bromham church cost, but this Thomas founded the parish library in the room over the south porch of the church where, it is said, he liked to work.[225] When he died, on March

22nd 1753, he was succeeded by his brother John who had been made a judge for Wales in 1724 and was MP for Woodstock in 1741 and 1747.[226] John married Elizabeth daughter of Sir Richard Steele, a noted essayist, but, like his elder brother, had only one daughter.[227] When he died, in London, on 27th September 1764, therefore, he was succeeded by his half brother Robert. Like his father and brothers, of course, Robert was descended from John Hampden. He, however, had become heir to the Hampden estates in Buckinghamshire and had already added to his name that of Hampden, after that of Trevor.[228] He was sent as British ambassador to Austria in 1737 and to The Hague in 1739. He was created the first Viscount Hampden in June 1776. He was a Fellow of the Society of Antiquaries and a Fellow of the Royal Society as well as a considerable classical scholar, writing a commentary on Horace and a number of poems in Latin which were published in a limited edition by his second son John in Parma in 1792. Among these was the lengthy *Villa Bromhamensis*.[229] He married in 1743 and had two sons and two daughters. He enjoyed fishing and was doing so at Bromham a week before his death on August 22nd 1783. Both his sons succeeded him in turn. Although both married (Thomas Trevor Hampden twice) both continued the family tradition of dying childless. Both died in 1824 and both titles died with John the third viscount and sixth baron.[230] The latter, like his father, had pursued a diplomatic career, being the British minister to the Elector Palatine and to the Court of Turin. John left the Bromham estates to his relative George Rice Rice-Trevor who, as we have seen, was to succeed as the fourth baron Dynevor. By that same will the estate passed to George's daughters on his accession to the title.[231] George himself did not die until 1868. According to Harvey[232] George frequently resided at Bromham and his youngest daughter Elianore, who remained unmarried, made it her permanent home. So, after more than two centuries, the lord of the manor of Bromham, and the owner of most of it, could be said to be in residence.

The Rice-Trevors and the last flourishing of the Estate

Of all the owners of the Bromham estates whom we have so far noted few could be said to be more than occasionally resident. Thomas, second baron Trevor, was an exception and his brother John clearly took an interest in the development of the village. But Elianore Mary Rice-Trevor, youngest daughter of the fourth baron Dynevor was of a wholly different type. She was not inclined to stay in Bromham in the winter and the resident housekeeper was left to deal with the fact that the river might well flow in the side entrance to the house. But in the summer she was very much in evidence. She paid for the renovation of a church badly in need of repair (and in the process had torn out some rather unfortunate earlier alterations).

As we have seen, not only did she pay for the school building but she listened to the teaching at the school, she gave annual parties for the children and their parents, she personally taught, and clothed, her select group of girls, she ran an "industrial" school and she saw to the distribution of coal in the winter and food and clothing at Christmas. Her death in Victoria's diamond jubilee year of 1897 ought to have left her tenants desolate for they would never again have a resident Lord of the Manor who took such an interest in them. In many ways the sale of the estate in 1924 was simply the inevitable result of her childless departure.

Elianore Mary Rice-Trevor was typical of Victorian landed gentry. She was just that. She was, indeed, the sixth largest landowner in Bedfordshire and although her 6,229 acres did not compare with the Duke of Bedford's lands they were not markedly less than those of the heiress of Earl Grey at Wrest.[233] Rev. CF Farrar[234] writes of her:

> "In my youth we never dared to steal by here in a boat, save in the early morning or late in the evening, for there dwelt here a stern lady, the Hon. Miss Rice Trevor, who had no use for boating folks intruding on her domain. She, like Miss Betsy Trotwood in pursuit of the donkey boys, would have rushed out of the drawing-room window and screamed herself hoarse at us for trespassers."

With respect, she would have done no such thing. She would have sent a servant to see them off.[235] Farrar is right, however, to imply that she expected respect, and why not, for the Dynevors descend directly from the princes of south Wales. Her tenants, no doubt, were on the whole content to provide her with that respect. We have seen that Arthur Mayhew, one of her farm-labouring tenants, did not share this general opinion when, in 1873, she evicted his family from their cottage because of his trade union activities on behalf of the Agricultural Labourers Union. These days a landlord who provided accommodation such as that enjoyed by the Mayhew family would be prosecuted for quite a number of offences, but 130 years ago their miserable cottage was a lot better than the hovels of many farm labourers in "unprotected" villages.

Most of her tenants were likely to have been quite genuine in their expressions of pleasure at her annual return in late Spring, usually from Bournemouth. The vicar certainly knew how to maintain his invitations to the Hall and had the church bells rung as, on those returns, her carriage came down Biddenham Hill. The "Bedford Mercury", assiduously every year reported the event[236] and the village girls, many in the summer uniform of her Sunday school class, decorated the park gates and stood in a line to curtsy as she passed. At the end of the tiring journey she would meet them at the Hall to hear how the winter had gone and to communicate her plans for the summer. Her annual treat for the school children in the gardens of the Hall was a sufficient event again for the "Mercury" not to miss it.[237] The adult members of the community were invited each year to an "At Home".[238] There were also parties for the old people.

Of course this was not revolutionary, although the fact that the local Press so regularly reported the events suggests they were not run of the mill. The second Lord Trevor, as we have said, had an annual party to celebrate the anniversary of his daughter's marriage to the second Duke of Marlborough. Cakes and ale for the tenantry were a common mark of the special family events of their landlords and these also continued through the nineteenth century. When two of her nephews came of age Miss Rice-Trevor gave receptions.[239] There is evidence that the previous generation of Dynevors had provided similar celebrations and distributed food and clothing. When George Rice-Trevor, in 1825, wrote indicating his intention to continue to pay £20 per year towards the salary of the schoolmaster he also indicated that he would "pay the percentage as before to the Benefit Society" and continue to provide the "Premiums" for the best gardens as before. The Bedford Times for 23rd October 1847 reports:

> "We had pleasure, in our last week's waper (sic) of reporting a dinner given by the Honourable George Rice-Trevor MP., for his tenantry and their wives; but during the past week, a scene, if possible far more interesting than that occurred at Bromham Hall. Although the famous had a treat, Mr and Mrs Trevor (whose ever watchful eyes are over the comforts and interest of the poor) have not forgotten them in the midst of their liberality, for every poor family in the three parishes of Bromham, Stagsden and Biddenham, have received at the hands of this truly benevolent family, gifts of the most useful description, comprising articles of clothing, and divers necessary household matters, according to the size and wants of their respective families; an event which will be far more lasting in their recollections than a mere dinner or tea drinking, and when they look for years to come, upon these useful articles, it will bring to their grateful remembrance, the noble benefactor and benefactress, from whom they received this mark of kindness. A Packet of Tea, was one of the gifts presented to nearly, if not all, the families, thus giving an opportunity to every poor old man and woman, in the three villages, in their own chimney corner, and in their own humble way, of enjoying the favourite beverage, and while drinking it, they would; with feelings of the greatest gratitude, most earnestly wish that the estate on which, in the order of a kind providence, it is their privilege to live, might long remain in that noble family."

Precisely so. One can understand Miss Rice-Trevor expecting the same sort of response as she contemplated the distribution, in her absence, of the annual Christmas bundle of food and clothing and the reporter whose uncritically fulsome comments cause modern readers to smile wryly, especially at the supposition that the poor had a chimney corner, was right in some ways because those of Miss Rice-Trevor's girls still alive in the 1950s remembered the bundles distributed in her day.[240] Miss Rice-Trevor did not forget either. On her death she bequeathed £400 of 2½% annuities producing £10 per year to continue provision for the poor. She also bequeathed an identical sum to continue the provision for her Sunday School Class.[241] These girls were her special care. She equipped them with both summer and winter uniforms: a print dress with a cross over top, a Holland cape bound with braid, boots and a white hat for the summer; a blue serge dress and a red astrakhan cape for the winter. She appears to have made a point of noticing and remembering. When Miss Pugh (later Mrs Webster) was newly a pupil at Bromham School she was forgotten in the prize giving. She also remembered in the 1950s that Miss Rice-Trevor had sent her a doll to make up for the omission. In this respect she was not untypical of many members of a now somewhat derided Victorian aristocracy.[242]

   Her standard of living must have amazed those of her tenants who came to work for her as domestic servants, especially if they came from the cottages of agricultural workers on her estates. She kept a butler, of course, a footman, four gardeners and a boy, three stablemen, an estate carpenter, a bricklayer and a steward; a lady's maid, three house maids, three kitchen maids, a stillroom maid, a between maid and a cook. A specialist brew man attended to the brewhouse next to the laundry during the annual brewing of beer. Presumably a number of these accompanied her to Bournemouth when Mrs Church acted as housekeeper in her absence. Naturally she kept a coach. Although the above list does not mention him specifically one of the stablemen must have been the coachman. Mr Jesse Gardener was the last coachman at the Hall. He retired and lived in Grange Lane into the late 1940s.

   Village life naturally responded to this sort of leadership and there were annual flower shows, usually then called cottage garden shows,[243] celebrations for May Day and the Annual Feast. The latter probably began as a sort of harvest supper and the villagers originally provided their own entertainment with local fiddlers leading the dancing. The tradition persisted, although in the twentieth century the entertainment was provided by an itinerant funfair. Numerous inter-village cricket matches are reported in the local Press. Miss Rice-Trevor would not wholly have approved of all the leisure activities of her tenants. One doubts whether she, or any other inhabitants, would have agreed that the village had ever deserved the critical comment of its state in 1814 made by a Methodist writer[244] that, "At this time, the parish of Bromham was, like many others, at that period, in a state of great darkness, both spiritually and socially. The people were in the grossest ignorance, drunkenness and profanity abounded." She had certainly taken any ignorance in hand and profanity would not have occurred in her presence. She kept drunkenness at a distance by ensuring that the public houses were on the Kempston boundary and her Bromham was certainly not socially dark.

Miss Rice-Trevor's tenants were not as subservient as the picture painted above might suggest. She would not have approved of Protestant non-conformists but some of her tenants were active Methodists who held meetings in the premises they rented.[245]

---

[173] *Magna Britannia (Bedfordshire):* D&S Lysons (1813) Cadell and Davies, London. at p.163. Lysons attributes the brass to Thomas Woodville, and, missing therefore the connection of that family with Bromham, suggests that the brass was moved from another church.

[174] The second Sir Lewis, in 1638 leased, from the Provost and College of Eton, the rectory and grange on condition that he supplied the parishioners with grass at Whitsun and straw at Christmas to strew the church floor.

[175] Godber at p.217.

[176] Godber at p.178.

[177] VCH Vol.2 p.96. See Appendix V, below, - "Field Names".

[178] English wool was the finest in Europe, much sought after, and the most important export.

[179] The grandson, who maintained that the attackers numbered sixteen or seventeen, names William Broughe, Lewis Simson, Thomas Smythe (yeoman), Henry Tommes (yeoman), Randolph Walton (yeoman), Brian Inglande (late of Clapham, yeoman), David Faldoe of Biddenham (gentleman), Edward Leader (yeoman) and William Deerye (of Biddenham, labourer). William Broughe ("a man of bad behaviour") was a particular buddy of John Dyve. It was he who had first said "there is noe remedye but we must fight it out".

[180] Godber at p.218 Bedfordshire and Luton Archive and record Service (BLARS) TW 1016.

[181] In the Parish Register for Bromham on 27th October 1623 Thomas Smith married a lady called Dennis.

[182] It is said that the first Sir Lewis had requested this on his deathbed. The property claims which had caused the dispute, however, were not yet resolved.

[183] The other godparents were Francis Godwin and Lord StJohn of Bletsoe whose succesors became parliamentarians, and so, enemies of Sir Lewis.

[184] Presumably it was her royalism that legally explained their sequestration after the Civil War, although Sir Lewis seems to have received all the rents.

[185] *Life and Letters of Sir Lewis Dyve 1599-1669:* HG Tibbutt (1946)Vol 27 BHRS. (Tibbutt)

[186] Tibbutt, above note 1, at pp.3-4.

[187] *The Thirty Years War:* CV Wedgwood (1938 Jonathan Cape) Folio Society Edition 1999 at p.162.

[188] That son, Lewis, is buried at Bromham.

[189] The first year of the reign of Charles I.

[190] The Dyves were among the very few royalist gentry in Bedfordshire. The Botelers of Biddenham were for parliament.

[191] Plenty of writers have subsequently repeated the story. The romantic CF Farrar can be relied on to do so in *Ouse's Silent Tide* (1921 Sidney Press Bedford) at p. 60 as does FG Emmerson, as fact, in his introduction to the Bromham entries in *Bedfordshire Parish Registers"* (1937 Bedford County Record Office). Tibbutt, however, is sceptical (pp. 24-5).

[192] The noted Bedford historian FW Kuhlicke (1947) 1 Bedfordshire Magazine 199 – reviewing Tibbutt – is unusually inventive in stating that Luke's troopers surrounded the Hall.

[193] See, Tibbutt at p.29.

[194] See, Tibbutt at p.33.

[195] See (1986) 65 BHRS at p.139.

[196] Of a family later to take a prominent part in the Gunpowder Plot.

[197] Tibbutt at p.37. But it seems likely that any royalist force would have done that in passing. FW Kuhlicke, however, (1947) 1 BM 199, is certain that Lewis was at Bedford on that occasion.

[198] Tibbutt at p.43.

[199] *The Tower of London Letter Book of Sir Lewis Dyve 1646-47:* Tibbutt, 38 BHRS pp.74 & 85. This collection includes a number of letters written by Lewis to the King in this period.

[200] One always seems, at this time, to encounter a heap of coals in any empty room.

[201] Which, it is suggested, had a rather more specific connotation than the general term "privie" by which the OED defines it. FW Kuhlicke (1947)1 BM 199 calls it a cloaca, which is a sewer, or the gutter connecting with a sewer. It is as well the guards had neglected their history. Slightly more than 100 years before, in January 1547, the Earl of Surrey had attempted, unsuccessfully, to escape from the Tower of London by the same means. It seems unlikely that others had not resorted to this obvious, if unpleasant, resource.

[202] Tibbutt at p. 98.

[203] *The Thirty Years War* (1938 Jonathan Cape.) 1999 Folio Society Edition at p.462.

[204] Rethel is in the Ardennes, north east of Reims on the Aisne. It is, currently, in France.

[205] Ross Lee, *Bedfordshire and the Civil War* (1986) 65 BHRS at p.125. The tenants are here listed by name.

[206] He was assessed for tax on 15 hearths in 1671 – (1934) 16 BHRS page 89 in the 1990 reprint.

[207] See Bell (Ed.) *Episcopal Visitations in Bedfordshire 1706-1720,* 81 BHRS (2002).

[208] At that time the four domesday manors of Bromham, Wakes, Bowles and Brayes were still separately identified – VCH iii 45.

[209] See Appendix V.

[210] VCH ii 60. Rev. Benjamin Rogers went frequently to Bromham and would have made a point of mentioning the presence of his lordship, had he been there. Such mentions as there are might suggest fairly fleeting visits. On the other hand Rogers received a lot of gifts from the second Lord Trevor which do not indicate an absentee, especially as he had no public business to cause him to live elsewhere. See Linnell (Ed), *The Diary of Benjamin Rogers* (1950) 30BHRS at pp.28, 51 & 73.

[211] Charted in detail by FW Kuhlicke (1967) 11 Beds Mag. 27.

[212] State Trials iii 1152.

[213] Kuhlicke, above n. 211, leaves the eldest son John out of his account, but his heirs are important to the history of Bromham.

[214] The lords of Dynefwr were princes of South Wales. A number of them are buried at Strata

Florida.

[215] Surprisingly it was offspring of one of George Rice's other sons by Baroness Dynevor who were also closely connected with Bedfordshire. This son, Edward, became Dean of Gloucester and his younger son Henry, became vicar of Biddenham while one of his numerous daughters married the rector of Carlton.

[216] Rice, incidentally, was an anglicisation of Rees, to which the Barons Dynevor have now reverted.

[217] One of her sisters became Countess of Longford and joined with her in building Bromham school.

[218] Burnet iv 344n.

[219] Foss, *The Judges of England* (Murray 1870) at p.676. is more charitable still, saying that Thomas probably reasoned that it would take a civil war to reinstate the Stuarts and that peace was preferable. Perhaps his principle was loyalty to the constitutional monarch.

[220] The author's first law tutor said that a Lord Keeper was what you appointed if you did not want to call someone Lord Chancellor. The Lord Keeper had all the powers of a Lord Chancellor and sometimes, subsequently, was appointed to the higher office. The Great Seal was frequently held in commission during an interlude between two Chancellors. Thomas actually did hold the Great Seal, briefly, between September 26th and October 19th 1710, as first commissioner. The Seal has not been held in commission since 1835.

[221] Foss, above n.40, says 31st December 1711. The alliance with Holland had, of course, been substantially William's war. Moreover, Ormond, who had succeeded Marlborough, had suffered a series of reverses and embarked the British army (from Dunkirk!) leaving the French to register a number of victories in Holland.

[222] Lord Campbell's *Lives of the Chancellors* iv 349.

[223] Above, n.211. Kuhlicke says that Thomas the second baron died in 1734 but this is incorrect.

[224] Perhaps it was the first of these which Benjamin Rogers missed in 1734 because he did not hear of it till the next morning. It seems unlikely that he would have missed it once established and he certainly attended the next year when her father was prevented by a cold from joining in.

[225] He also gave Mrs Rogers a lottery ticket on February 13th 1734 which her husband seems to have regarded as his when it won £10. See (1949) 30 BHRS at p.51.

[226] Might we suspect the support of the Duke of Marlborough?

[227] Diana born June 10th 1744.

[228] It is recorded that George I asked him why he allowed the name of Hampden to die out. He replied, incorrectly, that a peer could only change his name with the permission of the sovereign.

[229] A copy of this was in the parish library at Bromham. Mr Newman, a farmer from Stagsden, purchased the manuscript on the sale of the Bromham estate. It is believed that both are now in the Borough Library at Bedford.

[230] John liked hare coursing. See Godber at p.462.

[231] This provision of the will was subject to litigation which reached the House of Lords. See p.41 above.

[232] Ibid. at p.48.

[233] Godber at p.466.

[234] CF Farrar, *Ouse's Silent Tide* (Sidney Press, Bedford 1921) at p.60.

[235] How different things were under her successor Robert Skinner Esq. He came by on the old drive when the author and his brothers were borrowing his boat without his permission. Being the youngest, the author was sent to speak to him and he said that he would have helped clean it out save

that he had a bad arm.

[236] See e.g., The Bedford Mercury for 19th June 1880, 28th June 1882, 18th June 1887, 25th May 1893 and 1st June 1895.

[237] See e.g., The Bedford Mercury for 9th September 1876 and 8th September 1877.

[238] See e.g., The Bedford Mercury for 15th September 1888 and 1st November 1890.

[239] See The Bedford Mercury for 1st November 1890 and 6th October 1894.

[240] See the unpublished WI Scrapbook for 1965 for Bromham (Bedfordshire and Luton Archive and Record Service X535/3). Those girls included Miss Tebbutt, Mrs Webster – the daughter of Jesse Pugh, Mrs Cousins – the daughter of Mr Stafferton, the gardener at the Hall, and Miss Seamarks of the Millard family.

[241] One suspects the two may have been merged subsequently. In the 1950s the Skinner family at the Hall were still distributing goods at Christmas in accordance with these charitable bequests.

[242] See Christopher Hibbert, *The English* (Grafton Books 1987) Chap.48 – "Owners of Land".

[243] See e.g., The Bedford Mercury for 11th August 1894 and 3rd August 1895.

[244] In an undated extract from the "Methodist Messenger" Bedfordshire and Luton Archive and Record Service CRT180/295.

[245] See p.29 above.

Chapter VI
LATER LANDSCAPES

The End of the Estate

By reference back to the earlier accounts of the Dyves and Trevors[246] we have now traced the ownership of the Bromham lands from the Conquest to the end of the nineteenth century. It remains only to see the ending of the estate by sale in 1924 and 1926. Frances, the eldest daughter of the fourth baron Trevor, had married Edward Ffolliott Wingfield on May 1st 1848. He died, before Elianore Rice-Trevor (the 4th baron's youngest daughter) in 1865, but the Bromham estate passed to his grandson, Captain George Talbot Wingfield RN on the death of Elianore in 1897. The Wingfields had extensive property, including Ampthill House, and the Bromham estate was sold by auction in two sections in 1924 and 1926. The bulk (60 Lots covering an area of 1,560 acres) was sold in 1924, the auction being held at Bedford Town Hall. At that time the total rents amounted to about £2500. The sale catalogue separately identifies almost all the properties. It is unlikely to be widely available and so it will be worth looking at the more important items in some detail. Most of the description is taken from the catalogue but some comments have been added.[247]

<u>Berry Farm</u> (Bridge End) 80.357 acres (of which only 19 were in the parish of Bromham). There was a stone farmhouse with three sitting rooms, kitchen and scullery, four bedrooms a bathroom and two attic rooms. Part of this house had been built in the seventeenth century. The extensive farm buildings were mainly of stone.

It was noted that much of the land had road frontage and much of it was sold for building from the late 1950s. The farm was let to C and WE King at an annual rent of £120. It sold for £2750.

Bromham Grange (Opposite the western end of Grange Lane) 129.459 acres of arable and pasture, mostly in Bromham. This farm had been part of the property bequeathed to Cauldwell Priory and it passed to Eton College after the Dissolution. It was leased to the second Sir Lewis Dyve, but must have been purchased by the lord of the manor at some time.

In 1924 there was a relatively modern stone farmhouse with six bedrooms and two attic rooms. There was also a stone built, two bedroomed cottage and extensive stone built farm buildings, including a coach house. A stream that ran from the grounds of Bromham House crossed the Northampton Road and was dammed to form a pond beside the drive leading to the farmhouse. Here too was one of the major springs in the parish. Like Berry Farm at the time, the water for this farmhouse came from a well but in this case it was pumped to a tank said, in the catalogue, to be in the attic but in the author's recollection rather visibly on the roof. In 1786 this farm had been let to one of the Negus family, who appear, at that time, also to have occupied one of the other farms in the parish.[248] In 1924 this farm was let to GF Collins at an annual rent of £182.4s. It sold for £3750. It is believed that Mr Buckby senior bought this farm at that time, as well as "three capital cottages" facing the Green for £200. The largest of these cottages was later occupied by Mr Cyril Cooper who worked on that farm.

Mollivers Farm carrying with it the title of lord of the manor of Bromham and the attached rights over the Green and common land mainly lying between Stevington Lane and the Oakley Road. 432.159 acres of arable and pasture but including 9.339 acres of woodland, all in Bromham. The house was of brick and stone with an entrance hall, three principal reception rooms, five bedrooms and two attic rooms. Unusually in those days it had a full sized tennis court. It had the best kept of all the gardens of Bromham farms including partially walled kitchen and fruit gardens. The lot included two nearby stone built cottages with good gardens and a pump. It had two separate, but adjacent, sets of extensive and largely stone built farm buildings and a blacksmith's shop. The principal tenant was Mr B Howkins who paid an annual rent of £490 (another tenant paid a rent of £9.16s.). The author has to guess that the price would be around £15000. By 1940 this farm was owned by a Mr Cox. He was succeeded by Mr Brett. The present owner is Mr John Fensome whose family have long farmed at Stagsden. The excellent farmhouse, however, was not, and is not now, occupied by the farmer. During, and shortly after, the Second World War it was occupied by the then Chief Constable of Bedfordshire, Commander Willis.

Park Farm. The largest of Bromham's farms at that time. (The farmhouse is to the east of the Vicarage with a drive leading off the bend in the road by vicarage green. The farmland then occupied all the land east of that point within the bend of the river.) 529.404 acres, 67.5 acres of which are described as parkland, 153 acres as rich meadow and 291 acres as arable. 5.7 acres were in Clapham. Underlying much of the land were said to be deep beds of excellent quality gravel. The meadow and park had considerable river frontage. It sold for £16200. Within a couple of years Park Farm was resold in separate lots. Three separate farms were carved out, two of them lying off what came to be called Lower Farm Road, which was the old road to the ford at Clapham. In the 1940s and 50s Mr Bernard Stuart farmed the portion nearest to the Clapham river boundary and it was in this that most of the gravel production came to be concentrated. Inevitably it produced a waste land which, in recent years, has been developed as a nature park.

The house was sold separately and, in due course, in the 1950s, was occupied by General Sir Evelyn Barker, the last British governor of Palestine.

"*A Valuable Small Holding*" of 4.174 acres in a square bounded by the Hill and Grange Lane was sold to Mr Frederick Blythe for £450. He and his son farmed this, together with some other land they either purchased subsequently or rented, until 1953. This land was then sold (by the same firm as had conducted the sale of the estate). The land belonging to this smallholding south of Grange Lane, together with all other farm land between the Hill and Northampton Road and spreading south to Stagsden Road was built up within a very few years thereafter. But two small meadows and some allotment land now lying behind the village hall were acquired by the local authority and developed as a sports field. Before being flattened for this purpose one of these meadows had borne signs of a medieval field system. Not surprisingly, in view of its age as a meadow, it was covered with cowslips.

The Swan Inn. Bromham had had two public houses very close to each other in Bridge End, but the "Crown" was demolished to make room for widening of the Bridge at the beginning of the twentieth century, leaving only the "Swan", half in Kempston, facing a small triangle of grass known as the Swan Green. It was stone built with all the usual features of licensed premises. It was described as having a pretty tea garden, which soon became a car park. It was then let to the same tenants as the adjacent Berry Farm for £80 per annum. It sold for £1710. At one time thereafter it was owned by a Mr Jeffries. Coincidentally, a Thomas Jeffries had occupied it in 1786.[249] Not until 1957 did a second public house appear in the village. It is called "The Prince of Wales" and stands at the junction of the Northampton and Newport Pagnell roads.

House and Bakery. Lot 21 was withdrawn from the sale and, presumably, sold by private agreement. It was the best of the residential properties after those mentioned above, stone built and occupying, as the catalogue states, a commanding position overlooking the village green. Surprisingly, although it had a dining room, drawing room and sitting room on the ground floor it was listed as only having three bedrooms. Adjoining the house was the bakehouse, still with ovens, a tiled floor and a flour loft. On the north side there was a very pleasant paddock shaded from the Village Road with a line of mature trees (which, if the author remembers rightly were, unfortunately, elms). The whole property was let to Mr Bruty for an annual rent of £26.10s. During the Second World War this house was let to a cousin of the last Sultan of Turkey. After that it was owned by a family of Bedford brewers who proposed to convert it into a public house. Local opposition, for many reasons not all connected with temperance, prevented that.

"The Greenwood". This property, which may well be the oldest still standing in the village, is not so described in the catalogue but is called " a row of three capital cottages". (The catalogue alternates between "capital" and "pretty" as the adjective to describe cottages). Mrs Charles Church was the tenant of the first, which had one upstairs bedroom and a bedroom, living room and scullery downstairs. She paid £3.4s. annual rent. Mr A Church occupied the second which had "two rooms up and two and a pantry down". He paid an annual rent of £2.19s. The third with "one room up and two and a pantry down" was let to Mr EPF Harding, a gamekeeper, at a rent of £3.14s. The three were bought by the author's father for about £250. The author's father, fortunately, sold the house to Miss Thorne who tore out all the intrusive walls and floors of generations of cottagers and restored the central hall to its lofty medieval magnificence, removing, in the process four successive fireplaces, built one in front of the other from a sixteenth

century original. Miss Thorne's renovation revealed thirteenth century work in its hall. It was said that the beams in its roof, which run at knee height across at least one of its bedrooms, were from Viking longships. They might have come up the river as far as Kempston, but this story seems a bit fanciful. On the other hand, those beams had certainly been used somewhere before they were put in that roof. This particular bedroom is reached by a stair from the hall and so may have been the equivalent of a solar, or single bedroom for the owner and his family. The thatched roof obviously dates from a time when wattle and daub walls could not safely rise more than about six feet and it was advisable to have a very wide thatch overhang to keep rain off those walls.

Building plots. Many of the lots bordering on roads were advertised in the sale catalogue on the basis of their value as building plots. Much building in Grange Lane, Oakley Road, Bridge End and Stagsden Road did follow the sale. Some purchasers resisted the lure for quick return, however. Miss Carpenter purchased six acres of meadow, running down to the river, over the parish boundary in Kempston and adjoining her own house, for £435, expressly to prevent it being built on. By chance, next door to it and abutting on the south side of Bridgend, was a further six acres of market garden, also with a river frontage and a fine view of the bridge, advertised as an excellent site for the erection of good class houses. The property already had a substantial stone built house and was let at an annual rent of £35. The market gardener, Mr Witney, had a lease about to expire and intended to move out. Mr Statham bought the whole property for £800 and none of it was built on until his death. The catalogue had not mentioned a row of fine mature walnut trees on the Bridgend boundary. They were felled to make room for houses in the 1950s.

The Mill

There must have been many millers beside the Ouse at Bromham before the first recorded one we have mentioned (George Casse) in 1622. In the dispute between the Dyves and the Botelers regarding land holding at end of the sixteenth century one of the causes of complaint was that Sir Lewis Dyve's mill held back the river water and caused flooding of William Boteler's land. Sir John Dyve pointed out that if the water was indeed held back it was his land that was most likely to be flooded. Both sets of millstones are likely to have been in a building close to the present site. It would not have needed a river fed mill stream to supply power. A "raised pond" would suffice. So the absence of any indications elsewhere in the parish of signs of previous cuttings is no help in determining the position. However the power which supplied both medieval mills must have been on the river because of the need to pay that part of the rent which was in eels. Possibly a pond was still supplying the head of water in 1670 when Richard Jennings, or Jeyes, was washing his sheep in mid-summer at Bromham Mill and exchanged "an ew for an horned wether sheep". Washing sheep below the mill was, however, undertaken in the nineteenth century.

By 1698 Thomas Browne, who owned the windmill at Biddenham, was the tenant of the watermill at Bromham, and so he remained until his death in 1732. In 1708 he was paying an annual rent of £53.5s.4d. increased to £61.0s.5d. when the lease was renewed in 1719. There were then four separate sets of millstones. There were only two in 1924 but it is interesting to note that the rent then was only £84.2s.6d. In 1719 the miller rented, as well as the mill buildings, the old mill house, three acres of the "Miller's Holme" on the East side of the river and "the reed bed where the dam boote is usually digged". He additionally rented 8 acres known as the Mill Close, 7 acres of land between the Stagsden road and the Brook to the north and 8 acres called the Conygear . He was, therefore, a significant farmer as well. Presumably soon after this he gave up the lease of the conygear because this land, south of the church, was part of the Trevors' new park.

William Biggs was appointed Overseer of the Poor in Bromham in 1792 when he was already the miller. He succeeded a miller by the name of Willshire.[250] His son John Biggs took over the lease on his death. He extended the premises (and, as we have seen, got into trouble for creating a nuisance on the highway by the noise of his business). John prospered and bought property in Bedford and elsewhere. He undertook to supply a cart, two horses, and a driver in the event of national emergency during the Napoleonic Wars. He had sufficient capacity, even at harvest time, to agree to produce ten extra loads of flour per week, if necessary, and twenty loads per week after Michaelmas. His son William succeeded him in 1842. Thomas and Frederick Harrison took over the lease from William's son John. Harry and Walter Quenby (operating as R Quenby & Sons) took over the lease in 1905 and Walter and his family moved into the mill house.[251] They must also have prospered because, in 1918, they bought Oakley House and the Oakley estate from the Duke of Bedford. They also bought the Mill at Bromham in 1924 for £2300. In 1927 Harry and Walter decided to concentrate on farming and handed over Bromham Mill to Harry's eldest daughter, Walter's son (another Walter) and George Church (who had married Harry's younger daughter). George moved into the Mill House[252] in 1923 and was followed there by his son John from 1954 to 1968. The sister of Walter junior, who had taken over in 1927, moved back into the mill house in 1968 and remained there until 1992.[253] In 1940, however, the water board had forced the Quenby's to sell the mill,[254] which was then leased back on a 35 year lease. The Estate sale catalogue of 1924 seems much more interested in the mill house and the 14.9 acre smallholding (including an island between the river and the mill stream) that went with it. It describes "capital" farm buildings with cart and implement sheds, cow shed and storage. It also describes the "Water power corn mill" as a commodious building[255] of three floors built of brick, with slate roof and fitted with undershot and breast shot wheels. This latter, which replaced another undershot wheel, was of iron and was installed in 1908. It was restored in 1980 when the mill was opened as a tourist attraction and now drives two sets of millstones to produce flour for the first time since the Quenbys took over the business.[256]

A steam engine had been installed in the 1920s to replace water power when this was low. This was replaced by an oil driven engine in 1933. This, in turn, was replaced by electric power. In 1935 the water board imposed restrictions on the use of water power when the river was low. From time to time thereafter one could see the sluices open and the iron wheel turning by water power but commercial use of water had ceased well before 1943 when millstone grinding was finally totally abandoned.

The water board carried out £14000 worth of restoration work in 1961 but the Quenbys moved their business to Turvey in 1970 and the mill was purchased by the County Council in 1973. The building had become dilapidated and it looked as if Bromham might witness another act of official vandalism. Especially was this so when squatters, who had moved in and produced pottery and leather work, allowed fire to break out, destroying the roof and upper floor of the older eastern end. The building, however, was carefully restored and opened to the public in 1985. Five acres of meadow which had formed part of the smallholding, bounded by the mill stream (which now grows fine water lilies) and a tributary brook, with willow trees and areas of rough grass is available as a picnic site. In the author's opinion, next to the Moot Hall at Elstow, it is the best tourist attraction in North Bedfordshire.

Other Property

Bromham Hall. It seems strange to place the manor house, round which so much of the life of the village has revolved, under a miscellaneous heading. No detailed study of the building has ever been published, however. Harvey, who might have done so, concentrates on its contents. He writes of the structure only this;[257]

> "The manor house, about a quarter of a mile from the church, in beautiful timbered grounds, lies in a valley immediately adjacent to the river, so close that in former years it was liable to floods. It presents a diversity of architectural styles, having received additions at various times. The pointed doorway at the entrance (judiciously restored in 1868 by direction of the late Lord Dynevor) appears to have belonged to a much

more ancient edifice; ... The rooms are small but numerous; the staircase is very ancient and of rude workmanship, being constructed of rough blocks of oak."

It has to be said that it was still liable to flooding at least until 1941, although it was saved from deep flood water by the fact that the opposite bank fell away to the Bridge. The stable block stood to the north of the west front, abutting on the park. There had been a dovecot but this was demolished in 1710[258] almost immediately after the Trevors purchased the estate.[259] Carriages again drove through the park to the door of the Hall in 1983 when the BBC filmed the television production of Dickens' *Bleak House* with this house in the title role.

<u>The Park</u> has been an asset to Bromham. Bernard West summarised most of village history when he wrote of it:[260]

"A quiet backwater near Bedford. In spite of much modern building the village still preserves a rural atmosphere, and fortunately most of the modern cottages around the green are of excellent design.

The park, a magnificent stretch of country, is approached from the road through two gateways, each with a charming cottage lodge in the Victorian "romantic" style. It contains fine beeches near the hall, and ashes…..but the elms have become a prey of the dreaded elm disease.

Picturesquely embowered in trees by the river is the famous hall, an ancient building, quaint and rambling, with memories of the Dyves and Wydeviles, and in more recent times of the formidable Miss Rice Trevor."[261]

It had been first laid out by the first Lord Trevor, absorbing, in the process, the rabbit warren. He, originally, installed deer in it. They were removed when one of them frightened Lady Trevor. Presumably it was at this time that the old drive to the Hall from the ford at Clapham ceased to be used in favour of the new drive through the park from the bottom of the Hill.[262] This drive, which was tree-lined, mostly, as Bernard West says, with elm, curved round before the Hall gates and returned to the lower lodge. The more northerly branch, which was not tree lined, passed the church and forked off to the upper lodge. This section remains but the final stretch to the bottom gate was allowed to grass over after the death of Robert Skinner. In the 1930s attempts to shore up a massive oak tree near the bottom entrance failed and the "Old Oak" was a favourite place on which to play for the next twenty years. Harvey's drawing of the church shows how well cared for the park was in the late nineteenth century. Iron railings between the end of the churchyard wall and the Hall lent a distinctly manorial air of possession. The railings were uselessly sacrificed to the war effort in 1940.

Bromham House is not to be confused with Bromham Hall.[263] Bromham House was built on the Turvey boundary in 1897 by the architect WP Allen for WH Allen, who had founded the important Bedford engineering company of that name and who was at one time Sheriff of Bedfordshire. It was in mock tudor style and had a Norman & Beard organ in its tower. WH Allen purchased considerable land around the house, including several acres of woodland, and he began to landscape the eastern side of this. Most of it was farmed. There still are two lodges, the easternmost at the start of a lengthy drive. On the death of WH Allen the house passed to a trust which sold it, together with 135 acres of land, for £7500 in 1926 to the Bedfordshire, Northamptonshire and Northampton Borough Councils for the purpose of creating what was conceived of as a "colony" for those who, at that time, were known as mental defectives. The first patients were admitted on July 16th 1931 and lived, with the staff, in the house itself. They and the rapidly increasing numbers were not to stay long in this relative luxury but were moved into a number of barrack like two storey brick buildings. The house became the administrative building. Numbers of patients increased from 23 in 1937 to 77 in 1938 (29 female and 48 male) and 194 (114 female and 80 male) by March 31st 1939. This latter influx was composed of more than 100 patients evacuated from London hospitals. The overcrowding was worsened in 1941 when two of the four blocks were occupied by the Emergency Hospital Service. When the National Health Service took over in 1948 there were 280 patients (147 male and 133 female). Well before that a row of staff houses had been built on the Northampton road.

In 1948 the title "colony" was dropped in favour of "Bromham Hospital". In 1955 three new wards were built, adding 134 beds, and by 1979 there were fourteen wards. A new recreation hall and chapel, a central kitchen and a staff canteen were added in 1958. Later a craft centre and a centre for industrial therapy were created and in 1979 plans were afoot for a riding school in part of Salem Thrift. It might, therefore, not have seemed the most obvious move in 1982 to close the hospital. The public conscience moves inexorably onwards and the idea of "imprisoning" people, often for life, just because they were disabled by low intellectual levels ceased to be tolerable. The buildings were, thereafter, used for the "Rainbow School" for children with educational difficulties.

The early patients were high grade employable males and they, and some later admittees, came into the village to work, mostly gardening. They also worked on the colony's own farm run by Mr Benson who, prosaically, lived in a council house in Grange Lane. It was always the intention to provide other therapeutic activities and as early as 1934 the patients gave the first of a number of annual concerts. In 1935 they held their first annual sports day. Their families often lived considerable distances away and these events provided welcome opportunities to visit. Dr Marsh, who became the medical director in 1938, actively sought the involvement of the village and the wider community. Various drama groups put on plays and early in the second world war the Baptist Church devised a musical extravaganza specifically for the hospital named "The End of the Rainbow". Its enormous success led to its performance for the villagers in the chapel. A regular Sunday religious service was conducted both by the vicar and non-conformist preachers.

The Post Office. The rate book for 1926 describes one of the two semi-detached stone houses on the corner of Grange Lane opposite the park entrance as the Old Post Office. That must have been in the previous century because Mrs Odell had run it in the Bakery until 1914 when she moved, with her daughter, Mrs Purser, across the Green to one of a number of houses next to the Shop, several of which, thereafter, were to house it. It moved from there two houses down to Mr Frank Tysoe's home and then next door to his son's house.

The Village Hall. Unlike most of its neighbours Bromham did not possess any assembly building, such as a village hall or even a church room, until 1954. After the second World War Mr Robert Skinner gave land for such a building next to the schoolhouse and adjoining what became playing fields shortly thereafter, for the first village hall, which was a relatively simple structure with a few service rooms on either side of its entrance doors. It has recently been replaced by a more impressive, and well designed, building on the same site.

The Cattle Pound.[264] In 1652 there is a record of "a farmhouse abutting upon Church Lane there on the South and upon the Towne Greene and pound there on the North". In 1724 a terrier of church lands included, "3 little Houses by the Pound, 1acre 1rood." If a villager found a stray animal he or she had a duty to put it in this pound, from whence, if it was not claimed within a specified time, the finder might take it. It seems that it would have afforded little grazing in that time for the pound to which we here refer measured 18feet 3ins by 17feet.[265] The pound remained in existence at the western apex of the Green until the 1970s when it was swept away to permit entrance to a car park in front of a row of newly built shops. With a pound went a pinner; an officer whose duty it was to impound stray beasts. In 1854 John Inskip held this post and in April of that year was observed by John Perkins and Thomas White to be leading two donkeys, which they recognised, to the pound. There is not so much opportunity in modern times to rescue cars subjected to precisely this ancient system but Perkins and White thought it worth attempting to avoid the penalty they would have to pay to release the animals. So they attacked Mr Inskip and found themselves before the Bedford magistrates.[266] The charge was dismissed upon their promise to pay 8s.9d. each.

<u>A Nature Park.</u> If one amenity has gone another has recently appeared. In 1990 Bedfordshire County Council acquired the land of the former Council refuse disposal depot west of the railway and south of Lower Farm Road. This land had been part of Park Farm in the days of the estate and when it was sold the whole area was described as having rich deposits of gravel underlying it. They were ruthlessly exploited, particularly during the second World War, and no effort was made at that time to reinstate the land. The Council used various of the pits created by the extraction of the gravel for dumping refuse without much organisation of the operations. At another site off the same road but nearer to the village it emptied, in an uncovered and unprotected "lake", the contents of the tankers that, in the days before the installation of mains drainage, pumped out the household cesspits. The Council made amends for this lack of care for the environment by its purchase in 1990. The Nature Reserve which it then created under the terms of section 19 of the National Parks and Access to the Countryside Act 1949, extends over 25 acres of woodland and disused gravel working, flooded to form the lake. This gravel working was the last to be worked in the area and was opened after 1950.

The Waterways and Bridges of Bromham
Rivers and streams

Three streams of some significance flow within the parish. The River Ouse winds round the eastern boundary for about four miles from the bridge at Oakley, over the ford at Clapham to the Bridge and Mill on the Kempston boundary. It is crossed only by the two bridges, the one on the Oakley boundary and the other on the Biddenham boundary. The view across the water meadows from Bromham Bridge to the Mill on the west and the weirs south of the park was one of the most pleasant in Bedfordshire. The river below the weirs provided a pool, regarded by the author's brothers as a safe place unsuccessfully to teach him to swim, and a number of smaller pools where the fishing was easy and usually rewarding. The shallows across which the bridge ran provided excellent paddling.

It was, therefore, a matter of great importance when, in 1979, the relatively newly formed Anglian Water Authority proposed to excavate a thirty metre wide channel below the old weirs to bypass the old river and re-enter it at the bridge. The purpose was to lower the level of the river above the weir and provide a deep channel to take the winter flow and avoid flooding. The principal opportunity for this development was, no doubt, the cessation of normal operations at the Mill. Since it was apparent that the flooding, largely absorbed by the adjacent flood meadow, appeared to do little harm considerable opposition on environmental grounds rapidly developed. It was, however, disastrously disorganised. A public meeting had been held at the Mill on January 19th 1979, but this was largely concerned with the concurrent proposals to develop the Mill as an amenity. The County Planning Department used these proposals to support an objection that the lowering of the water level would make it impossible to operate the mill wheels for demonstration purposes and it devoted some energy to successfully refuting the claim made at the public meeting that operation of the machinery would create vibration which would damage the structure of the Mill. Quite why this should have been so after more than 200 years is not apparent. The Arts and Recreation Officer of the Council, who had shown that the fitting of new bearings would eliminate all vibration, complained that his own Planning Department's objection that the proposal to fill in the old channel with the soil excavated from the new would leave a backwater which would fill with rubbish, stagnant water and algae. He was rather sharply told that it was not for his department to deal directly with the AWA. The Planning Department was concerned that the infilling would destroy even that part of the river bank vegetation that survived incorporation in the new cut. Both departments were concerned with the effect on the island between the mill stream and the old river course, which had recently been declared a nature reserve and from which it would cease to be possible to exclude the public. The Arts and Recreation Officer perceptively envisaged the public walking to the island across the top of a new weir the AWA proposed at the confluence of the mill stream and what he referred to as the Stagsden Brook (and the Planning Department, with even less historic support, referred to as the Crawley Brook).[267] The County Architect saw the effect of the proposal as the creation of something like the "Hundred Foot Drain" in the Fens, which the Duke of Bedford had created before the age of public objection. He pointed out that reduction of the water level in the river above the weir by 300 millimetres, as proposed, would lead to the destruction of the wetland vegetation in the flood meadow. He drew attention to the reference by the Bedfordshire and Huntingdonshire Naturalist Trust to the river upstream from Bedford as "a choice site of natural history interest", and to Dooney's rather less fulsome description in "Flora Bedfordiensis" of it as "one of the more interesting parts of the County". He concluded that completion of the proposed works would produce "an unacceptable landscape out of harmony with the valley". He proposed that the new channel should not be straight but should "curve as naturally as possible", and that the old course of the river should be retained and fed from the mill stream (which seems an obvious solution to the stagnant waters objection). The AWA had proposed what they thought was a rather tasteful sloping of the banks of the new cut. He pointed out that "aquatic marginals" do not establish themselves on such orderly banks. He was also concerned to conserve an island below the bridge which must always have been in danger of being swept away had the mill outflow operated to full capacity, or the new cut discharged its flow directed straight at the island. The AWA, which had offered to dig a "surpentine channel",obtained planning permission on July 27th 1979 and the energies of objectors were, thereafter, largely diverted to preventing access to the works through the mill rather than across the flood meadow. The opposition would have been better advised to keep up the pressure on the performance of the works because, on October 26th 1979, the Regional Controller of the Department of Transport forbade access through the mill land.

Children, of course, now have better things to do than paddle in rivers but the activities of the same water authority have, if nothing else, destroyed this facility, which we once extensively used both at Oakley and Bromham Bridges.[268]

The Brook[269] still flows in from the west being the confluence of three separate streams, two rising in Stagsden and a third just over the County boundary in North Crawley. It joins the River Ouse at the head of the millstream. It is rarely "an inoffensive trickle" as the editor of the Bedfordshire Magazine described it in 1983.[270] It had also, as she suspected, never till that time been called the River Stag.[271] She states that it had flooded in the last three years, but long-term residents of Bromham will know that it flooded the whole of the low lying meadow between Northampton Road and the hill (known as The Slype) virtually every year. In 1944 Italian prisoners of war, for want of something better for them to do, dug out and straightened this length, thus destroying its gravel bed and all the plant life on the steep banks, without any significant effect on the flooding. The third stream flows from the grounds of Bromham House under the Northampton Road to supply the pond at Grange Farm from which it flows out to join Bromham Brook as it crosses the other arm of Northampton Road.[272] The water from this stream, mainly coming from the springs near Grange Farm, was approved by the County Council for use by its steam rollers, which filled up through a suction pipe lowered down its steep bank just before it joined the Brook. The waters of the Brook were not so approved.

The Bridges

The Brook has four bridges now within the parish. The most westerly takes the road from Stagsden over an arch of medieval origin. Simco and McKeague[273] suggest this may date from the fifteenth century. It was widened (in limestone as originally) by the turnpike trust, probably in 1817, and again, in concrete, in 1937. They note that originally it was 7ft 6in. wide but is now 32ft wide. The brick bridge on the Northampton Road was replaced with a more functional, but more ugly, bridge in the 1950s. The third bridge crosses the stream at the foot of Bromham

Hill and provided one of the best known scenic views of Bromham looking towards the bottom lodge. The fourth is a wooden footbridge taking the footpath, known now as Millfields, from Bridgend, by the old forge, into the park.

It was once common to refer to the principal river bridge on the Bedford to Northampton (the A428) road as "Roman". It is about a thousand years later than this that it was first built; but long enough before 1224 to need repairing in that year at a cost, recorded in the Pipe Rolls, of 4s.[274] Simco and Mc Keague[275] say that before the bridge there was not even a track to this crossing place. The crossing place next below Clapham was probably served by an extension of the road that now ends at Biddenham church. The present route was constructed through the field system of Biddenham presumably at the same time as the bridge was built. The river was shallow at this point until the new weir was constructed, but this may only have been the case after the old weir was constructed north of the bridge. There seems no reason to suppose there would ever have been a ford at this point. There can be little doubt, however, that the construction of the bridge made this the strategic crossing. In 1646 Henry Lowens had stretched a chain across it in what one assumes would have been a vain attempt to prevent the passage of parliamentary troops, who, earlier, would have used it on their way to garrison Newport Pagnell. The same idea occurred to the authorities in the Second World War when six rows of sockets were inserted at the Biddenham end to hold vehicle barriers.

This bridge was one of a number of similar medieval stone crossings of the Ouse in Bedfordshire.[276] It was in need of repair again after 1281 when, following a severe frost, it gave way. A woman on it at the time was carried on an ice floe as far as Bedford, where she was last seen. Those who crossed the bridge in the severe winter of 1947-8 and saw similar ice floes sweep across the flooded meadows to crash against the cutwaters will understand the collapse 634 years before. It was common for the cost of repairing bridges to fall on the lord of the manor. Repair of the river arches appears initially to have been the responsibility of the chantry. The deed of sequestration of the lands of Sir Lewis Dyve in 1661 contains a reminder that the estate was committed to the cost of repair of the first of the two river arches. Both the causeways seem to have been a charge on surrounding parishes. In 1383 Stagsden, Stevington and Turvey were called upon to contribute and Turvey, reasonably, objected on the ground that it had a bridge of its own to look after. Simco and McKeague say that the cost of the river arches would have continued to fall upon the income of the chantry.[277] It was also common for inhabitants of parishes which made use of a particular bridge to leave money by will for its upkeep. So far as Biddenham bridge is concerned in 1508 John Howden left 8d.[278] and widow Joan Poley left 20d. in 1509.[279] Nicholas Skypwith, rector of

Biddenham left 20s. in 1492. In 1501 one Fyssher of Stevington left three measures of barley for its upkeep.[280] Similarly Goditha Wodyll of Stagsden in 1507 left the chantry priest "sir Thomas" (Ibbott)[281] two measures of barley towards its repair.[282] William Boteler of Biddenham, citizen and alderman of London, included in a very lengthy list of charitable bequests in 1528, provision "Towards the repairing and supportacon of Biddenham bridge £10. Exors. to call unto them good counsel with the advice of 6 of the most substantial men of that town to see and ordain that the said £10 be bestowed in the best manner for the maintaining of the said long bridge and this to be done within 4 years after my death."

No doubt many repairs great and small have been carried out in the 800 years that Bromham bridge carried all the traffic between Bedford and Northampton and Newport Pagnell. A plaque, discovered in 1966 and now over the first arch, records that it was repaired in 1685. One hundred cartloads of stone were required to repair it in 1724 after a serious flood[283] and 44 loads of gravel at 4d. per load were needed a few years later. On this latter occasion the bridge was paved with stone from Stagsden. It is not clear what sort of repairs a blacksmith carried out in 1738 and 1742 but in 1752 a carpenter charged £6.10s. to make the wooden support for the construction of a new arch. This arch was one over the mill tail because a temporary bridge was made there whilst the repairs were made.

Until 1812 the bridge presented a very different appearance than it does today. Maps of 1794 and 1798 show that after four river arches 11ft wide a cart bridge branched off at the fifth span, to the south, bending round to rejoin the road at the Biddenham end. Something like the line of the present bridge was occupied by a foot and horse bridge 6ft wide over 22 arches which met with the cart bridge to cross the river. The horse and foot bridge was carried on arches, but that for carts used a solid causeway, sloping up, on arches, to join the other at the river bank. In 1793 it was noted that "five collateral arches be added for safer passage of carriages over deepest parts of the meadow at high water." Bringing a cart from Bedford to Bromham in some Februarys must have been a hazardous undertaking. The cart bridge was certainly under water as early as September in 1797.

Already, by 1769, the cart bridge was too narrow and Quarter Sessions, in that year, sought an estimate for widening the horse and foot bridge. In 1791 a stonemason carried out £80 worth of repairs and a sum not exceeding £100 was authorised for improvements in 1792. It is likely that this only went as far as raising the cart track and building the five flood arches. Traces of two of those arches could be seen, until extensive changes controlling the flow of the river at this point were completed in 1981, on the banks of the small stream (or "drain") which led off the river opposite Bromham Hall and rejoined the river just south of the bridges. In 1812 Robert Salmon, the Duke of Bedford's estate agent, was asked to survey the bridge, but he was too busy and the survey was carried out by Henry Provis. He produced plans for the continuation of two, wider, bridges and a new roadway at a cost of £8226. Not surprisingly, this estimate was regarded as excessive. John Wing, who was, at the time, the architect for the new Bedford bridge produced an estimate of £3780. But Wing's estimate for Bedford bridge had been considerably exceeded and this may be why his estimate for Bromham bridge was rejected. On June 24th Robert Salmon at last had time to look at the bridge and did so in the company of local magistrates, producing, as a result, an estimate for £3840 for rebuilding the foot and horse bridge and repairing the cart bridge. The rebuilt bridge, paradoxically, was 17ft wide and so, for the next 89 years after completion of the work in 1814 met up with a significantly narrower river crossing. The new arches mostly had a span of 12ft 6ins, with limestone inverts which have recently been restored by the removal of concrete overlays. But every fourth arch has a span of 15ft 5ins. The span of arch 21 which joins the old river crossing is, however, 21ft 4ins. The narrower piers of the medieval bridge were incorporated into the widened bridge from arches 10 to 21 but from arch 9 to the Biddenham end the new line veered away slightly to the south.

Simco and McKeague deduce that Salmon must have used some inferior stone and repairs were required almost every year from 1823 to 1855. In 1850 the County Surveyor reported that "a worse constructed Bridge and with worse Materials could not have been built". Quarter Sessions in 1855 notes that the Bromham quarries had lately begun to produce the harder stone, for which they had been waiting.

A committee of the County Council reported at the beginning of the twentieth century that it was quite impossible for two carts to pass and that it was unsafe for a horseman, cyclist or pedestrian to pass a vehicle in motion. The Chairman of the Parish Council reported that a trap had collided with a carrier's cart and a boy had been thrown off his bicycle and almost fallen in the river.[284] As a result the river arches were widened in 1902 by building extensions on each of the existing arches. Two pedestrian refuges were added.[285]

At the end of the nineteenth century a census revealed that 1021 passers by used the bridge each day, rising to 1795 on Saturdays. In 1985 an average of 2,700 heavy lorries and 12,300 other vehicles crossed it daily. It then carried what was supposed to be the Felixstowe to Weedon A428 Trunk Road. Not only did this mean that the parapet was often knocked off by vehicles attempting to squeeze past each other but, more seriously, the infill of the piers of the arches began to move forming holes within the structure.[286] This posed a prospect of imminent collapse. There was no feasible prospect of closing the bridge while repairs were undertaken. Until the bypass and new bridge were constructed there was no realistic route for diversion of the traffic on this major road. Surprisingly, on this occasion the wonders of modern civil engineering techniques enabled the work to be done in two weeks for no more than £3000. Drill holes were bored into the piers between the arches and a semi liquid "grout", which dried in four hours, was pumped in.

Well before that there had been discussion of a bypass.[287] By 1983 this had been finally decided upon, but the residents of Bromham were complaining about the environmentally unsatisfactory plans.[288] In the event the new bridge is approached by roads which run between the turning to Biddenham beyond Bromham bridge and a point very close to the Turvey boundary.[289] The new Bromham bridge, of course, is in Kempston!

Springs

There are many springs in Bromham. Harvey[290] mentions four. Of the spring, or "holy well", at the mill we have already spoken. Farrar[291] devotes a whole chapter to a reverie while sitting on its "worn stone steps". Alas, those steps, and the stone arch over them, were built when the bridge was widened in 1902 and the parapet at the mill end was splayed out over the spring to provide a better approach. For all that, the spring probably did provide water, and even a focal point for travellers and the chantry after the Norman Conquest.

The first Viscount Hampden built an arch over a second spring, now largely forgotten, just south of the lower drive to the Hall and at the eastern end of an enclosure long known as the osier beds. Harvey noted that the water was very pure and was said to heal fresh wounds.[292] In at least one period of drought in the nineteenth century this spring provided drinking water for much of the village but its real importance lies in wasting its waters. It has cut no stream to the nearby river but sustains the band of wetland on the northern bank behind the weirs. Harvey mentions a third which he is unable to place, called the "roaring spring". In Stevington a spring of the same name is said to be so called because its waters bubble. In Bromham it is a name which would aptly describe the spring at Grange Farm, which Harvey separately mentions. This spring has not been known to run dry and during a prolonged drought in about 1700 it supplied a wide area. Since Harvey does not apply the name to that spring it may well have referred to another, a short distance to the east of it, the water from which also ran into the same stream. In the author's youth there was a very active spring to the east of Bowles Wood about 150 yards north of Grange Lane. It fed a little stream which wandered down to meet that through Grange Farm's pond. There was another feeding a shallow well in the garden of one of the two cottages immediately beyond the paddock that belonged to the Old Bakery on the Green. Yet another spring provided water in

Grange Lane until the late 1930s. It rose immediately outside the gate to no.18 and the author's brother remembers that one clambered down to it with a bucket. If one lost the bucket the water was too deep to wade in but Mr Hillyard, who occupied no.18, would provide a pole with a hook on the end. This spring was bricked in and covered with concrete slabs over which the footpath ran. Its waters probably still run into the main drainage system. There was also a spring in the field North West of the Green (which may also have supplied the well from which the pumped water was drawn). This spring also supplied a stone arched "horsewell".

The farms and a few other properties listed in the 1924 sale catalogue were described as possessing their own wells. A number of structures having all the appearance of wells were, however, essentially tanks to which water was piped and which seem to have been placed where they could serve more than the property in which they were located. That at "The Greenwood", for instance, stood by the front gate. It was fed by a pipe leading from a pumping house which stood roughly where the eastern end of a row of modern shops was located in the 1960s and which was a short distance behind the "Greenwood". This pumping house was built over a deep "well" or tank which drew its water from the same sources as an adjacent pond. Power was originally provided by a small windmill on the roof. Evidence that this system was still regarded as operative during the second World war is provided by replacement of the wind pump with an electric pump at that time but it is doubtful if it was then supplying domestic water. No doubt this pump house also supplied the water for the tank under the three lime trees that stood on the village green until after the second world war. They were known as the "pump trees" because a pump was erected above this tank. Its pipe was cut off at ground level before Bromham's well water was declared not fit for drinking in the late 1930s, and it is to be assumed that the tank was filled, probably in 1929, well before the trees shading it were felled. The author is unaware of what other "wells" were supplied by this piped water but he has been told that it ran as far as the crest of the Hill on the eastern side of the road. The well in the garden of the three cottages that stood on that crest, however, was a genuine deep well. So was that by the front gate of the group of cottages on the other side of the road, one of which was the farmhouse of the smallholding described in the property sales above. There was, however, in the 1940s, a deep square pit just inside the park gate by the "top lodge" and this may have been the site of another supplied tank. It is not surprising that this pumped water was eventually said to be unfit to drink. A large colony of great crested newts, no doubt of a cleanly turn of mind, lived in the pumping house tank while it was operative.

A similar piped supply provided water to Mollivers Farm. That depended on a rectangular, and obviously man made, pond at the north eastern corner of Bowles wood. This pond, similarly, had a spring on its eastern side. In this instance the storage tanks at the farm were gravity fed, the pond being deliberately sited at one of the higher points in the village. Despite its relative height this spring overflowed in times of heavy rain, its waters running down Stevington (Mollivers) Lane.

A well about 50ft deep in New Road, Thistley Green, which then appeared to be of relatively recent construction was still in regular use in the 1940s. The condemnation of all well water resulted in the provision of cast iron stand pipes by the road side but in the author's memory these only continued to exist into the 1950s in Thistley Green. Because of the prevalence of limestone the water in Bromham's wells was analysed as being twice as "hard" as that in the river.

There were also a number of ponds. Many of these were largely seasonal like that at the eastern end of the bridle way through the narrow middle of Bowles wood. Some of them were hollows[293] which simply filled with water in the winter. These ponds have mostly been filled in. In any event a number of them would probably have dried with the general drying of the ground in the village following the installation of main drainage in or around 1950. They took with them, among other things, large numbers of the great crested newt, which had been common but is now extinct in the parish.[294]

Roads and Railways
Roads

Immediately after the end of the Second World War the road plan of Bromham was simple. A rough square was formed by the Hill and Northampton Road to the east and west and by Stagsden Road and Grange Lane to the south and north. Roads ran from each of the four corners of this square. In the south-east the main A 428 ran through Bridgend over the Bridge to Bedford. Forking from it south across the front of Berry Farm and The Swan ran the road to Kempston. At the north east corner was the main village road running past the school and the Green, with a right angle bend at the Vicarage to Oakley and Stevington. It is important to realise that before 1924 the village, as such, lay entirely to the north east of the square of roads here described. The sale catalogue of that year describes a property on the corner of Grange Lane and the top of the hill as being "on the outskirts of the village". No through roads led off the village road. Stevington Lane ran through the middle of the Green but was, for almost all its course, a green lane.[295] None but farm vehicles used more than about 400 yards of it at the village end. Beyond the Vicarage, Lower Farm Road was the pre-Conquest ridge route from the West to the ford at Clapham, but no vehicles would have used that ford in the twentieth century. From the south-west corner of the square the former toll road led, over Bromham Brook, to Stagsden and Newport Pagnell. At the north west corner Northampton Road turned at right angles and proceeded via Turvey and Olney. The Normans would have recognised this pattern. By no means all the road frontages had been built up. Most pre-estate sale buildings were concentrated along the Village Road and round the Green between Grange Lane and the Vicarage. In the 1930s about half the frontage onto Grange Lane had been built (including twelve of the ugliest council houses in the County). The north side of Bridgend and rather more than half of both sides of the southern boundary of the square had also been built upon, but there was virtually no building on the eastern side of that square. Beyond the square there had been considerable building on the road to Stagsden and on the northern side of the road beyond the vicarage green.

Of the older property there were, as there still are, a significant number of thatched houses. In the nineteenth century the estate had added some attractive stone built properties. Since the 1950s virtually the whole of the centre of the square has been filled in with housing and most of the land from Stevington (Mollivers) Lane to Oakley Road has been built up. Many new roads have thus been created. There has been significant building elsewhere. The centre of Bromham is now, officially, a built-up area.

In the 1940s Bromham had two remaining stretches of green lane; that is to say, carriageway that had never been tarred. The best of these was Stevington Lane west of the apex of the Green. Eventually, if one opened the farm gate across it, this opened out, at the north west corner of Bowles Wood, into a track across what had once been common land[296] to Stevington. But for two or three hundred yards the road ran through high banks bordered with mature elms. The elms were felled in the late 1940s, the banks were levelled and the first of the post-war housing in Bromham bordered it. The other green lane was Thistley Green Lane at the point where the Stagsden and Turvey roads divided. It was, in reality, the start of two recognised footpaths which had, no doubt, been widened to two or three eighteenth century cottages. It opened out into a track over "The Box" to join the Kempston road with a branch towards Hanger's Wood on the Stagsden boundary.

Turnpike trusts

Two of the roads mentioned above had been the subject of Turnpike Trusts, both first created in 1754. Before this road maintenance was the responsibility of the parish from 1555 and this responsibility continued in respect of non-toll roads[297] until the general Highways Act of 1835. Two parish surveyors of highways had to see that the parishioners turned out for four (later six) days each year to repair the roads. One trust dealt with the whole route from Bedford to Sherington Field where the road joined that between Olney and Newport. There was a gate on this near the Swan. The second dealt with the road branching off this in Bromham and running through Turvey to Lavenden where it joined the Olney to Wellingborough Road and so provided the route to Northampton.[298] A turnpike keeper from Bromham was buried in 1760 so there was, presumably, a keeper's house. In 1790 a new trust was established by Act of Parliament covering the road from the Biddenham end of Bromham Bridge to the Olney-Wellingborough road. The Act does not provide for the termination of the former trusts, each covering part of this route, so they must have simply ceased to exist They do not seem to have been a great success.[299] The gate at the Swan does not reappear. The Turvey-Lavenden road had a keeper's house next to Grange Farm by 1796. In that year it was auctioned at the Bull Inn Olney, which the trustees had wisely designated the location for the annual auction of gates, the rent then being the considerable amount of £120 per year. The lease of the Bromham gate would include the side gates at the bottom of Grange Lane and on the Stevington and Stagsden turns off the main Olney road. The Bedford-Newport Pagnell road was without a trust from whenever the former trust had ceased until 1814. This now left the other turnpike at the Bromham turn, rather than vice versa. The toll keeper's house on the Newport road in Bromham was called the "Stagsden Gate", for the very good reason that it was then in the parish of Stagsden, and is shown on a Map of 1826. It is still standing.

The rent of the Bromham gate, on the Turvey-Lavenden road, and its side gates was usually the highest on the route. In 1831 and in 1832 it was £173 and £163 respectively and in the final years of the trust around £200 per year was bid, whilst in 1864, when, for some reason the lease was only for ten months and the Bromham gate went for £207 the Lavenden gate was secured by a bid of £144 and the Ravenstone gate for £77. It seems that organised toll contractors, rather than individual toll keepers, normally secured the leases. They provided the names of securities and usually deposited the first month's rent. This probably suited the trustees in preference to the bankruptcy of the toll keeper at Bromham in 1863. In the last year of the trust Samuel Baker, a toll contractor operating from the Woburn Sands gate of another trust, successfully bid £205 for the Bromham and Lavenden gates together and deposited £17.1s.8d.[300]

Payment of the toll entitled one to pass through the gate at any time in the next twenty four hours. The charges on the Bromham-Lavenden turnpike included 2 shillings for any sort of carriage drawn by six or more beasts. The charge reduced as the number of draught animals reduced; one shilling and sixpence for five or four, one shilling and threepence for three, one shilling for two and sixpence for one. One penny a head was charged for single animals, laden or unladen, but not drawing a vehicle, whilst herds were charged by the score. It might be useful to combine a trip with a visit to church because this was free, as were funerals. In practice there was a certain amount of variation on these formulae. Edwin Ransom of Kempston Mill complained, on November 26th 1868, of overcharging by the Bromham keeper, Edwin Preston. He pointed out that the toll for a one horse van should have been 6d. He was being charged seven pence halfpenny. He maintained that, apart from their weight, the only difference between his and other one horse vehicles was that the latter had springs. So far as weight was concerned he claimed that the load in his vans was between 1½ and 2½ tons whereas hosiers' vans, although they looked light, might weigh 3 tons. He refused to pay, was summoned before the magistrates and fined "the normal fine". The magistrates took the view, which on the evidence here seems to lack support, that the toll was determined by weight. Not surprisingly, the clerk to the trust received a letter from Ransom's agent saying that as the fine was less than 40 shillings he had no right of appeal but the next time he was charged the extra amount he intended to summon the trust for overcharging. This would enable him to appeal to Quarter Sessions if the magistrates continued to be against him. Perhaps the threat was an empty one because there is no record of him doing so. Confusingly, the Stagsden gate's scale of charges, as displayed in 1846,[301] was based on different criteria. Four wheeled carriages paid one shilling and two wheeled carriages sixpence. Animals were charged separately. Coach horses were charged sixpence each whilst those drawing wagons paid fourpence. Apparently commuting the individual toll was permitted. The inhabitants of Lavenden, for a nominal one shilling per year, secured free passage of cattle and carriages between the village and the mill. The inhabitants of Ravenstone paid 2 shillings and sixpence for a similar right at their sidegate. But John Whitchurch, a farmer from Turvey paid 35 shillings a year for use of the road and William Pike of Steventon paid 25 shillings for passage through the Stevington sidegate.

When the trusts ceased to operate in 1874 the trustees of the Bedford-Newport Pagnell turnpike offered Miss Rice-Trevor the chance to purchase the cottage at Thistley Green, and she did so. William Golding wrote on her behalf on 19th November 1874 to the Bromham-Olney trust asking that she be given the same opportunity to purchase the cottage at the Bromham gate. In fact that was sold a month later to Eton College for £40. Highway authorities replaced the turnpikes which had maintained the roads in better condition than the former parish surveyors but, as will be appreciated from the amount of their income from letting the gates, had not overcome Arthur Young's objections of a century before.

Railways

In the mid-nineteenth century almost everyone would have liked to build a railway and eight routes were surveyed through Bromham. Most of these were concerned to travel from Bedford northwards and they would have crossed the parish at the far eastern end close to the Clapham boundary. Only the Midland Railway Company built any lines. It had built the line from Leicester to Hitchin (via St John's station in Bedford) which did not cross Bromham. At Hitchin passengers for London would travel on the Great Northern line into King's Cross station. In 1861, however, the Great Northern excluded Midland trains from the London terminal and the Midland Railway, in 1863, obtained an Act of Parliament empowering it to extend its line south from Bedford through Luton and St Albans. The line to St Pancras station was opened on October 1st 1868. The Midland line crosses the Ouse six times between Wellingborough and Bedford. The crossing at the Bromham boundary is, like all the others, a fine piece of Victorian engineering in steel. The first diesel electric locomotives used to haul main line trains in the United Kingdom were run on this line. There were two massive black trial locomotives which were then more exciting than the familiar steam engines and which we waited patiently on the road bridge to see. At first we saw them one at a time, but it was rumoured that they could not climb Shap Fell (trains then ran from St Pancras to Scotland) and so they were linked together.

No station was ever proposed in Bromham. The first station north after Bedford was at Oakley and so it was that when the last of Bedfordshire's railways was constructed from Bromham to Northampton in 1872[302] the point at which it branched west from the main line was called Oakley Junction and a signal box was erected facing the new branch line. It is remarkable how much care was taken in the building of this line. It crossed the old ridge road between Bromham and Stevington where it was not even a through track for vehicles, yet a house for a crossing keeper was built.[303] This line was a triumph of enthusiasm over good business sense, although it was the result of a long cherished scheme for an east to west line. Northampton was adequately served by more direct routes and, apart from Olney (which had some significant industry), the branch line served only a few villages. Had the east-west project ever reached the East Anglian ports it might have succeeded but this part of it closed in March 1962. The sight of the "Turvey Flyer" (the two hourly passenger service on this line) on the embankment leading to the bridges over the Oakley and Stevington roads was one to stir the soul, even then. Railway enthusiasts would now pay enough to make the line viable if that sight could only be restored. The line, however, has become a footpath and the bridges have gone.

[246] See ch V above.

[247] The author's copy of the catalogue contains pencilled notes of the price realised for many of the lots and these prices are given in the text without any guarantee that they are invariably correct. The catalogue indicates the annual tithe charge payable at that time on a number of the properties.

[248] Harvey at p.75

[249] Harvey at p.75.

[250] Harvey at p.75.

[251] Eve Church, *Kempston Memories* (1993) 23 BM 322 states that they bought the mill then but it is clear that they did not, in fact, purchase it until 1924.

[252] The old mill house, pictured, in Harvey, thatched and with seven bedrooms and three staircases, had been demolished when the bridge was widened in 1902. The last traces of the stonework of the chantry disappeared with it.

[253] Stuart Antrobus, *The Quenby Family at Bromham Mill* (1999) 26 BM 331 – This was the last issue of BM.

[254] It seems that compulsory purchase was threatened and an agreement reached as a result.

[255] The older part of the building is the eastern end next to the river, which is brick and timber on a stone base, bearing the dates 1695 and 1722. The western end, built entirely of stone, was added in 1858.

[256] The wooden undershot wheel fell to pieces in 1939 and was not replaced, there being no regular use of water power after 1935. There was an ancient eel trap beside the iron wheel which once caught 1½ cwts (about 75 kgs) of eels in one night. It was destroyed when the sluices were widened in 1961.

[257] Harvey at p.48. He copies the estimate of the age of the door from D & S Lysons' *Magna Britannia – Bedfordshire* (London 1813) at p.61 but Lysons describes the house as "small and inconvenient".

[258] Alan Whitworth, *Dovecots and Pigeon Houses of Bedfordshire* (1996) 25 BM at p.93.

[259] See Appendix V "Field names-the dovecot".

[260] Bernard West *A Bedfordshire Sketch-Book VI* (1948) 1 BM 230.

[261] It is not entirely clear to which "modern" cottages around the Green Mr West refers. There was a nineteenth century house occupied at that time by the church organist (Miss Everest) and one modern semi-detached house. The only other modern buildings round the Green at that time were three thoroughly incongruous pastel coloured square boxes packed into a small site in front of "The Greenwood" in the 1930s by a builder from Biddenham called Prior.

[262] The old drive is still in existence and although the entrance gates have long gone the piers on which they were hung remain.

[263] Although it was so called, for maximum effect, by Henry Longhurst (the golf correspondent. He lived in a large house called Crossmead lying off the Village Road and overlooking the park.) who, in an autobiographical account, complained of its transformation into a mental hospital as the typical fate of manor houses.

[264] There is a photograph of the Pound in the Bedfordshire Historical Record Society's Survey of Ancient Buildings 1936 Volume III figure 21.

[265] These are measurements taken by the author in 1953. At that time the oak beams which barred its entrance were still in place.

[266] See The Bedford Times 22nd April 1854.

[267] The Brook rises in the parish of Crawley in Buckinghamshire.

[268] Destruction of the shallows at Bromham Bridge also removed the habitat of a rare water bug. See Nau, Boon and Knowles (Eds) *Bedfordshire Wildlife* (1987 Bedfordshire Natural History Society) p.74.

[269] We are about to collect a sixth alternative name for this anonymous stream, in descending order of probability, they are: Aldwick, Lye, Stagebrooke, Stagsden, Crawley and Serpentine.

[270] (1983) 19 BM 62.

[271] The people of Stagsden may well object to the name Bromham Brook which this stream had previously borne but that village has nothing to do with stags. Its domesday name was Stachedene. It seems unlikely that, even if the stream was called the Stache, it would have been sufficiently significant for the village to bear the name of its valley.

[272] It grew excellent water cress which we regularly gathered oblivious of the fact that much of the water came from the private sewage farm at Bromham House. Perhaps it was fortunate that this supply was augmented by the powerful spring which flowed in below the farm pond.

[273] Simco and McKeague, n.275 below, at p.45, referring to the stream as "Serpentine Brook", name this as Tymsill Bridge.

[274] Which leads Simco and McKeague (n.275 below) to suggest that this repair was paid for by the sheriff on behalf of the Crown.

[275] Angela Simco and Peter Mc Keague, *Bridges of Bedfordshire*, Bedfordshire Archaeological Occasional Monograph Series No2 1997 at p.39.

[276] The others were Turvey, Harrold, Stafford, Bedford, Barford and St.Neots.

[277] Which is supported by Godytha Wodyll's bequest. Godber, at p. 319, says that the County had taken it over "at an early date", by which she appears to mean before the seventeenth century. Rather strangely, the inhabitants of Biddenham remained responsible, in about 1630, for repair of the "high" arch where the foot bridge and the cart bridge joined

[278] (1966) 45 BHRS p.91. He also left 20d to repair the way at the end of the "vill", although this would no longer have led to the principal river crossing.

[279] (1966) 45 BHRS p.51.

[280] (1966) 45 BHRS 22. He also left two measures of barley for Harrold Bridge.

[281] Not in Harvey's list, which is incomplete at this period.

[282] (1966) 45 BHRS p.89. She left the same amount for the repair of Tymsill Bridge.

[283] Cartloads of stone were presumably used on the cart bridge. One can understand the havoc a winter's flood could wreak on this. But this particular flood had also damaged the river bridge for a payment was made for gathering up the coping stones from the river.

[284] This was on the then unwidened river end. In 1954 the present writer met a similar fate nearer the Biddenham end.

[285] Interestingly, Salmon had thought of this because the wall of his widened bridge bends outwards on both sides of each pier.

[286] It also meant queues of traffic in the morning rush of workers to Bedford stretching back from the bridge to beyond the junction of Grange Lane and the Northampton Road.

[287] See (1964) 9 BM 119. This had been shelved by 1978 (see, 16 BM 64) when widening at a cost in excess of £350,000 was being discussed.

[288] (1983) 18 BM 307-8.

[289] The material on Tymsill and Bromham Bridges has largely been drawn from: Simco and McKeague, *Bridges of Bedfordshire* (1997) pp.39-45; Paul Tritton (1985) 20 BM 34-38; and Peter McKeague, (1988) 21 BM 205-8.

[290] At p. 29.
[291] CF Farrar, *Ouse's Silent Tide* (The Sidney Press Bedford 1921) at pp.61-64.
[292] The author's family knew this as the "wishing well". The arch was intact in the 1950s although it was threatened by the roots of an ancient yew tree which Lord Trevor had probably planted to provide shade.
[293] They seem unlikely to have been stone quarries. The known sites of these in Bromham all indicate cutting from the open side of a hill.
[294] Not the sort of reptile one wishes to tread on in a dark kitchen, as, surprisingly, we quite frequently did at 16 Grange Lane. The trick was not to turn it over because it had a rather off-putting bright yellow underside. The author's mother would pick it up on the coal shovel and put it outside the back door.
[295] Although the County Council declared the section (which it did then call Stevington Lane) from the end of the Green to the gate at the the end of the metalled section near Bowels Wood a "new street" in February 1937. Use of the word metalled seems a little optimistic for a road with a broad band of grass along almost the whole length and no curbs to its shrub covered banks.
[296] The common, (sometimes called "The Moor") covered around 120 acres, was crossed by the continuation of Stevington Lane. Around that time one would often see unmanned gliders flown from it because it was the highest point in Bromham. Because it was left wild it was a rich source of plant and bird life. At the outset of the Second World War it was covered with iron stakes to prevent an airborne landing. When the danger of that receded it was ploughed. An RAF "Mosquito", on a proving flight, made a crash landing on it in 1944.
[297] But it should be noted that the inhabitants of villages had long been entitled to charge a toll from strangers travelling on the village roads.
[298] For some of the information here given on the turnpike roads see FG Emmison, *Turnpike Roads and Toll gates of Bedfordshire* in BHRS Survey of Ancient Buildings Vol. III. 1-26.
[299] Arthur Young, *A Six Months' Tour through the North of England* (1770) complains of the state of the Bedford-Newport road.
[300] See record number GA/276/250/2 – Bedford and Luton Archive and Record Service
[301] The board is on display at the Bedford Museum.
[302] There was a later proposal in 1885 for a line from Bedford to Peterborough.
[303] Last occupied by a family called Dart. The author last saw it roofless but it would have made a very attractive rural retreat with a view of Stevington windmill.

Chapter VII
WILDLIFE

Bedfordshire, since the abolition of Rutland, Middlesex and Huntingdon and the early death of Avon, is the smallest surviving county in England. It also has one of the lowest rainfalls and it is primarily lowland. The area covered by the parish of Bromham rises only to 300 feet on the Stevington border. Most of the County's woodland lies in a band across the north east corner and another band, partly plantation, diagonally across the central lower greensand ridge. Within the parish of Bromham there are only three areas of woodland of any size, totalling just over 39 acres. Bromham and the North-east of the County are dominated by the valley of the river Ouse which cuts through the Oxford Clay, and its overlay of Boulder Clay, spreading across the rest of that area. Great Oolite clay and Great Oolite limestone line this valley in which the river has deposited very extensive beds of Pleistocene gravel. These are between 10 and 25 feet deep and, below Oakley can extend two to four miles in width. The soil of Bromham is, therefore, primarily calcareous, although one strikes a promontory of clay in the north west of the parish. By nature the area is rich in wild plants, save where extensive gravel working occurred in the twentieth century mostly in the land in the east of the parish bounded by the bend of the river.

The commonest fish in the river Ouse in Bedfordshire was the bream. A 9lb bream was caught at Bromham in 1898. But it seems to have become scarce at Bromham since the author's brother never saw one when he fished the river from 1943 to 1949. Pike are sufficiently numerous to be caught frequently by fishermen using small fish as bait. A 28½lb pike has been caught at Kempston and one weighing 20lbs at Oakley. Other common fish are the perch, roach, rudd, gudgeon, chub, dace, bleak and, of course, sufficient eels to pay feudal rents.

It is to be feared that the Large Blue butterfly long ago deserted the "Big Field" beyond Bowels Wood when the latter was ploughed. The same is true of the Larks and Plovers that frequented this 120 or so acres of uncultivated land before the 1940s. Tree creepers and Nuthatches are reported in the park, attracted, no doubt, by the older trees. Most birdwatchers would be surprised by the presence of Nightingales, but the author listened to them on the eastern edge of Bowels Wood in the late 1960s. At that time the small pipistrelle bat was common. Many lived in the hornbeam tree then in the front garden of number 18 Grange Lane. Our porch floor was covered each morning with the wings of the moths they caught.

As this history will have revealed, Bedfordshire is very rich in historical records, and this applies no less to flora. In 1798 Dr Abbot published in Bedford his *Flora*

Bedfordiensis. The first work of its kind in England, it was based on his own collection of its plants. This inspired continuing interest and between 1876 and 1879 the Bedfordshire Natural History Society's proceedings record some seven hundred species. Dr Abbot noted locations from time to time. James Saunders, in *The Field Flowers of Bedfordshire*[304] noted almost 1000 species, again recording one or more locations for most of them. In 1976, however, John G Dony, in his *Bedfordshire Plant Atlas,*[305] published eight hundred maps of the entire county recording, species by species, in two kilometre squares, the survey conducted by his wife and himself between the years 1970 and 1975. It is that survey which is the primary source of information for the following section. Where Bromham is specifically mentioned as a site by either Saunders or the Victoria County History this fact is noted against Dony's record. There is one snag in that the two kilometre squares into which Dony divides the standard Ordnance Survey ten kilometre squares do not, of course, correspond with the parish boundaries. Within the ten kilometre square 05 the two "Tetrads" (2 kilometre squares) that cover the vast majority of the parish are those at the extreme left hand bottom corner (which Dony numbers 05A) and the square diagonally above it. (05G). Some of 05A is in Kempston and Stagsden but 05G is entirely within Bromham. It is intended, however, to list as to be found in Bromham during the period 1970 to 1975 those subspecies shown in both the 4 square kilometres covered by 05A and 05G. Two hundred and ninety of those that follow are in 05G.

Horsetail	*Equisetum*	*-fluviatile*	(water)	
		-palustre	(marsh)	
		-arvense	(field)	
		-telemateia	(giant)	
Wall-rue	*Asplenium*	ruta-muraria		
Male-fern	*Dryopteris*	filix-mas		
Polypody	*Polypodium*	vulgare – interjectum		scarce outside NE Beds
Marsh-marigold	*Caltha*	*palustris*		partic. Mill meadow
Traveller's joy	*Clematis*	*vitalba*		
Buttercup	*Ranunculus*	-acris	(meadow)	
		-repens	(creeping)	
		-bulbosus	(bulbous)	
		-sardous	(hairy)	only site in County
		-auricomus	(goldilocks)	
		-sceleratus	(celery-leaved)	
Water-crowfoot		-fluitans	(river water crowfoot)	

Celandine		-*ficaria*	(lesser celandine)	
	Chelidonium	*majus*	(greater)	
Meadow-rue	*Thalictrum*	*flavum*	(common)	scarce, largely N Beds
Yellow Water-lilly	*Nuphar*	*lutea*		all along R. Ouse
Hornwort	*Ceratophyllum*	*demersum*	(rigid)	
Poppy	*Papaver*	-*rhoeas*	(common)	
		-*dubium*	(long-headed)	
		-*hybridum*	(rough)	rare in Beds
		-*argemone*	(prickly)	
Fumitory	*Fumaria*	*officinalis*	(common)	
Black mustard	*Brassica*	*nigra*		
White mustard	*Sinapis*	-*alba*		
Charlock		-*arvensis*		
Wall-rocket	*Diplotaxis*	-*muralis*	(annual)	
Wild radish	*Raphanus*	*raphanistrum*		
Cress	*Coronopus*	*squamatus*	(swine)	
	Thlaspi	*arvense*	(Field penny-cress)	
Shepherd's purse	*Capsella*	*bursa pastoris*		
Whitlowgrass	*Erophila*	*verna*	(common)	
Horse radish	*Armoracia*	*rusticana*		
Cuckooflower	*Cardamine*	-*pratensis*		
Wavy bitter-cress		-*flexuosa*		
Hairy bitter-cress		-*hirsuta*		*Saunders* records in B
Cress	*Barbarea*	*vulgaris*	(winter)	*Saunders* "locally plentiful"
	Rorippa	-*microphylla*	(water)	Grange farm stream
		-*islandica*	(marsh yellow)	
		-*amphibia*	(great yellow)	All along R.Ouse
	Arabidopsis	*thaliana*	(Thale cress)	
Mustard	*Alliaria*	*petiolata*	(garlic mustard)	
	Sisymbrium	-*officinale*	(hedge mustard)	
Rocket		-*orientale*	(eastern)	
Weld	*Reseda*	-*luteola*		
Mignonette		-*lutea*	(wild)	
Violet	*Viola*	-*odorata*	(sweet)	
		-*reichenbachiana*	(early dog-)	
		-*arvensis*	(Field pansy)	
St John's Wort	*Hypericum*	*perforatum*	(perforate)	
		-*tetrapterum*	(square stalked)	
		-*hirsutum*	(hairy)	
Campion	*Silene*	-*vulgaris*	(bladder)	
		-*alba*	(white)	
Ragged Robin	*Lychnis*	*flos-cuculi*		

Mouse-ear	*Cerastium*	*-holosteoides*	(common)	
		-glomeratum	(sticky)	
		-diffusum	(sea)	Scarce in Beds
		-pumilum	(dwarf)	Scarce in Beds
Chickweed	*Myosoton*	*aquaticum*	(water)	
	Stellaria	*-media*	(common)	
Stitchwort		*-holostea*	(greater)	
		-graminea	(lesser)	
Pearlwort	*Sagina*	*-procumbens*	(procumbent)	
		-annual	(annual)	
Sandwort	*Moehringia*	*trinervia*	(three-nerved)	
	Arenaria	*-serpyllifolia*	(thyme-leaved)	
		-leptoclados	(slender)	
Goosefoot	*Chenopodium*	*-polyspermum*	(many-seeded)	
		-album	(Fat-hen)	
		-ficifolium	(fig-leaved)	Thinly scattered
		-murale	(nettle-leaved)	Rare in Beds
		-hybridum	(maple-leaved)	Scarce, scattered
		-rubrum	(red)	
Orache	*Atriplex*	*-patula*	(common)	
		-hastate	(spear-leaved)	
Mallow	*Malva*	*-sylvestris*	(common)	
		-neglecta	(dwarf)	
Fairy Flax	*Linum*	*catharticum*		
Crane's-bill	*Geranium*	*-pratense*	(meadow)	
		-pyrenaicum	(hedgerow)	
		-dissectum	(cut-leaved)	
		-molle	(dove's-foot)	
Herb-Robert		*-robertianum*		
Balsam	*Impatiens*	*-capensis*	(orange)	Along R. Ouse
Sycamore	*Acer*	*-pseudoplatanus*		
Maple		*-campestre*	(field)	
Holly	*Ilex*	*aquifolium*		
Spindle	*Euonymus*	*europaeus*		
Buckthorn	*Rhamnus*	*catharticus*		
Restharrow	*Ononis*	*repens*		
Lucerne	*Medicago*	*-sativa*		
Medick		*-lupulina*	(black)	
Melilot	*Melilotus*	*-altissima*	(tall)	
		-officinalis	(ribbed)	
Clover	*Trifolium*	*-pratense*	(red)	
		-hybridum	(alsike)	from cultivated
		-repens	(white)	
		-fragiferum	(strawberry)	
		-campestre	(Hop trefoil)	
		-dubium	(lesser trefoil)	

Bird's-foot trefoil	*Lotus*	*corniculatus*		
Tare	*Vicia*	*-hirsuta*	(hairy)	
		-tetrasperma	(smooth)	
Vetch		*-cracca*	(tufted)	
		-sepium	(bush)	
		-sativa	(common)	from cultivated
		-angustifolia	(narrow-leaved)	
Vetchling	*Lathyrus*	*pratensis*	(meadow)	
Meadowsweet	*Filipendula*	*ulmaria*		
Dewberry	*Rubus*	*caesius*		
Silverweed	*Potentilla*	*-anserina*		
Cinquefoil		*-reptans*	(creeping)	
Avens	*Geum*	*urbanum*	(wood)	
Agrimony	*Agrimonia*	*eupatoria*		
Parsley-piert	*Aphanes*	*arvensis*		
Burnet	*Poterium*	*sanguisorba*	(salad)	*Saunders* lists Great Burnet at B. (*s.officinalis*)
Rose	*Rosa*	*-arvensis*	(field)	
		-canina	(dog)	
Blackthorn	*Prunus*	*-spinosa*		
Cherry Plum		*-cerasifera*		Scarce, partic. N Beds
Wild Cherry		*-avium*		
Hawthorn	*Crataegus*	*-monogyna*		
		-laevigata	(midland)	
Crab apple	*Malus*	*sylvestris*		
Stonecrop	*Sedum*	*acre*		
Saxifrage	*Saxifraga*	*tridactylites*	(Rue-leaved)	
Red currant	*Ribes*	*-rubrum*		
Black currant		*-nigrum*		
Purple-loosestrife	*Lythrum*	*salicaria*		
Willowherb	*Epilobium*	*-hirsutum*	(great)	
		-parviflorum	(hoary)	
		-montanum	(broad leaved)	
		-adenocaulon	(American)	
		-tetragonum	(square stalked)	
		-angustifolium	(rosebay)	
Enchanter's nightshade	*Circaea*	*-lutetiana*		
Milfoil	*Myriophyllum*	*-spicatum*	(spikes water-)	
		-verticillatum	(whorled water-)	Pre-1970 Rare
Mare's tail	*Hippuris*	*vulgaris*		Pre-1970 Rare
Starwort	*Callitriche*	*stagnalis*	(common water-)	
Mistletoe	*Viscum*	*album*		Scattered

Dogwood	*Cornus*	*sanguinea*		
Ivy	*Hedera*	*helix*		
Chervil	*Chaerophyllum*	*temulentum*	(rough)	
Cow parsley	*Anthriscus*	*sylvestris*		
Shepherd's needle	*Scandix*	*pectin-veneris*		Pre-1970 Rare
Hedge parsley	*Torilis*	*japonica*	(upright)	
Hemlock	*Conium*	*maculatum*		
Fool's water-cress	*Apium*	*nodiflorum*		
Stone parsley	*Sison*	*amomum*		
Pignut	*Conopodium*	*majus*		
Burnet-saxifrage	*Pimpinella*	*-saxifraga*	(saxifrage)	
		-major	(greater…saxifrage)	
Pepper-saxifrage	*Silaum*	*silaus*		
Ground elder	*Aegopodium*	*podagraria*		
Water-parsnip	*Sium*	*latifolium*	(greater)	Pre-1970 Rare
	Berula	*erecta*	(lesser)	Scattered
Water-dropwort	*Oenanthe*	*fistulosa*	(tubular)	Scarce
Fool's parsley	*Aethusa*	*cynapium*		
Fennel	*Foeniculum*	*vulgare*		Scarce
Wild Angelica	*Angelica*	*sylvestris*		
Wild parsnip	*Pastinaca*	*sativa*		
Hogweed	*Heracleum*	*sphondylium*		
Wild Carrot	*Daucus*	*carota*		
White Bryony	*Bryonia*	*dioica*		
Dog's Mercury	*Mercurialis*	*perennis*		
		annua	(annual)	Scarce, scattered
Spurge	*Euphorbia*	*-peplus*	(petty)	
		-exigua	(dwarf)	
		-helioscopia	(sun)	
Knotgrass	*Polygonum*	*-aviculare*		
		-aequale		
		-amphibium	(amphibious Bistort)	
Redshank		*-persicaria*		
Persicaria		*-lapathifolium*	(pale)	
Water-pepper		*-hydropiper*		
		-mite	(tasteless)	Along R.Ouse
Black-bindweed		*-convolvulus*		
Sorrel	*Rumex*	*-acetosella*	(sheep's)	
		-acetosa	(common)	
Dock		*-hydrolapathum*	(water)	
		-crispus	(curled0	
		-obtusifolius	(broad-leaved)	
		-pulcher	(fiddle)	
		-sanguineus	(wood)	
		-conglomeratus	(clustered)	

Pellitory-of-the-wall	*Parietaria*	*judaica*		
Nettle	*Urtica*	-*dioica*	(common)	
		-*urens*	(small)	
Hop	*Humulus*	*lupulus*		
Elm	*Ulmus*	-*glabra*	(wych)	
		-*procera*	(English)	Probably wiped out
		-*carpinifolia*	(small-leaved)	
Silver Birch	*Betula*	*pendula*		
Alder	*Alnus*	*glutinosa*		
Hornbeam	*Carpinus*	*betulus*		
Hazel	*Corylus*	*avellana*		
Oak	*Quercus*	*robur*	(pedunculate)	
Italian Poplar	*Populus*	*canadensis*		
Willow	*Salix*	-*alba*	(white)	
		-*fragilis*	(crack)	
		-*triandra*	(almond)	Scattered[306]
		-*purpurea*	(purple)	
		-*caprea*	(goat)	
		-*cinerea, sensu l.*	(grey)	
Osier		-*viminalis*		*Saunders* lists in B[307]
Cowslip	*Primula*	-*veris*		
Primrose		-*vulgaris*		
Creeping-Jenny	*Lysimachia*	-*nummularia*		
Yellow Loosestrife		-*vulgaris*		Scarce in Beds
Scarlet Pimpernel	*Anagallis*	-*arvensis*		
Brookweed	*Samolus*	-*valerandi*		*Saunders* "plentiful in Ditches near B bridge" Scarce
Ash	*Fraxinus*	*excelsior*		
Privet	*Ligustrum*	*vulgare*		
Comfrey	*Symphytum*	x *uplandicum*	(Russian)	
Forget-me-not	*Myosotis*	-*scorpiodes*	(water)	
		-*arvensis*	(field)	
Bindweed	*Convolvulus*	*arvensis*	(field)	
	Calystegia	-*sepium*	(hedge)	
		-*sylvatica*	(large)	
Greater Dodder	*Cuscuta*	*europaea*		Scarce in Beds
Nightshade	*Atropa*	*belladonna*	(deadly)	Rare. *VCH* lists in B
	Solanum	-*nigrum*	(black)	
Bittersweet		-*dulcamara*		
Thorn-apple	*Datura*	*stramonium*		Scarce
Mullein	*Verbascum*	*thapsus*	(great)	

Toadflax	*Linaria*	*vulgaris*	(common)	
	Cymbalaria	*muralis*	(ivy-leaved)	
Figwort	*Scrophularia*	*auticulata*	(water)	
Brooklime	*Veronica*	*-beccabunga*[308]		
Speedwell		*-catenata*	(pink, water)	
		-chamaedrys	(Germander)	
		-arvensis	(wall)	
		-hederifolia	(ivy-leaved)	
		-serpyllifolia	(thyme-leaved)	
		-persica	(common, field)	
		-filiformis	(slender)	
Red Bartsia	*Odontites*	*verna*		
Water mint	*Mentha*	*aquatica*		
Gipsywort	*Lycopus*	*europaeus*		
Calamint	*Calamintha*	*ascendens*	(Common)	Scarce, scattered
Clary	*Salvia*	*horminoides*	(wild)	
Selfheal	*Prunella*	*vulgaris*		
Woundwort	*Stachys*	*-palustris*	(marsh)	
		-sylvatica[309]	(hedge)	
Horehound	*Ballota*	*nigra*	(black)	
Dead-nettle	*Lamium*	*-amplexicaule*	(henbit)	
		-hybridum	(cut-leaved)	
		-purpureum	(red)	
		-album	(white)	
Hemp-nettle	*Galeopsis*	*angustifolia*	(common)	
Ground-ivy	*Glechoma*	*nederacea*		
Skullcap	*Scutellaria*	*galericulata*		
Bugle	*Ajuga*	*reptans*		
Plantain	*Plantago*	*-major*	(greater)	
		-media	(hoary)	
		-lanceolata	(ribwort)	
Field Madder	*Sherardia*	*arvensis*		
Bedstraw	*Galium*	*-mollugo*	(hedge)	
		-verum	(lady's)	
		-palustre	(common marsh)	
Cleavers		*-aparine*		
Elder	*Sambucus*	*nigra*		
Wayfaring-tree	*Viburnum*	*-lantana*		
Guelder-rose		*opulus*		
Honeysuckle	*Lonicera*	*periclymenum*		
Cornsalad	*Valerianella*	*-locusta*	(common)	
Valerian		*-officinalis*	(common)	
Teasel	*Dipsacus*	*fullonum*		
Scabious	*Knautia*	*arvensis*	(field)	
Bur-marigold	*Bidens*	*-cernua*	(nodding)	Scarce, scattered
		-tripartita	(trifid)	

Ragwort	*Senecio*	*-jacobaea*	(common)	
		-aquaticus	(marsh)	Scarce
		-erocifolius	(hoary)	
		-squalidus	(Oxford)[310]	
Groundsel		*-viscosus*	(sticky)	
		-vulgaris		
Colt's-foot	*Tussilago*	*farfara*		
Butterbur	*Petasites*	*hybridus*		
Fleabane	*Pulicaria*	*dysenterica*	(common)[311]	
	Erigeron	*acer*	(blue)	
	Conyza	*Canadensis*	(Canadian)	
Daisy	*Bellis*	*perennis*		
Hemp-agrimony	*Eupatorium*	*cannabinum*		
Yarrow	*Achillea*	*-millefolium*		
Sneezewort		*-ptarmica*		Mainly upper Ouse
Mayweed	*Matricaria*	*maritima*	(scentless)	
		-recutita	(scented)	
Pineappleweed		*-matricarioides*[312]		
Ox-eye Daisy	*Leucanthemum*	*vulgare*		
Tansy	*Tanacetum*	*vulgare*		*Abbott,VCH,* "at Grange Farm".
Mugwort	*Artemisia*	*vulgaris*		
Burdock	*Arctium*	*-lappa*	(greater)	
		-minus	(lesser)	
Thistle	*Carduus*	*-nutans*	(musk)	
		-acanthoides	(welted)	
	Cirsium	*-vulgare*	(spear)	
		-arvense	(creeping)	
Knapweed	*Centaurea*	*-scabiosa*	(greater)	*Saunders* at B, Common.
		-nigra	(common)	
Nipplewort	*Lapsana*	*communis*		
Cats-ear	*Hypochoeris*	*radicata*		
Hawkbit	*Leontodon*	*-autumnalis*	(Autumn)	
		-hispidus	(rough)	
Oxtongue	*Picris*	*echioides*	(bristly)	
Goat's-beard	*Tragopogon*	*pratensis*		
Prickly lettuce	*Lactuca*	*serriola*		
Sow-thistle	*Sonchus*	*-arvensis*	(perennial)	
		-oleraceus	(smooth)	
		-asper	(prickly)	
Mouse-ear Hawkweed	*Pilosella*	*officinarum*[313]		
Hawk's-beard	*Crepis*	*-vesicaria*	(beaked)	
		-capillaris	(smooth)	

Dandelion	*Taraxacum*	*officinale*		
Water-plantain	*Alisma*	*plantago-aquatica*		
Flowering-rush	*Butomus*	*umbellatus*		Mainly upper Ouse
Canadian Waterweed	*Elodea*	*Canadensis*		
Pondweed	*Potamogeton*	*-natans*	(broad-leaved)	
		-pusillus		Scarce
		-pectinatus	(fennel)	
Bluebell	*Endymion*	*non-scriptus*		
Rush	*Juncus*	*-compressus*	(round-fruited)	Scarce, scattered
		-bufonius	(toad)	
		-inflexus	(hard)	
		-effusus	(soft)	
		-articulartus	(jointed)	
Wood-rush	*Luzula*	*campestris*	(field)	
Wild Onion	*Allium*	*vineale*		
Iris	*Iris*	*-foetidissima*	(stinking)[314]	*Saunders* at B and Stevington. Scarce
		-pseudacorus	(yellow)	
Black Bryony	*Tamus*	*communis*		
Orchid	*Orchis*	*morio*	(green-winged)	Orchids scarce in Beds. Pre-1970 site only one in B Ouse valley below B
Sweet flag	*Acorus*	*calamus*		
Lords-and-Ladies	*Arum*	*maculatum*		
Duckweed	*Lemna*	*-trisulca*	(ivy-leaved)	
		-minor	(common)	
Bur-reed	*Sparganium*	*erectum*	(branched)	
Club rush	*Scirpus*	*lacustris*	(common)	
Spike-rush	*Eleocharis*	*uniglumis*	(common)	
Sedge	*Carex*	*-sylvatica*	(wood)	
		-riparia	(greater pond)	
		-acutiformis	(lesser pond)	
		-flacca	(glaucous)	
		-hirta	(hairy)	
		-acuta	(slender tufted)	Along R.Ouse
		-otrubae	(false fox)	
		-spicata	(spiked)	
		-remota	(remote)	
Common reed	*Phragmites*	*communis*		
Sweet-grass	*Glyceria*	*-fluitans*	(floating)	
		-maxima	(reed)	

Fescue	*Festuca*	*-pratensis*	(meadow)	
		-arundinacea	(tall)	
		-gigantea	(giant)	
		-rubra	(red)	
	Vulpia	*bromoides*	(squirreltail)	
Rye-grass	*Lolium*	*-perenne*	(perennial)	
		-multiflorum	(Itailian)	
Fern-grass	*Catapodium*	*rigidum*		
Meadow-grass	*Poa*	*-annua*	(annual)	
		-compressa	(flattened)	
		-pratensis	(smooth)	
		-angustifolia	(narrow-leaved)	
		-trivialis	(rough)	
Cock's-foot	*Dactylis*	*glomerata*		
Crested Dog's-tail	*Cynosurus*	*cristatus*		
Melick	*Melica*	*uniflora*	(wood)	
Brome	*Bromus*	*-erectus*	(upright)	
		-ramosus	(hairy)	
		-sterilis	(barren)	
		-mollis	(soft)	
		-commutatus	(meadow)	*VCH* for B
False-brome	*Brachypodium*	*sylvaticum*		
Couch	*Agropyron*	*-caninum*	(bearded)	
		-repens	(common)	
Barley	*Hordeum*	*-secalinum*	(meadow)	
		-murinum	(wall)[315]	
Oat-grass	*Trisetum*	*flavescens*	(yellow)	
	Helictotrichon	*pubescens*	(downy)	
False oat-grass	*Arrhenatherum*	*elatius*		
Wild-oat	*Avena*	*fatua*		
Yorkshire-fog	*Holcus*	*lanatus*		
Hair-grass	*Deschampia*	*caespitosa*[316]	(tufted)	
Small-reed	*Calamagrostis*	*epigejos*	(wood)	
Bent	*Agrostis*	*-tenuis*	(common)	
		-gigantea	(black)	
		-stolonifera	(creeping)	
Cat's-tail	*Phleum*	*-bertolonii*		
Timothy		*-pratense*		
Black-grass	*Alopecurus*	*-myosuroides*		
Foxtail		*-geniculatus*	(marsh)	
		-pratensis	(meadow)	
Wood Millet	*Millium*	*effusum*[317]		
Sweet Vernal-grass	*Anthoxanthum*	*odoratum*		
Canary-grass	*Phalaris*	*-arundinacea*	(reed)	
		-canariensis		

Impressive as this list may appear it must be borne in mind that since 1970-75 building in Bromham will have destroyed many sites. The biggest loss will be the elms, the loss of which is, of course, not the fault of housing. Dony does not list the walnuts, which were.

It is scarcely surprising that some species specifically said by Abbot to be at or near Bromham are, after more than 200 years, no longer to be found there. *Blackstonia perfoliata* (Yellow-wort); *Utricularia vulgaris* (Lesser Bladderwort – now only one site in Bedfordshire); *Fritillarai meleagris* (Fritillary – now probably extinct in Bedfordshire); and *Sieglingia decumbens* (Heath grass – now confined to the south of the County) are all casualties since Abbot. He found *Caucalis daucoides* and *C latifolia* (both described by Saunders as rare) at Oakley, but the latter was last recorded there in 1920. *Trifolium medium* (Zig-zag clover), which Saunders described as rare and of which he sought a recent record, is scarce, but still in Oakley, however. The same is true of *Astragalis glycyphyllos* (Milk vetch). *Phyllitis scolopendrium* (Harts tongue), which Abbot found near Bromham but Saunders considered rare, seems to have recovered somewhat and is still near Bromham. On the other hand Saunders considered *Sium latifolium* (the greater Water Parsnip) to be plentiful in the Ouse valley but Dony found it only in one site, although he hopes earlier sightings suggest its survival at Bromham. The VCH says that the Stinking Hellebore – *Helleborus foetidus,* Dwarf Elder – *Sambucus ebulus* – and Meadow Brome – *Bromus commutatus* – were to be found at Bromham but it is so no longer, and the first two are rare in the County. The VCH record of Soapwort – *Saponaria officianalis* at Bromham could be confirmed by Dony if it is near Bridgend, but this is one of only two sites in the north of the County. Wild Liquorice – *Astragalus danicus* – found both by Abbot and the VCH, may still be around Oakley bridge. Of those Saunders specifically located at Bromham *Lathyrus nissolia* (Grass vetchling), also listed by the VCH, is mapped by Dony in square 05F and so, again, may be near Bromham bridge. Dony found the Wild Strawberry – *Fragaria vesca* – in square 05B. The author hopes this site is still beside the Northampton Road west of Grange Farm where he and his family picked them in the 1940s. It is pleasant to find the Stinking Iris – *Iris foetidissima* – which Saunders considered rare, still in place at Bromham and Stevington, where he had found it.

[304] Eyre and Spottiswoode, 1911
[305] Borough of Luton Museum and Art Gallery, 1976.
[306] Used for basket making.
[307] Basket making and fencing.
[308] Prevents scurvy.
[309] As its name suggests it was used to heal wounds.
[310] Introduced in 1794.
[311] As it says, deters fleas (and is a treatment for dysentery).
[312] Introduced in 1871.
[313] Treats jaundice.
[314] A purgative.
[315] This is what children use for darts.
[316] This has sharp leaves which can cut fingers.
[317] Sometimes deliberately sown for game birds.

Appendix I Tenants under the Crown of Bromham lands

Hugon de Belchamp (known as Beauchamp)
Baron of Bedford castle
Descent through Beauchamp line (with short depossessions) to
William de Beauchamp
|
John de Beauchamp
(killed at the battle of Evesham 1265)
lands forfeited to crown and given to Prince Edward
reassigned to Amicia, wife of William de Beauchamp
died 1278
|
Divided between John's three sisters

Countess Judith[1]

[Hugh Beauchamp is mesne tenant)
Descent uncertain until about 1250

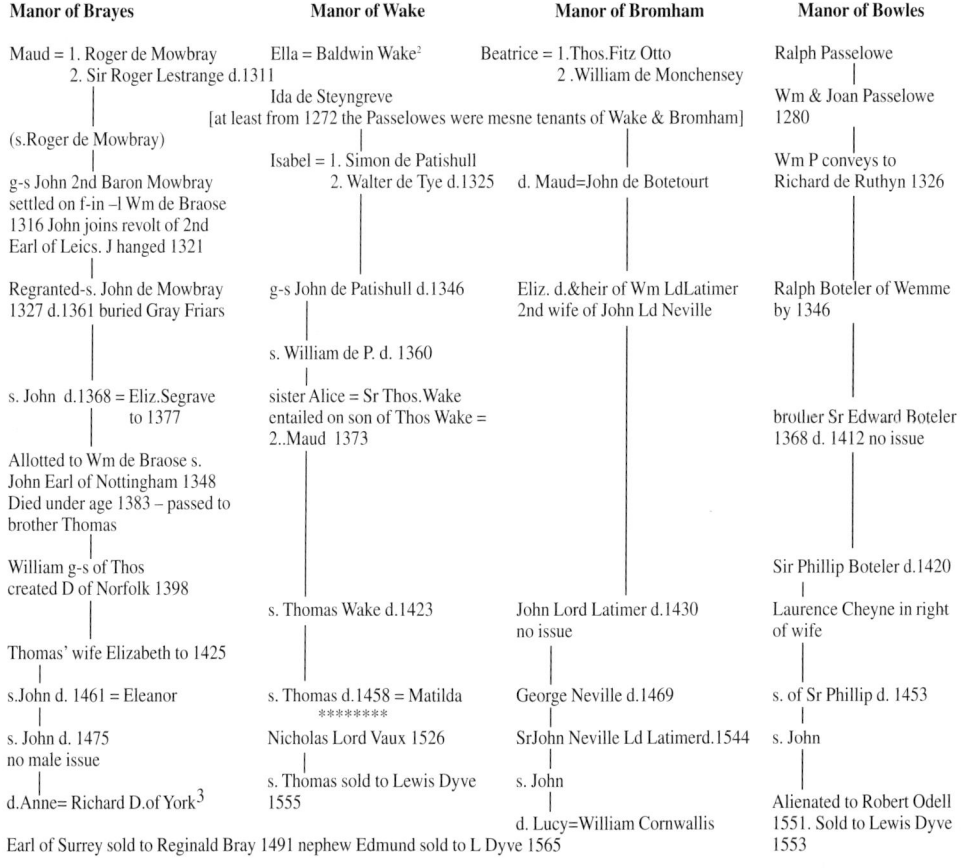

Manor of Brayes	Manor of Wake	Manor of Bromham	Manor of Bowles
Maud = 1. Roger de Mowbray 2. Sir Roger Lestrange d.1311	Ella = Baldwin Wake[2] Ida de Steyngreve [at least from 1272 the Passelowes were mesne tenants of Wake & Bromham]	Beatrice = 1.Thos.Fitz Otto 2 .William de Monchensey	Ralph Passelowe
(s.Roger de Mowbray) g-s John 2nd Baron Mowbray settled on f-in –l Wm de Braose 1316 John joins revolt of 2nd Earl of Leics. J hanged 1321	Isabel = 1. Simon de Patishull 2. Walter de Tye d.1325	d. Maud=John de Botetourt	Wm & Joan Passelowe 1280 Wm P conveys to Richard de Ruthyn 1326
Regranted-s. John de Mowbray 1327 d.1361 buried Gray Friars	g-s John de Patishull d.1346 s. William de P. d. 1360	Eliz. d.&heir of Wm LdLatimer 2nd wife of John Ld Neville	Ralph Boteler of Wemme by 1346
s. John d.1368 = Eliz.Segrave to 1377 Allotted to Wm de Braose s. John Earl of Nottingham 1348 Died under age 1383 – passed to brother Thomas William g-s of Thos created D of Norfolk 1398 Thomas' wife Elizabeth to 1425	sister Alice = Sr Thos.Wake entailed on son of Thos Wake = 2..Maud 1373		brother Sr Edward Boteler 1368 d. 1412 no issue Sir Phillip Boteler d.1420 Laurence Cheyne in right of wife
s.John d. 1461 = Eleanor	s. Thomas Wake d.1423 s. Thomas d.1458 = Matilda ******** Nicholas Lord Vaux 1526 s. Thomas sold to Lewis Dyve 1555	John Lord Latimer d.1430 no issue George Neville d.1469 SrJohn Neville Ld Latimer d.1544 s. John d. Lucy=William Cornwallis	s. of Sr Phillip d. 1453 s. John Alienated to Robert Odell 1551. Sold to Lewis Dyve 1553
s. John d. 1475 no male issue d.Anne= Richard D.of York[3] Earl of Surrey sold to Reginald Bray 1491	nephew Edmund sold to L Dyve 1565		

[1] Count Eustace also held one and a half hides on the Stevington border. Arnulf of Adres, Count of Guines was the mesne tenant of all the lands of Count Eustace in North Bedfordshire.
[2] Other property of Ella Beauchamp in Bromham passed (a) to 2nd d. Elizabeth and became merged with the holding of John de Patishull; (b) to 3rd d. Joan and from her to John Picot. Trace of this is lost after 1335.
[3] Richard Duke of York was the younger son of Edward IV and is said to have been murdered in the Tower of London on the orders of Richard III in 1483. Anne was five years old when she married him. His lands were divided between William Viscount Berkeley (Earl of Nottingham) and D. of Norfolk. The latter, to whom this manor passed on death of former, was killed at Bosworth in 1485 but this manor passed to his son (Earl of Surrey) who sold it to Sir Reginald Bray in 1491.

Appendix II

Harvey's list of Incumbents and Chantry Priests

Incumbents of St Andrew /St Owen   Priests of the Chantry of St Mary

mid-12th C	William de Brumham		
1235-1257	{Radulph de Bedford		
	{F…………..		
1258-1279	Ralphe de Bedeford	1324-	Simon Wolston or Wulstan
1280-1299	Roger de Graveby	1334-1339	John de Oseberton
		1340-1347	John Becke
1363-1397	{John Hayle	1347-	Richard de Wombewell
	{Pbr William Wandesford	-1360	Pbr John Wrabet de Naresby
	{Pbr Elias Witenford		
	{Robert Boregh		
	{Pbr John Wryghte	1363-	Pbr John Wrughte
		-1397	Robert Burgh
1456-1470	{Thomas George	1398-1450	{John Cook
	{Richard Lounde		{Robert Baldock
1471-1479	John Faune	1450-1456	John T……..
1480-1494	William Alen	1471-1479	Nicholas Skypwith[1]
1495-1513	{John Wryght	1480-1494	Robert Halytreholm
	{William Aby		
		c1507	Thomas Ibbott
1521-1546	{Thomas Mendar	c1530	Pbr Henry Atkinson
	{John Patynson	1536	Henry Boswell
		1539-1548	Peter Weyver
	{Alexander Clerke		
c1556	Henry King[2]		
1560-	Thomas Symons[3]		
1564-	David Vaughan		
1588-	Richard Maddocks	Before 1546 the patron was Cauldwell Priory
1597-	Nicholas Barton[4]		
1605-	George Daniel MA[5]		
1608-	John Stokes MA[6]		
1633-1643	Anthony Waters MA[7] (Oliver Thorowgood – curate)		
	Nicholas East (Grobie – curate 1638)		
1661-	Andrew Cater	From 1661 (with one exception by lapse to the
1671/2-1688	Robert Whitehead MA	Bishop of Lincoln in 1671) the patron was Eton College.

129

1688-1712	Simon Gale MA (also of Oakley)
1712-1758	Robert Richards MA
1758-1769	Wyat Francis MA
1769-1799	Thomas Richards BA
1799-1827	Robert Measham MA (also Oakley from May 1818)

Vicars of Bromham andOakley

1827-1866	James Joseph Goodall MA
1866-	Alfred James Coleridge BA
Twentieth century – Canon Browning	Rev. Evans
	Canon Burns
	E Denby Gilbert MA

[1] Rector of Biddenham. d.1492. Bequeathed 20s. to repair bridge.
[2] Patron – Lewis Dyve.
[3] Patron by lapse – Bishop of Lincoln.
[4] Patron – John Dyve.
[5] Patron – Sir Richard Dyer of Great Staughton, Huntingdonshire.
[6] Patron – Dame Beatrice Dyve, widow of John Dyve.
[7] Patron – John Digby, Earl of Bristol (by right of wife Beatrice).

Appendix IIIA

Genealogy – Dyve

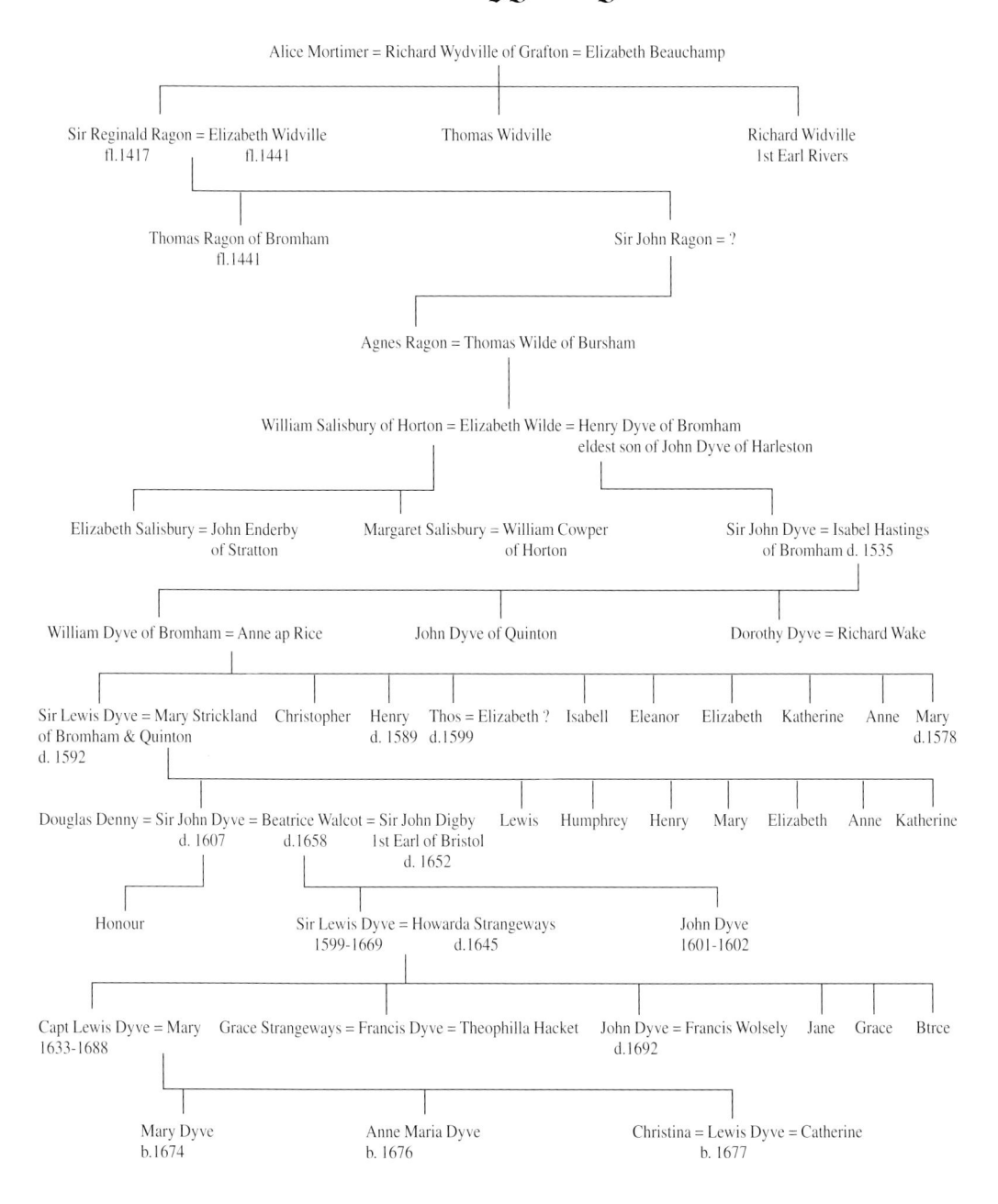

Alice Mortimer = Richard Wydville of Grafton = Elizabeth Beauchamp

- Sir Reginald Ragon = Elizabeth Widville
  fl.1417   fl.1441
- Thomas Widville
- Richard Widville
  1st Earl Rivers

- Thomas Ragon of Bromham
  fl.1441
- Sir John Ragon = ?

Agnes Ragon = Thomas Wilde of Bursham

William Salisbury of Horton = Elizabeth Wilde = Henry Dyve of Bromham
eldest son of John Dyve of Harleston

- Elizabeth Salisbury = John Enderby of Stratton
- Margaret Salisbury = William Cowper of Horton
- Sir John Dyve = Isabel Hastings of Bromham d. 1535

- William Dyve of Bromham = Anne ap Rice
- John Dyve of Quinton
- Dorothy Dyve = Richard Wake

- Sir Lewis Dyve = Mary Strickland
  of Bromham & Quinton
  d. 1592
- Christopher
- Henry d. 1589
- Thos = Elizabeth ? d.1599
- Isabell
- Eleanor
- Elizabeth
- Katherine
- Anne
- Mary d.1578

- Douglas Denny = Sir John Dyve = Beatrice Walcot = Sir John Digby
  d. 1607   d.1658   1st Earl of Bristol
                                        d. 1652
- Lewis
- Humphrey
- Henry
- Mary
- Elizabeth
- Anne
- Katherine

- Honour
- Sir Lewis Dyve = Howarda Strangeways
  1599-1669   d.1645
- John Dyve
  1601-1602

- Capt Lewis Dyve = Mary
  1633-1688
- Grace Strangeways = Francis Dyve = Theophilla Hacket
- John Dyve = Francis Wolsely
  d.1692
- Jane
- Grace
- Btrce

- Mary Dyve
  b.1674
- Anne Maria Dyve
  b. 1676
- Christina = Lewis Dyve = Catherine
              b. 1677

This table is a simplified adaptation from Harvey, The History and Antiquities of the Hundred of Willey (Nicholl –London 1872)

Appendix IIIB
Genealogy – Trevor and Rice-Trevor

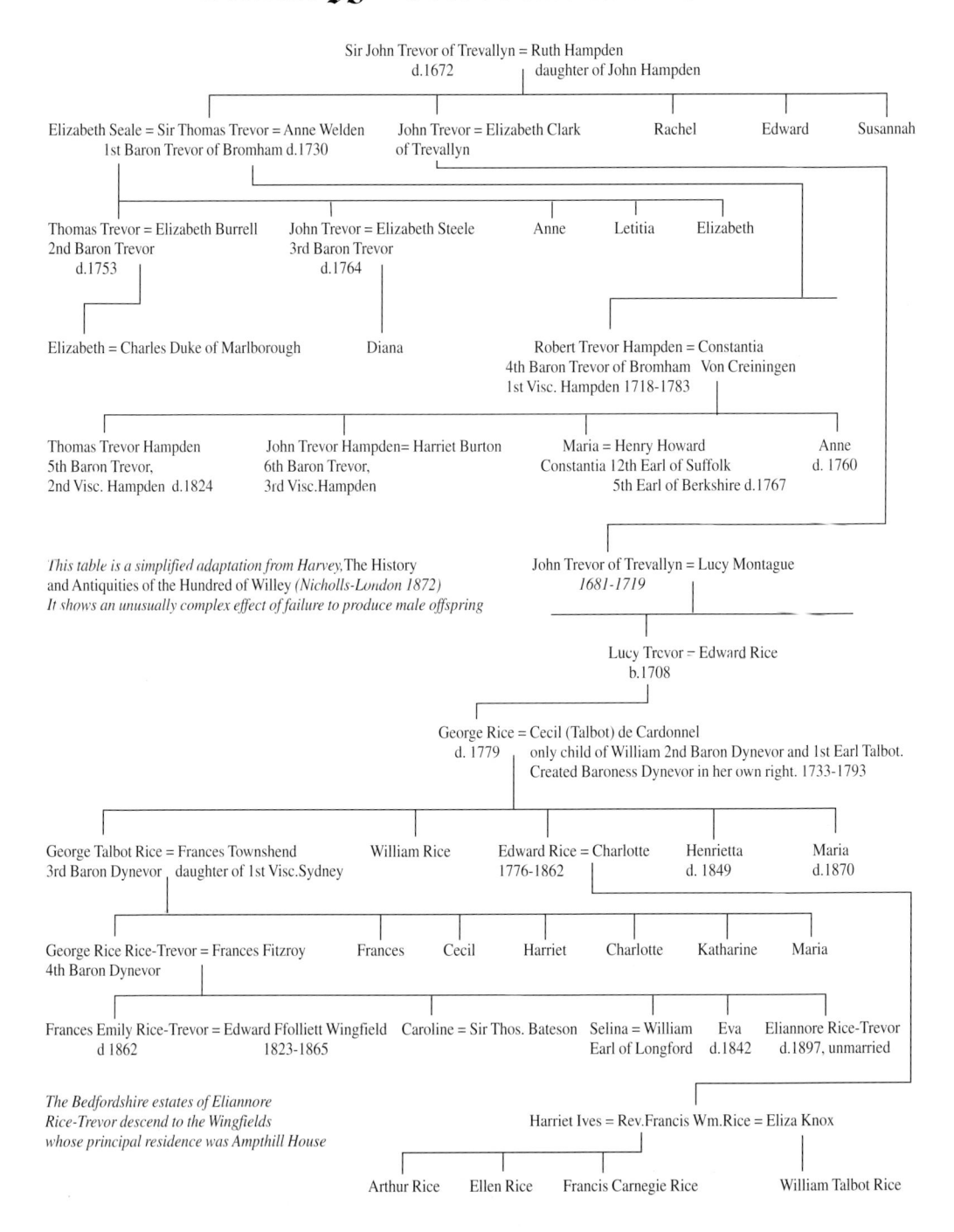

```
                    Sir John Trevor of Trevallyn = Ruth Hampden
                              d.1672              daughter of John Hampden
   ┌───────────────────────────┬──────────────────────────┬──────────┬──────────┬──────────┐
Elizabeth Seale = Sir Thomas Trevor = Anne Welden   John Trevor = Elizabeth Clark   Rachel   Edward   Susannah
                  1st Baron Trevor of Bromham d.1730    of Trevallyn
          ┌────────────────────┬─────────────────────┬──────────┬──────────┐
   Thomas Trevor = Elizabeth Burrell   John Trevor = Elizabeth Steele   Anne   Letitia   Elizabeth
   2nd Baron Trevor                    3rd Baron Trevor
      d.1753                              d.1764
          │                                  │                              ┌────────────┴────────────┐
   Elizabeth = Charles Duke of Marlborough   Diana                 Robert Trevor Hampden = Constantia
                                                                  4th Baron Trevor of Bromham  Von Creiningen
                                                                  1st Visc. Hampden 1718-1783
   ┌──────────────────────────┬────────────────────────────┬─────────────────────────────┬────────────┐
Thomas Trevor Hampden       John Trevor Hampden= Harriet Burton    Maria = Henry Howard              Anne
5th Baron Trevor,           6th Baron Trevor,               Constantia 12th Earl of Suffolk          d. 1760
2nd Visc. Hampden d.1824    3rd Visc.Hampden                      5th Earl of Berkshire d.1767
```

This table is a simplified adaptation from Harvey,The History and Antiquities of the Hundred of Willey (Nicholls-London 1872) It shows an unusually complex effect of failure to produce male offspring

```
                       John Trevor of Trevallyn = Lucy Montague
                                1681-1719
                                    │
                         Lucy Trevor = Edward Rice
                                b.1708
                                    │
                    George Rice = Cecil (Talbot) de Cardonnel
                        d. 1779   only child of William 2nd Baron Dynevor and 1st Earl Talbot.
                                  Created Baroness Dynevor in her own right. 1733-1793
   ┌──────────────────────────┬──────────────┬────────────────────┬──────────────┬──────────┐
George Talbot Rice = Frances Townshend   William Rice   Edward Rice = Charlotte   Henrietta   Maria
3rd Baron Dynevor  daughter of 1st Visc.Sydney              1776-1862                d. 1849     d.1870
        │                                                         │
George Rice Rice-Trevor = Frances Fitzroy   Frances   Cecil   Harriet   Charlotte   Katharine   Maria
4th Baron Dynevor
   ┌──────────────────────────────────┬────────────────────┬──────────────┬──────────┬────────────────┐
Frances Emily Rice-Trevor = Edward Ffolliett Wingfield  Caroline = Sir Thos. Bateson  Selina = William  Eva  Eliannore Rice-Trevor
         d 1862                      1823-1865                                    Earl of Longford  d.1842  d.1897, unmarried
```

The Bedfordshire estates of Eliannore Rice-Trevor descend to the Wingfields whose principal residence was Ampthill House

```
                                          Harriet Ives = Rev.Francis Wm.Rice = Eliza Knox
                             ┌──────────────┬──────────────┐                    │
                        Arthur Rice   Ellen Rice   Francis Carnegie Rice    William Talbot Rice
```

132

Appendix IV   The Bromham May Song[1]

It was the Church family of Biddenham who first brought home to me the fact that there were other versions of this carol still known, and sometimes still sung, in Bedfordshire. Mrs. E. Church gave me the one she used to sing in Kimbolton and the villages on the Bedfordshire border with Huntingdonshire. Her father-in-law, Walter 'Paddy' Church, told me that when he was a boy in Bromham (c. 1880) the custom was for the young men to gather thorn branches the night before May Day, and these they planted in front of the door of all the unmarried women of the village. During May Day morning they went round again, this time to collect their reward in the form of money and sometimes beer or food. They sang on each of these perambulations, using the same tune, but having two sets of words.

BROMHAM MAY SONG

W. Church
Biddenham. 1952.

NIGHT SONG

We've been a-rambling all the night
And the rest part of the day
And now we are returning back again
We've brought you a branch of May.

[1] See also *Folk Song Journal*, No. 4 (1902), p. 182. A Night Song and Day Song collected at Fowlmere in Cambridgeshire are also given in this *Journal*, p. 180. *FSJ*, No. 7 (1905) gives a May carol from Rushden, Northants, and a note on the procession associated with the carol at Southill, Bedfordshire. Further notes on May carols and customs are printed in *FSJ*, No. 14 (1910).

A branch of May so fine and gay
And at your door it stands
It's nothing but a sprout but it's well budded out
By the work of our Lord's hands.

Arise, arise you pretty fair maids
And take your May bush in
Or else in the morning it should be gone
You'll say we've never been.

Arise, arise you pretty fair maids
And wake from your drowsy dream
And step into your dairy house
And fetch a cup of cream.

If not a cup of your cold cream
A jug of your brown ale
And if we should live to tarry in the town
We'll call on you next year.

The clock strikes one
It's time to be gone
No longer can we stay,
God bless you all both little great and small
And send you a happy May.

DAY SONG

Remember us for May is here
And now we do begin
For to lead a life into righteousness
For fear we should die in sin.

Repent, repent you wicked men of all
Repent before you die
Or how do you think that you are to repent
When in the grave you lie.

The hedges and fields are closed (sic) all round
With several sorts of green
Our heavenly Father he waters them
With his heavenly showers of rain.

Take a Bible in your hand
And read a chapter through
And when the day of judgment comes
The Lord will think on you.

I have a purse in my pocket
Drawn up with a silken thread (string)
And all that it wants is a little silver
To line it well within.

[1] From an article by F.B.Hamer in the Journal of the English Folk Dance and Song Society – Volume IX No.2 p.81

Appendix V

Field Names

The value of information derived from field names and locations contained mainly in deeds of conveyance cannot be more clearly demonstrated than by reference to the most historic of them so far as Bromham is concerned. The conveyance of 1651[1] of the sequestrated lands of Sir Lewis Dyve by the Parliamentary Commissioners to his father-in-law, Sir John Strangwaies includes "land between Leybrooke on the north and the Bedford-Northampton road on the south". The Tithe Commissioners records of 1844 refer to that land as Leyside and this name (as Lyeside) had appeared in 1576[2] and subsequently (when it was said to contain stone quarries)[3]. "The Brook" was clearly referred to as Aldwick Brook in 1576 and again in legal documents around 1600. In both sources it is precisely identified as next to land abutting on the Bedford-Stagsden Road. This land is called "Lye side" both then and in 1844 but it is unlikely that this was the name of the brook. The same word describes a piece of land beside the river near Clapham. Aldicks is preserved as a name for land to the north of the brook beween the Hill and Grange Lane, in 1844. To confuse the issue, however, the 1844 survey contains a reference to "Stage brocke fields". We are presented, therefore, with three possible names. "Ley" seems most likely to have been a mistake by those who did not know the local names, since it is almost immediately contradicted. "Stag" appears only to have this single reference to justify its much later adoption as "the river Stag" by late 20th century ordnance surveys. Possibly the people of Bromham in that century showed more sense in not reviving forgotten memories and calling the stream simply "The Brook". However that may be we see clearly that it did once have a distinctive title.

Some field names became of long standing in Bromham, although one has to be careful in identifying them. The "Burnt Meadow" of 1347 is not the "Burnt close" of 1844. The former was said to be "near the chapel" and deeds of 1708 state that it came to be called Brodemede. The latter lies to the south east of Grange Lane. It is often the case that parcels of land come to bear the name of some former owner and the WI scrapbook of 1956 for Bromham notes Burr, Galloways, Harrison's and Georgie Morris's as such. But none of these appear in the Tithe Commissioners' list of 1844, nor do any of these surnames appear in that list of landowners. Such names must have been attached, therefore, little earlier than the end of the nineteenth century and are probably no more than recollections of the names individuals used to identify land. The modern King's Close was named by Robert Skinner Esq., when he erected four estate houses there between the two world wars on a part of Gibbin's Close. This latter name existed in 1707 and survives in the house name given by its first owners to a residence built on the eastern end of that close. There was a King's Close in 1609 and in 1701. It was then 10 acres in extent and could be the King's Field which, in 1844 is listed as part of what later became known as the "Big Field", north of Bowels Wood. That surname is one of the oldest in Bromham and the field name is more likely to have derived from it than from the sovereign who was only ever the ultimate feudal overlord of Bromham land. Perhaps, because its size was that of the square furlong it was, the piece of land the Kings received when Sir Lewis Dyve persuaded them to part with their strips. There are a number of field names in the 1844 list which are obviously, or probably, the names of people. Webbs certainly identifies the former tenant of a small piece of land on the west side of the Hill. The Gibbins family was still resident in the village in 1844 (though not tenants of the piece of land of that name). White, Savage, Hawford (?) and Aldick likewise probably refer to former occupants. If Hennies is derived from a surname it is of some antiquity. It appears as Hinneys in 1608. Blakes Hill sounds a likely candidate but appears to come down from the Blakynhyll of 1442. But these are comparatively few examples and it is possible that the fact that all occupants would have been no more than tenants inhibited designation to them. Beware of "Canvin's Meadow", extensively referred to in reference to the new river cut in 1979 (and actually in Biddenham). This name derives only from a hoarding erected, as a form of advertisement, by the Bedford butchers of that name when they purchased the land in the 1950s. A number of names of long standing appear in the 1844 list and one, at least, survived in 1956. The Slype (ors.Slipe) was then said always to have referred to the strip of land at the foot, and to the west of, the Hill, north of the Brook.

Farm names tend to be of long standing and the oldest of these is Maulivers (presently Mollivers). Berry Farm[4], however, is not referred to by name in 1709 or 1728 when leases of it exist, and "Grange Farm", despite the fact that it always was Glebe land is not usually given that name. Salem Thrift[5], Bowels Wood and Mollivers Wood are among the oldest of all the land names to survive today. Walnut Tree Close figures prominently in the land dispute between the Dyves and the Botelers because it appears that it was actually in dispute. It was somewhere near the church and was, therefore, probably absorbed into the park. Cow Pasture and Sheep Pasture appear in 1609 and still in 1844. The Hurstpytfeld of 1442 and the Huspitt feilde of 1576 still exists in 1844. A number of the early names are those of "furlongs". A furlong was originally the length of the furrow in the common field and came to be applied, in theory, to a square of land of about 10 acres, the sides of which were roughly a "furlong" in length. It should be remembered that these named pieces of land were not necessarily bounded by clear hedgerows (let alone fences), especially shortly after the sort of enclosure that the first Sir Lewis Dyve had indulged in.[6] The descriptions of the disputed lands around the year 1600 frequently refer to them as marked by stones at the corners, and even by poles. In consequence, many of these early names would have disappeared as the land they described was absorbed into larger areas. Typical of the lost names are: Lobbeswick Field, Woodfield (which we can identify since it is said to be towards Steventon Crosse and thus likely to be close to the north end of Bowels Wood), Blacknelfield, Buryehill, Brewsters Yate, Longland, Shortmede furlong, Dedland, Achemere and Verins. The new fields are referred to in the papers of the land dispute as those enclosed by Sir Lewis Dyve and in 1844 we see them extending from Mollivers farmhouse round Mollivers wood.

The cottages by the roadsides of the 1844 survey are not given names but one interesting strip of roadside land in what is now Lower Farm Road, which was then occupied by Samuel King, and was actually church land, is specifically described as "Roadside". It was not always easy to find a spare bit of land on which to build a cottage without the objection of some landowner. Cottages built on strips of land by modern roads appear in other parts of Bedfordshire. Perhaps a benevolent vicar had not raised an objection when, at an earlier date, some homeless family had moved in. If so the new tenants would have discovered that residence on church land had the distinct advantage of avoiding liability to pay tithes.

There follows a selection of names taken mostly from conveyances but also from terriers and other official records. In some cases acreage is recorded. Unfortunately none of these records is accompanied by a reference map and the actual location of the land can normally only be a matter of conjecture. As we have already seen, however, a few of the names survive into the age of maps.

****

A document the present writer has not traced[7], said to be dated 1228, records the names Wulnescroft and Brotherputes. Another of 1290 is said to contain the names Mariespoll and a road called shortfurlong way. The road to the Bridge was, by this time, normally called The King's Highway.

In 1347[8] a terrier was compiled of lands in Biddenham and "on the Bromham side" cultivated on the open field system. It lists the ownership of strips of land in the fields. A few of the field names survive into the nineteenth century as, for instance, meadow called "le Lake" which recurs in 1609, 1701 and 8 and 1844. Sometimes the land has no specific name and is recorded as "pasture next the Fullyngmylne below the Wal" and "pasture le Conhelm at the pond up to the willows". Otherwise the names are clear, though now long forgotten. Bonewode and Malerbes were both pastures with spinneys. In the dispute between the Dyves and the Botelers at the end of the 16th century the latter regarded Malerbes as a particularly fertile piece of land. There was a Pytul at Sarlefryth.[9] Large strip fields included Longehul and Shorthul, Palyshul, Stokewellelcone and le Longyerde near the chapel. There were meadowlands le Figers, Hykkesholm and Burnt meadow.

Some of these names, slightly amended, may recur in a document dated 1442.[10] Eatsfield, Lynchfurlong, Langmede, Langmadedych, Achemershfurlong, le Hurst, Harlewene, Stonyfurlong, Clyppyscroft, Nether Watelond, Shortfurlong, Blakynhythfeld, Malemede and Blakynhyll. We can, at least, locate Clapham Dam at the ford at the end of Lower Farm Road.

Bridgende is first mentioned in 1576 and there is a reference to "a messuage called the Vyne" which is then described as an Inne and seems to have been Bromham's first public house. Oate Close is mentioned in documents relating to the Dyve-Boteler dispute as being in the East Field. The latter must have been one of the common fields of pre-enclosure. The former is probably carved out of it by that enclosure.

A post mortem inquisition of the property of Sir Lewis Dyve in Bromham, Stagsden and Steventon in 1609[11] has already been remarked upon as containing the names Cow Pasture, Sheep Pasture, King's Close and Pasture called Maliavers. So has the historic conveyance to Sir John Strangwaies in 1651.[12] Salem Thrift and Mollivers Wood are mentioned in this, as is a Blartnell Close "abutting on Grange Lane". So one of the minor thoroughfares receives a surprisingly early mention. This conveyance notes that Eton College owns the Grange, which is then in the occupation of John Abbeny and exempt from the sequestration. It also records that the estate is committed to paying annually 6 shillings to St John's Hospital, Bedford and 10 shillings "to repair the first arch of the Stone Bridge over part of the River Ouse". Sir John paid £4970.13s.2d for the Bromham estate.

The closing days of the Dyve's possession of the estate generated a large quantity of parchments and probably some profit to lawyers because the family never recovered from its losses in the civil war and was driven to mortgage its property. In 1700/1[13] Lewis Dyve mortgaged the Bromham estate to Sir Thomas Trevor for £3650. In 1707 he surrendered his equity of redemption for £1000 and in 1707/8 he conveyed the legal title to Sir Thomas for a further £5713.8s.7d.[14] Many of the names in those documents are supported by a long and full "note" of the extent of the estate, prepared in 1707. Since these documents record the size of the various parcels of land some of those we have already named will be repeated. Newfields is obviously what became the large undivided "Big Field" of the mid-twentieth century. Since it is described in 1707 as covering 240 acres it must then have referred to the whole of the Big Field. Folklore in the mid-twentieth century had it that this was once the common. It was, of course, like most of the land, once held in common and cultivated in strips. But a good deal, if not the whole, of it had been appropriated by Sir Lewis Dyve in the sixteenth century. Savages Close, of 7 acres, adjoined it on the Stevington boundary. By 1844 this area had been subdivided into numerous individual parcels of land, as had the other large areas such as Lornd pasture (70 acres), Old Warren and Oates Close (62 acres), and the Lake meadow (33 acres). Forty Acre and Twenty Acre meadows explain themselves. Sheep Close was of 40 acres. Small areas included The Lawne (7 acres), Huspitt close (5 acres), Smith's Ground (4 acres, and also already a subdivided part of what became the Big Field), Broad Close (5 acres) and a one acre plot "north of the Church" which was to become the old cricket field. Salem Thrift and Bowels Wood, at 13 acres and 15 acres respectively, were much their present size, although the tithe map of 1844 indicates Bowels Wood not extending as far as the track to Stevington. Something seems to have happened to King's Close, which was said to be of ten acres when it was leased to George Read in 1701[15] but to be of 4 acres in 1708. Not surprisingly some of the 1707 names do not recur in 1844.[16]

The Trevors leased individual properties, as we shall see in the case of Berry Farm, but did not sell any large portions of their estate. The next extensive account of property in Bromham is that prepared by the Tithe Commissioners in 1844. Early in the nineteenth century, as an agricultural society increasingly gave place to industry, payment of tithes in kind was seen as an outdated and burdensome anomaly. It did not occur to anyone, of course, simply to abolish them. The Commutation of Tithes Act made provision for the payment in kind to be commuted to a rentcharge, payable in money, the amount of which was assessed on the value of fixed quantities of wheat, oats and barley established by an average of the previous seven year's prices. (In the case of Bromham this was 7s.0¼d. for wheat, 3s.11½d. for barley and 2s.9d for oats.) Parties might agree by 1838 on a permanent commutation after which, if no agreement had been reached, Commissioners would make an award based on the seven years preceding 1835. Happily, no agreement was reached in Bromham and the survey by an assistant commissioner (Thomas Smith Woolley of South Collingham, Notts) of all land holding in that time is of sufficient information value for it to be set out in full. His map, (property names added), is attached. The Duke of Bedford, Eton College, the Vicar and one or two others own individual property. Otherwise the landowner, in all cases, was the Honourable George Rice-Trevor. The total area covered was 1798 acres 10 perches, of which 707 acres 1 rood were arable and 779 acres and 21 perches were meadow or pasture. Woodland covered 74 acres 2 roods and 24 perches; 24 acres were occupied with houses and gardens and domestic buildings, 60 acres were roads and waste and 153 acres 1 perch was Glebe land. Tithes were payable in most cases both to the Vicar, and to Eton College as the owners of the advowson. The total annual value assessed was £350.11s.5d. to Eton College and £220 to the Vicar. In the following list is set out the map reference number, the names of the fields referred to, the name of the tenant and the amounts of each of the two tithes. Rather inconveniently, the commissioner established the amount of tithe per tenant, which must have meant a certain amount of recalculation every time a part of each tenancy was subsequently re-let (or ultimately sold), and which makes it almost impossible to compare amounts with those payable in 1924 (although where this is possible it is done). A tenant's total tithe is, therefore, stated in the case of the first property he holds on the list.

Enclosure

Much later enclosure of village common lands was authorised by private Acts of Parliament and is therefore, fully recorded. There is no record of enclosure in Bromham and the inference has been that it was "early". The inference, of course, is that the Dyves did it, with or without compensation. This is verified by evidence given in the legal proceedings at the beginning of the seventeenth century concerning the land in Biddenham and Bromham in dispute between the Botelers and the Dyves. From these the first Sir Lewis Dyve would certainly seem to have been addicted to appropriating any land he could lay his hands on. He is accused of stopping up a number of rights of way (to which his answer is that he provided more convenient ways). William Boteler says; "As to the enclosing of common meadows in Bromham by Sir Lewis 40 years previously, defendant has heard that before the enclosure his father kept a great number of cattle in the common fields of Bromham, which since the enclosure he has ceased to do." There is specific reference to some of this land such as the "New Close", the Lake and Fullake, as well as an "excellent" piece of land apparently next to Sir Lewis' pastures known as Malherbis. Sir John Dyve seems to have admitted as much for he says, ". . . his father did take in certen Lands that were auncient arrable lands in Bromham for which the Lord Latimers tenaunts had or might have had as he thinketh commons in the same inclosed lands . . ." Sir Lewis is said to have persuaded the commoners to exchange their strips by reminding them of the greater ease of transporting produce from a single piece of land.

It is interesting to note that Biddenham and Stagsden, although substantially wholly owned by the Trevors since the early seventeenth century, were not enclosed until 1828; a very late date for such action. The Dyves, of course, had been in no position to enclose Biddenham because the Botelers owned most of it.

One must assume that the lack of enthusiasm for the project, specifically stated by the last Viscount Hampden, was shared by his predecessors in title. He died in 1824 and the Rice family obviously lost no time in reaping the advantages of enclosure to the principal landowner.

Public Houses

The Swan Inn has been referred to in the account of the sale of the estate in 1924. It was the only public house in Bromham for the first half of the twentieth century and even that was qualified by the fact that it was half in Kempston. But earlier in the village history there had been others. The Vyne is the earliest to be mentioned. Its name appears in deeds of 1576 and 1600. The Dyve/Boteler settlement around that time describes it as in Bridgend. In 1709 it is referred to as The Vyne Tree when it is leased to William Staines for £57.12s.3d. It is referred to as in Bromham and Kempston and is, therefore, obviously, The Swan by an earlier name. Certainly an inn was called The Swan in 1853.[17] On an estate map later in the century The Swan is shown as leased to (probably a later) William Staines. Kelly's Directory for 1869 says that the Judges on the Norfolk circuit (later the Midland circuit) met the sheriff of Bedford here. A map of 1798 shows a toll gate here. This is probably a side gate to Bromham. In 1823 the licensee was Anthony Chibnall, John Hart had succeeded him by 1864 and Samuel Harrison in 1869. He is still the occupier in 1891 and his widow seems to have continued the licence until 1903. It is interesting to note that R Quenby and Sons took over the lease of the Mill in 1905 from Frederick Chibnall Harrison and in 1919 and 1924 George Quenby is recorded as licensee of The Swan. In 1903 the brewers Newland & Nash leased the premises from the executors of Miss Rice-Trevor. They had been the brewers for The Crown, which closed in 1904 when it was demolished to permit the widening of the Bridge. Its last landlord was James Rust. There is a reference in 1810 to "The Leathern Bottle" and it seems likely that this was an earlier name for The Crown.

The Dovecot

Alan Whitworth[18] says that the dovecot in Bromham was demolished in 1710. This was, in fact, the dovecot erected by Sir Lewis Dyve shortly before 1605. In legal papers relating to the resolution of the dispute between him and William Boteler of Biddenham there is a reference to the dovehouse newly built by Sir Lewis Dyve in his Conygrave. In that same set of papers it is said, in 1595, that this Conygrave almost surrounded the house of John Dyve. A conygrave is a rabbit warren[19]. This one was otherwise called the Churchfield when it was conveyed to Sir Thomas Trevor as part of the direct lands of Bromham Hall in April 1708 and it lay to the south of the churchyard. It is not clear why Sir Thomas Trevor demolished this dovecot. The land in question became part of the park sometime after 1710 so it may have interfered with the view envisaged by this development. Alternatively it may have been near enough to the house for the pigeons to sit on the roof and block the gutters. It may be that the old dovehouse was in need of refurbishment in the light of Elizabeth Boteler's impressive new one built at Biddenham in 1706.[20]

Whatever the reason it was demolished and re-erected in the field immediately west of Berry Farm house beside the Bedford-Northampton road (which is called "dovehouse close" in 1844 although no building is shown upon it at that time). The oldest part of that farmhouse today has the date 1664 on an eave facing the bridge. The farm does not seem always to have been part of the estate. In 1635 farmland at Bridge End and Box End was bought by John Malcott of Newport Pagnell. By the time it was conveyed to Henry Cater, a London merchant, in 1661 there was a farmhouse, not mentioned earlier. In 1684 sixty acres of the land was said not to be grazed. Possibly this was the Moor from which Moor End derives its name. By 1710, however, the Trevors had acquired the farm[21] and Sir Thomas leased it for 12 years to Joseph Holt at an annual rent for the first four years and then for £180 for the last eight years. That lease records that the rent should include "one young fatte turkey and one young fatte goose" on 25th December each year. It also requires the tenant to supply "all such young pidgeons as the said Lord Chief Justice shall have occasion to use or think fit to spend in his or their family during the time of his or their dwelling at Bromham and soe many young pidgeons more as he or they shall think fitt to send for to London for his or their use there". The lease gave leave to the tenant to pull down the "old dovehouse standing in the said Warren". It seems likely, therefore, that the intention was that the tenant should use the materials from one dovecot to build another. He would certainly need one in order to comply with the terms of the lease and its existence is confirmed when Berry Farm was again let, on that occasion to Thomas Clark (for £140), in 1728. The tenant covenants to preserve "the flight of pidgeons" in the dovehouse.[22]

---

[1] DDWW15. The references to these documents in this section are those used by the Bedfordshire and Luton Archive and Record Service. They may be consulted at its offices at the County Hall, Bedford.
[2] TW 11/86.
[3] As in the legal documents relating to the Dyve – Boteler land dispute.
[4] It is not Bury Farm, as it is so often misnamed. That is in Stagsden.
[5] Appearing in 1707 as Sallow Thrift, but this seems a temporary aberration.
[6] See below.
[7] But in the manuscript list he has seen its reference given as F6 vi 74.

[8] CRT 130 Bid 5.
[9] A phygtle (modern spelling – pightle) is simply a small plot of land and in 1707, for instance, describes at least one two acre orchard.
[10] TW11/77.
[11] DDWW 388.
[12] DDWW 15.
[13] DDWW 17.
[14] DDWW 20 and 23. Names in this deed still used in 1844 are marked with an asterisk on the table of the Tithe Commissioners' survey which is attached.
[15] DDWW 389.
[16] For example, Nether pasture, Tardy Piece, Broome close, Beare Lane spinney, Pixleys spinney, Marches and Blacknall close.
[17] See The Bedford Times 24th September 1853.
[18] *Dovecots and Pigeon Houses of Bedfordshire* (1996) 25 BM at p.93.
[19] The word is variously spelt. Conynger, conygie and conyger are all alternatives. All would have been pronounced to rhyme with "honey". So would "coney", until the nineteenth century. This pronunciation makes the derivation from the Latin even more obviously direct. The Romans called a rabbit cuniculus. The scientific name is still "lapis cuniculus". Ever economic in words they used the same word to describe an underground burrow. "Warren" had replaced it by the time of the conveyances around 1700.
[20] This was restored in 1932. It was demolished in 1960.
[21] Sir Thomas Trevor also acquired, by lease in 1705, originally for ten years, the Glebe land of Grange Farm (together with the rectory). That farm had been part of the lands of Cauldwell Priory and passed to Eton College at the dissolution. In 1721 Lord Trevor leased that farm for 12 years initially to the brothers George and John Negus – DDWW 218 and 219.
[22] DDWW 74 and DDWW 85.

Appendix VI

The 1844 Tithe Commission Valuation

Map ref	Property	Type	Tenant	Vicars tithe	Eton College	Comments
1	Cobblers*	grass	David Henman	Rectoral glebe		with 6; 7;8;9;12;55;83
2	Cobblers*	grass	William Poole	£1. 10s. 0d		Owned by William Whitworth
3	Cobblers*	grass	Richard Barker	£4. 14s. 0d	£15. 6s. 0d	with 15
4	Little Huinies and Great Huinies	grass	Thomas Gregory	£5. 6s. 0d		
5	10 acres, 8 acres*,14 acres*, Bromham close, Paine*, Slade* & Sheep Walk	arable & grass	Richard Barker	see 3		
6	Dead Woman Willow Close	arable & grass	David Henman	see 7 & 8		
7 & 8	Homestead and garden Road side	grass	David Henman	£14. 6s. 0d	£10. 14s. 0d	with 6;7;8;9;12;55;83
9	Newlands & peas close	ar & gr.	David Henman	see 7		
10	Salem Thrift wood*	wood	Mary,Jane etc. Trevor	17s. 6d		
11	Salem Thrift wood	wood	Hon Geo Rice Trevor	£13. 3s. 6d	£6. 7s. 0d	with 16;28;40;71
12	Three Corner Close, Pooles Close Meadow Close*, Pecks Close, Cow Pasture*, Fern Close, 8 Acres, Sandys Piece Spinnies and 7 Acres	mixed	David Henman	see 7 & 8		
13	Stevington Cross* Close & Long Baulk	arable	John Lavender	£29. 9s. 6d	£50. 0s. 0d	with 14;42;59
14	Hawfords, Bunnies field* & Savages*	arable	John Lavender	see 13		
15	Lady Close	arable	William Biggs	£16. 7s. 0d	£21. 8s. 0d	with 19;25;33;69;75;76
16	Bowels* (wood)	wood	Hon Geo Rice Trevor	see 11		
17	Bowels	grass	William Scammell	£3.10s. 0d	£8. 7s. 0d	with 78;80;82
18	Spinney	wood	John Rogers	In 1924 17 = Lot 42 tithe £2. 6s. 8d £49. 17s. 0d	£122. 11s. 0d	with 26;29;36;38;45;54;56;58
19	Bowels, Little Bowels* & (Stephen) Earles Close*	pasture	William Biggs	see 15		
20	Cottage and garden		John Brockett			
21	Gardens		John Inskip & others	1s. 6d		
22	Part of Bowels*	grass	John Garner	13s. 6d	6d	with 85
23	Garden		Henry Islip	1s. 6d		
24	Cottage and garden		Matthew Tebbut	1s. 3d		
25	Horse Close, Smiths Ground* Nottingham Close* & L'lle Hawfords		William Biggs	see 15		

143

No.	Field name	Type	Occupier/Owner	Value/Tithe	Notes
26	Swine Pits*, Nunsfield, Park Close Hard Ground, Kings field*?, Barn Close*, & Three Corner Close		John Rogers	see 18	
27	Homestead, Spinney, Little New Field* Great New Field*	arable & grass	Amos Maxey	£14. 0s. 6d £19. 16s. 0d see 11 see 18	with 41 and 44 This is Mollivers Farm. Tithe in 1924 £69. 1s. 5d
28	Maulivers* Wood	wood	Hon Geo Rice Trevor		
29	Maulivers Reeds Close, orchard and homestead	grass	John Rogers		
30	Cottage and garden		Thomas Maxey	2s. 9d	Part of this is Lot 14 in 1924. Tithe 6s. 6d
31	Cottage and garden		Thomas King	5s. 6d	
32	Cottages and gardens		Henry Islip & others	17s. 0d	
33	Pightle		William Biggs	see 15	Part of this is Lot 17 in 1924. Tithe 6s. 4d.
34	Cottages and gardens		John Islip & others	13s. 0d	
35	Cow pasture, the lawns & Oakley	arable & wood	John Rogers	£12. 0s. 0d see 18	This forms, in 1924, Lots 21 (7s.8d), 23 (The Greenwood – 4s.), 24 (1s.8d) and 25 (2s.8d)
36	Long Hills and Spinney	grass	Charles Roger	£2. 12s. 0d	Owned by Duke of Bedford
37	meadow near Oakley			6d	2s. 0d
38	Long Hills north, meadow & spinney				
39	Whites Meadow	grass	Samuel King	£9. 6s. 0d	
40	Spinney in Whites Meadow	wood	Hon Geo Rice Trevor	see 11	£3. 14s. 0d with47;65
41	Blake Hill pasture*?, & 7 Acres*	ar.& gr	Amos Maxey	see 27	
42	Wet Lands, Ley Close*, Sheep Pasture* & Spinney		John Lavender	see 13	
43	Parsons Hard Ground		Robert Hulat		
44	Reeds Home Close	grass	Amos Maxey	see 27	
45	Parkes Home Close	grass	John Rogers	see 15	Vicarial glebe – no tithe
46	Glebe Close	grass	Joseph Goohall		Tithe in 1924 – 11s.
47	Wheat Lands	grass	Sammuel King	see 39	
48	Great Meadow, Home Close, Long Grounds, Great Huspits*Plantation Little Ploughed Ground*, Cockyard* & Great Corn Ground	arable & grass	Henry Gibbins	£32. 1s. 6d	£67. 12s. 0d with 49;64;64a all church land occupied by the vicar
49	Parsons Meadow	grass	Joseph Goohall		with 53;57;62 church land
50	Parsons Meadow	grass	Samuel King		church land
51	Spinney in plowed Huspits	wood	Hon Geo Rice Trevor		see 11
52	Church Ground*		Samuel King		church land

144

53	Cottages, Meadow, Further Asplins Middle Asplins & Hither Asplins	arable & grass	Henry Gibbins	see 48	(possibly after William Aspland who is named in 1700)
54	26 Acres & hard ground	arable	John Rogers	see 18	
55	Mauns Meadow and Leys	grass	David Henman		Glebe Land belonging to Eton College
56	Ford Meadow	grass	John Rogers	see 18	
57	Great Meadow	grass	Henry Gibbins	see 48	
58	Ford Meadow, 26 Acres, 15 Acres homestead garden, 12 Acres, Ox Yard*, Home Close*, Lake Meadow* and 26 Acres Meadow	arable & grass	John Rogers	see 18	
59	Lake Meadow*	grass	John Lavender	see 13	church land
60	Cottage, pightle and roadside	grass	Samuel King	see 13	
61	Parks		John Lavender	see 48	
62	Homestead & pightle	grass	Henry Gibbins	see 13	
63	Homestead, Orchard & Fawn furlong Plantation		John Lavender		church land
63a	Vicarage House and garden and close		John Lavender		church land with 46;49;64a
64	Church and Churchyard		Joseph Goohall		
64a			Joseph Goohall		
65	Gibbins Close*	grass	Samuel King	see 39	then of 6 acres
66	Cottages and gardens and pightle		John Norse & others	17s. 6d	
67	Cottages and gardens		George Orpin	4s. 6d	
68	Cottage and garden		John King	6d	
69	Homestead and orchard		William Biggs	see 15	
70	Gardens		John Brockett&others	5s. 9d	
71	Church ground, grove, barrow.		Hon Geo Rice Trevor	see 11 for non-church ground	property underlined is church land
72	Mead pleasure grounds, Mansion Courtyard, kitchen garden Stable and dairy yard		Hon Geo Rice Trevor	see 11	
73	Ozier Bed and wood		Miller Golding	£4. 14s. 0d	£6. 7s. 0d with 74
74	Part of the park and marshes part of the park and Home close		Miller Golding		
75	Mill Holme*		William Biggs	see 15	
76	Mill house, Mill and close		William Biggs	see 15	
77	Blacksmiths shop and pightle		John Prudden	Tithe in 1924 £2. 9s. 4d 2s. 6d	No tithe in 1924 – not surprisingly
78	Cow yard* Cottage & Godfreys Close*	grass	William Scammell	see 17	One lot in 1924 Tithe 8s. 0d

No.	Field	Owner	Type	Tithe	Notes
79	Part of the Swan Inn	Anthony Chibnall		£1. 9s. 0d	with 81 and 86 (the other part in Kempston) Note no other Inn appears. No ref. to The Vine
80	Dove House close and One Land	William Scammell	ar. & gr.	see 17	
81	Bridge End Close, pits and cottage	Anthony Chibnall	ar. & gr.	see 79	£6. 2s. 3d Apart from the then police house this was Lot 47 in 1924. Tithe 7s. 9d
82	Ley side*	William Scammell	arable	see 17	
83	Peartree Close, Aldicks* and meadow	David Henman	arable		Glebe land – Eton College This name is attached to different land over time
84	Burnt Close	David Henman		see 7 & 8	With apart of 83 (no tithe) all 84 and 85 is Lot 38 in 1924. Tithe 12s.1d
85	Cottages, garden and pightle	John Garner	grass	see 22	
86	Slipe baulk* and Webbs Close	Anthony Chibnall	ar&gr	see 79 Lot 45 in 1924. Tithe 10	

146

The Tithe Commissioners' Survey 1844

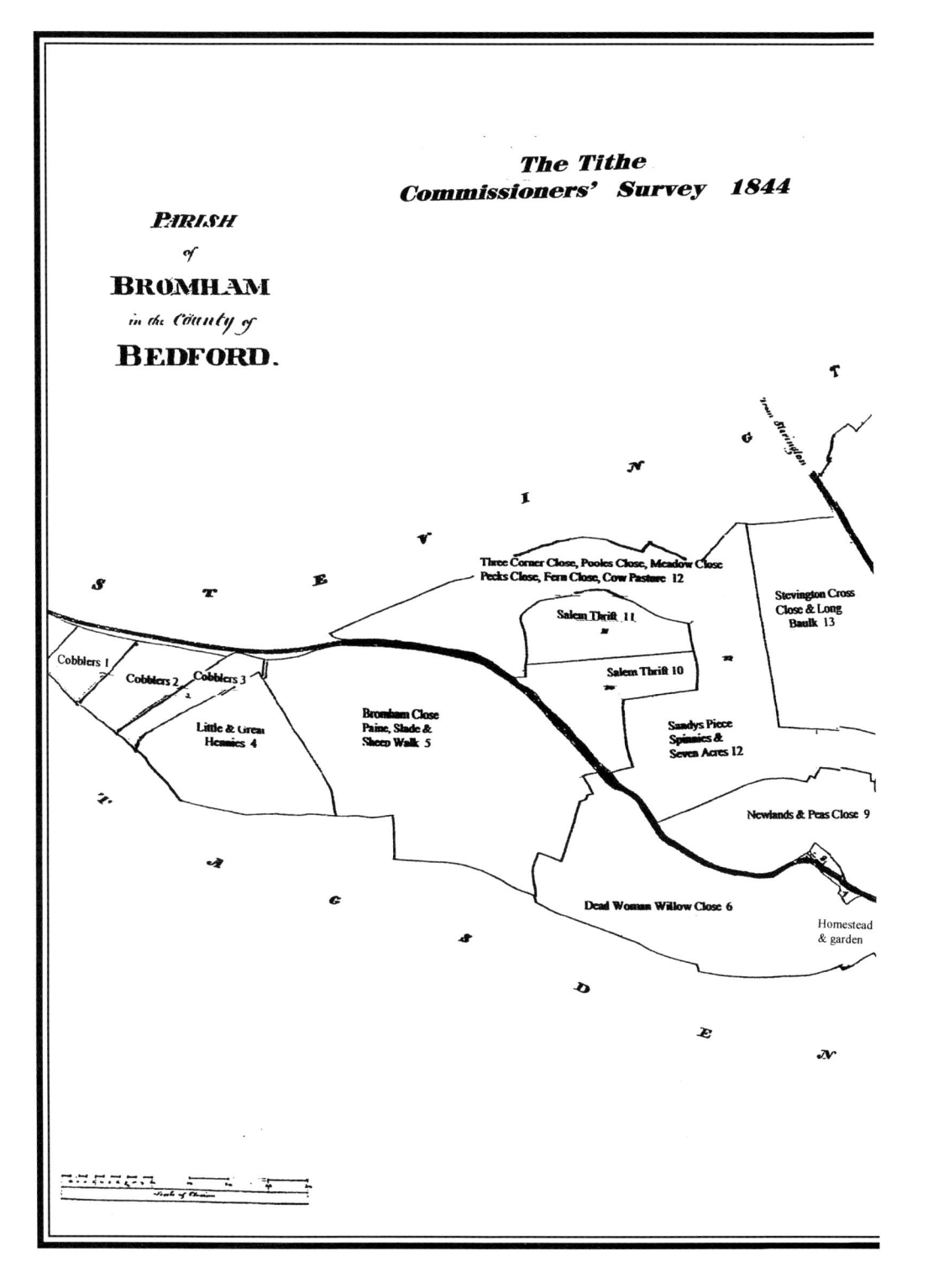

PARISH of BROMHAM in the County of BEDFORD.

Three Corner Close, Pooles Close, Meadow Close, Pecks Close, Fern Close, Cow Pasture 12

Stevington Cross Close & Long Baulk 13

Salem Thrift 11

Salem Thrift 10

Cobblers 1
Cobblers 2
Cobblers 3

Little & Great Hennies 4

Bromham Close Paine, Slade & Sheep Walk 5

Sandys Piece Spinnies & Seven Acres 12

Newlands & Peas Close 9

Dead Woman Willow Close 6

Homestead & garden

Map of fields with labels:

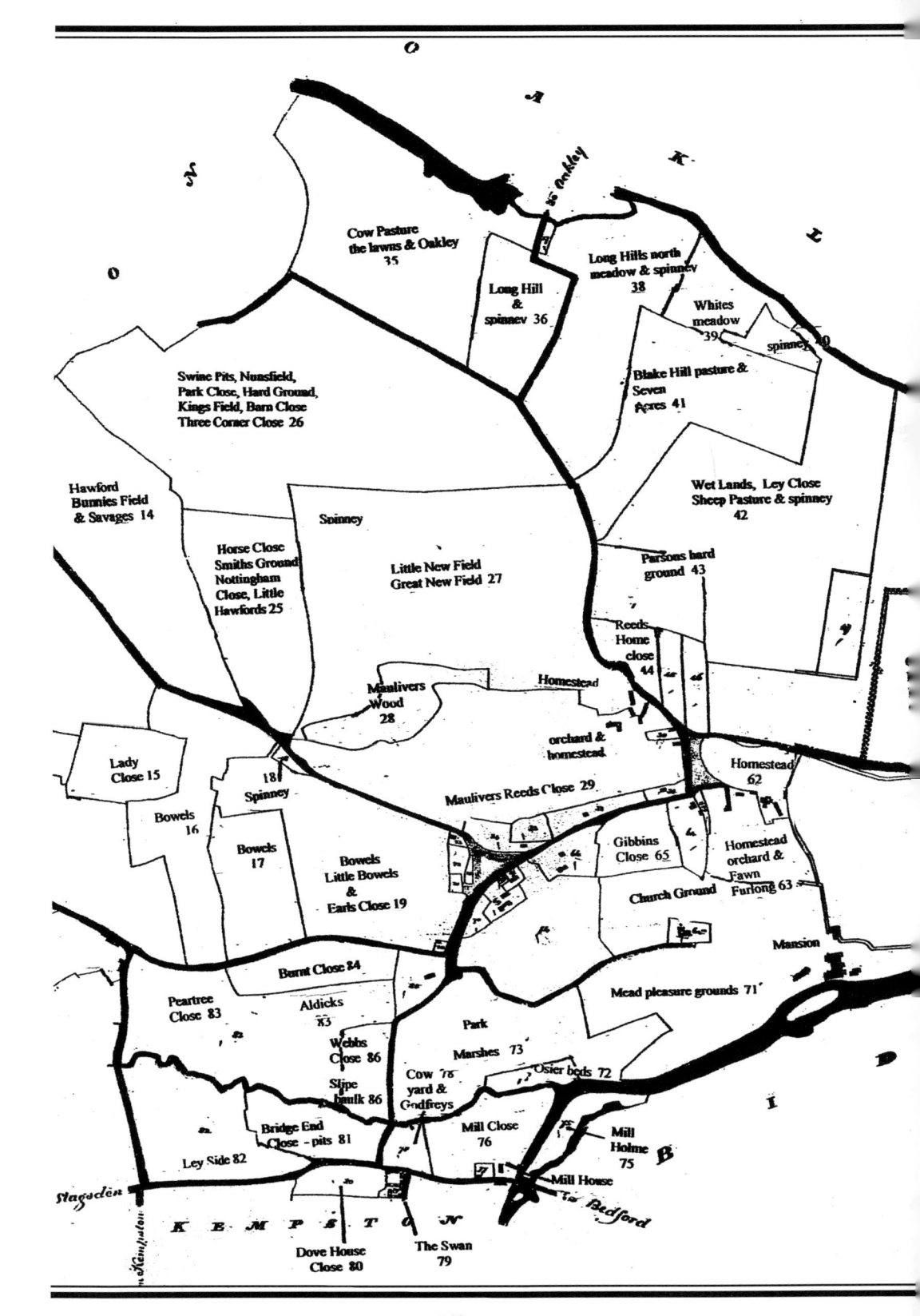

- to Oakley
- Cow Pasture the lawns & Oakley 35
- Long Hill & spinney 36
- Long Hills north meadow & spinney 38
- Whites meadow 39
- spinney 40
- Swine Pits, Nunsfield, Park Close, Hard Ground, Kings Field, Barn Close Three Corner Close 26
- Blake Hill pasture & Seven Acres 41
- Hawford Bunnies Field & Savages 14
- Horse Close Smiths Ground Nottingham Close, Little Hawfords 25
- Spinney
- Little New Field Great New Field 27
- Wet Lands, Ley Close Sheep Pasture & spinney 42
- Parsons hard ground 43
- Reeds Home close 44
- Maulivers Wood 28
- Homestead
- orchard & homestead
- Lady Close 15
- Spinney 18
- Homestead 62
- Bowels 16
- Maulivers Reeds Close 29
- Bowels 17
- Bowels Little Bowels & Earls Close 19
- Gibbins Close 65
- Homestead orchard & Fawn Furlong 63
- Church Ground
- Mansion
- Burnt Close 84
- Peartree Close 83
- Aldicks 85
- Mead pleasure grounds 71
- Webbs Close 86
- Park Marshes 73
- Slipe baulk 86
- Cow yard & Godfreys
- Osier beds 72
- Bridge End Close - pits 81
- Mill Close 76
- Mill Holme 75
- Ley Side 82
- Mill House
- to Bedford
- Stagsden
- to Kempston
- KEMPSTON
- Dove House Close 80
- The Swan 79

148

Parsons Meadow 49 & 50

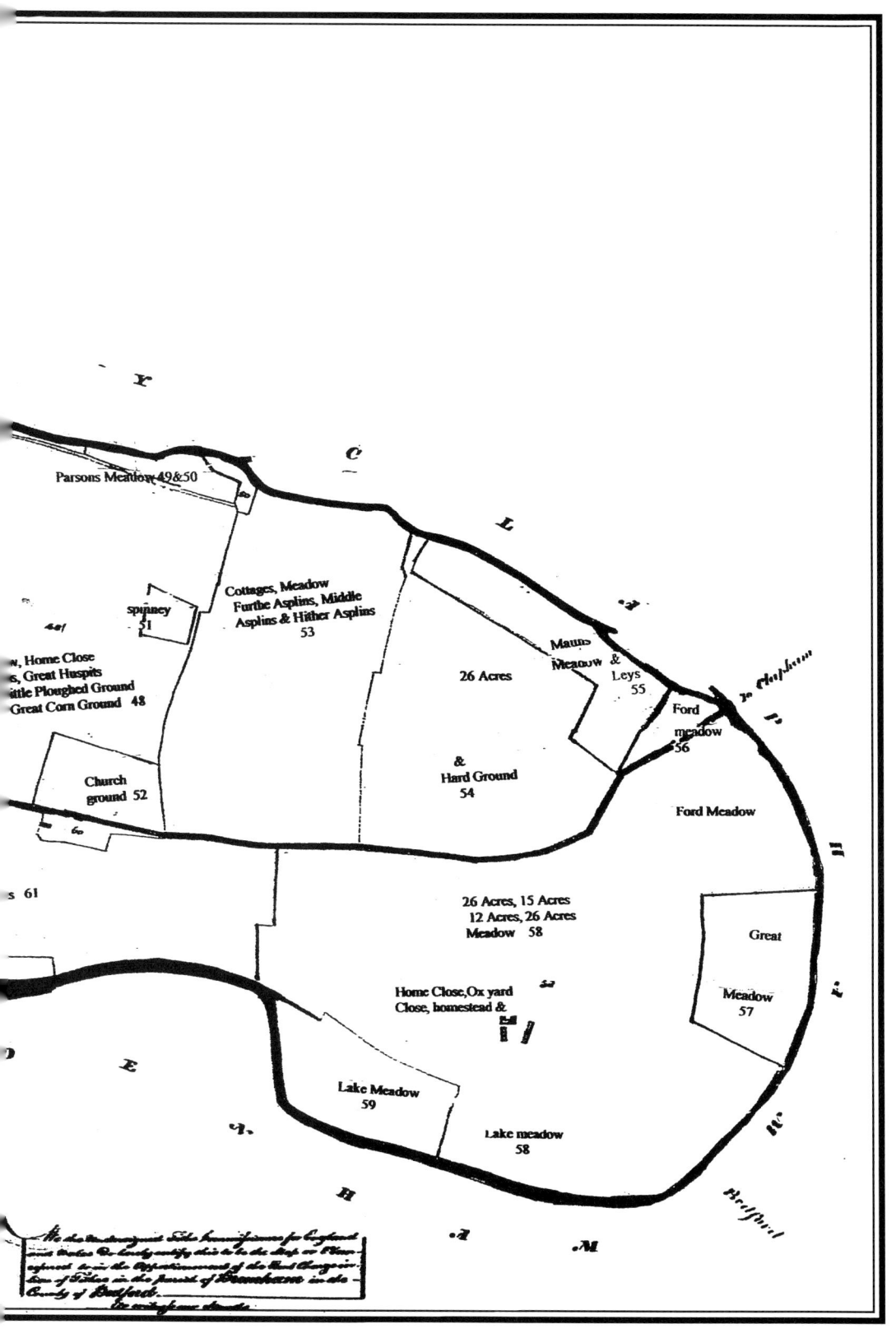

spinney 51

Cottages, Meadow
Furthe Asplins, Middle
Asplins & Hither Asplins
53

w, Home Close
s, Great Huspits
ittle Ploughed Ground
Great Corn Ground 48

26 Acres

Maults Meadow & Leys 55

Ford meadow 56

& Hard Ground 54

Church ground 52

Ford Meadow

s 61

26 Acres, 15 Acres
12 Acres, 26 Acres
Meadow 58

Great Meadow 57

Home Close, Ox yard
Close, homestead &

Lake Meadow 59

Lake meadow 58

149

Appendix VII

The Rate Account Book for 1928[1]

This is, in a sense, a random year to choose to look at property occupation in Bromham. Annual rate account books are held by the office of the Bedford and Luton Archive Service for every year from 1920. This one was chosen because it shows where the last estate tenants settled down, as well as recording long standing names before "new" residents flooded in.

Comments in brackets have been added.

Name of householder	Name of Property	Nominal Value £	Rate £	s	d
Church GAR	Mill House	22	5	8	2
Prudden Wm	Smithy	11	2	14	1
Smith G	Police House	9	2	4	3
Lock & Co	Garage	38	9	6	10
		18	4	8	6
Gibbard Mrs EJ	Newlands	18	4	8	6
Quenby George	The Swan	32	7	17	4
Millard JT	Bottom Lodge	7	1	14	5
Waller Henry	The Hill	6	1	9	6
Robinson John	The Hill	6	1	9	6
Blythe F	Hillside [smallholding]	8	1	19	4
Summerton Miss M	2.3. Belvedere	3 (each)		14	9
Johnson A	1 Belvedere	3		14	9
Mortimer Mrs G	The Old Post Office	5	1	4	7
Woodham	The Hill [Grange L corner]	6	1	9	6
Bird F	Woodside [Grange Lane]	11	2	14	1
Gough Mary	Fairhaven [Grange Lane]	11	2	14	1
Dale H (to Gardner Jesse)	Restmore [Grange Lane]	17	4	3	7
Henson F (to George MsCA)	[thatched-corner Grange L]	2		9	10
Chambers James	[allotment ?]	4		19	8
Grandy John	Schoolhouse	11	2	14	1
Orpin	The Green [school garden 1945]	6	1	9	6
Seamarks	The Green	5	1	4	7
Inskip	The Green	10	2	9	2
Mortimer	row of	5	1	4	7
Tysoe	cottages east of	4		19	8
Mortimer Thos.	Green	3		14	9
Tebbutt Miss JA	The Green	3		14	9
Curtis Samuel	[Stevington] Lane	4		19	8
Gee WH	[Stevington] Lane	3		14	9

Name of householder	Name of Property	Nominal Value £	Rate £	s	d
Chambers WC	[Stevington] Lane	5	1	4	6
Rideout ES	[The Greenwood] 3	3 (each)		14	9
Bruty Charles	The Bakery	26	6	7	10
Seamarks William	Village	4		19	8
Hewlatt Charles	Village	5	1	5	7
Poole John	Village	5	1	4	7
Barclay	"Kinnard" (newly built)	11	2	14	1
Hyde WB	Vine Cottages	4		19	8
WM Peacock (owner)	(two were vacant)				
Pepper Frank		5	1	4	7
Harrison Ms Fanny	The Cottage	17	4	3	7
Mortimer AE	Cottage in Park Farm	6	1	9	6
Peacock WM	Park Cottage	68	16	14	4
	Park Cottage land	2		9	10
Burne Rev. AE	Vicarage	48	11	16	0
Freeman James	cottages owned by	5	1	4	7
Smith	GH Brierly adjoining	4		19	8
Brierly GH	Woodstock	19	4	13	5
Longhurst HW	Crossmead	84	20	13	0
Inskip James	⎧ cottages two of which	4		19	8
Tysoe Arthur	⎨ later became	4		19	8
Wallinger Thomas	⎩ post offices	4		19	8
Purser	The Post Office	5	1	4	7
Poole George	[between PO and shop]	18	4	8	6
Webster John	Village shop	22	5	8	2
Cousins George	⎧ thatched cottages lying	5	1	4	7
Stafferton William	⎩ back from shop	6	1	9	6
Metcalf Mrs C	Park View	6	1	9	6
Ledward J	Top Lodge	5	1	4	7
Gough Frederick	⎧ possibly in	4		19	8
Maxey Elizabeth	⎨ Hall	4		19	8
Tysoe Sydney	⎩ grounds	3		14	9
Green Leonard	(middle of Park)	64	15	14	8
(Vacant)	Lower Farm Cottage (later HQ of ARP)	2		9	10
Bull William	Grange Cottage (Gr. Farm)	3		14	9
	2 cottages at Mollivers Fm	4 (each)		19	8
Skinner Robert	Bromham Hall	188	46	4	4
	Bromham land	19	4	13	5
Trustees of WH Allen	Bromham House	191	46	19	1
	grounds of Bromham H	69	16	19	0

Name of householder	Name of Property	Nominal Value £	Rate £	s	d
Quenby & Sons	The Mill	40	9	16	8
	land at mill	5	1	4	7
Trsts of Ben Hawkins	Mollivers Farm house	30	7	7	6
	Mollivers Farm land	20	4	18	4
Oakley Jncn Gravel Co	Park Farm	250	61	9	2
Barcock R	London Barn Farm	5	1	4	7
		1		4	11
	London barn Farm land	18	4	8	6
Buckby	Grange Farm house	2 ?		9	10
	Grange Farm house land	24	5	18	0
Jeffery HA	Berry Farm house	1		4	11
	Berry Farm land	4		19	8
	[farm houses appear to have low rateable value. Much of Berry farm land would be in Kempston]				
(Vacant – had been King WR)	Park House	4		19	8
Skinner Miss M	Park House land	4		19	8
(Vacant)	Park Farm house	30	7	7	6

Other land holding

Quenby George	(next to police house – 2 plots)				
Peacock WM	(on Hill)				
Longhurst	(in Bromham Park)	8	1	19	4
Phipps	(next to Bowels Wood)	4		19	8
	and Bowels Wood	2		9	10
Blyth F		1		4	11
Bruty Charles	(in Grange Lane)	1		4	11

Recently built houses

Wilkerson	The Chalet (opposite school)	26	6	7	10
Hillyard EJ	(now 18 Grange Lane)	16	3	18	8
Everest Ernest	⎧ council houses				
White George	⎪ in Grange				
Robinson Miss A	⎨ Lane – all at	8	1	19	4
Harding Edward	⎪ value of £8;				
Seamarks Harry	⎪ there were eventually				
Tysoe Sidney	⎩ twelve of these				

Appendix VIII

Teaching staff at Bromham School

Headmasters	Assistant teacher	Monitresses
1861 – Sammuel Harrison		
	1869 – Miss Henkin	
1871 – Frederick Perkins		
1882 – Joseph Carrier		
		1883 – Emma Church
	1887-96 – Elizabeth Ham	?-1887 – Nellie Tebbutt
		1887 – Nellie Odell
	1890-1904 – Mrs Carrier (sewing)	
	1890 – Carrie Gardner	
		1891-2 – Lizzie Cooper
		1892 – Lucretia Brockett
		1892-1900 – Cissie Carrier
		1893 – Cissie Cooper
		1894 – Eva Carrier
1896-1929 John Grandy	1896-7 – Louisa Brockett	
	1899 – Miss J Willan	
	1900 – Augusta Bayley	
	1904-5 – Charlotte Pridmore	1904 – Miss Stafferton
	1905 – Amy Boston	
	1907-08 – Amy Frances Elliott	
	1908 – Georgina Lizzie Perkins	
	1913-14 – Miss DG Hassall	1913 – Madge Grandey
	Miss ML Seaman	
	1914-17 – Miss ALT Powney	1914 – Florence Tysoe
		1915 – Janet Askew
		1915-19 – Millicent Mayo
	1916 – Annie Elizabeth Beard	
	Lillian Matilda Russell	
	1917 – Mabel Grace Ebden	
		?-1918 – Sybil Field
	1919 – Gladys Evelyn Traster	
	1920 – Alice May Hurley	
	1921-35 – Lily Woolston (Truphet)	
1929-43 – Maud Lucy Prickett		
	1931 – Olive Nolley	
	1935 – Mrs DM Morse	
	1937 – Beatrice Waller	
	1937-58 – Miss F Walton	

Headmasters	**Assistant teacher**
	1940 – Miss Pull (Willesden)
	Miss Allen (Froebel trained)
	1941-3 – Miss SS Williams
1944 (Jan) – Estelle Bruton (acting)	
1944-60 – Mary Markham	1944-5 – Miss Riddy
	1952 – Miss Malliphant
	1952-5 – Miss L Linden
	1957-8 – Mrs Barrett
	1958 – Mrs Jordan
	Miss Spindler
	1959 – Mrs Dickenson
	Miss Dear
	Miss Jennings
1960 – Gladys Hart (acting)	
1961 – Andrew Ellison	

Moves to Rice Trevor Junior School when this school renamed St Owen's Infant School in 1965.

Appendix IX
Comparative populations of neighbouring villages from 1801

	Bromham	Clapham	Biddenham	Oakley	Stevington	Stagsden	Kempston	
1801	297	157	252	265	415	492	1035	
1811	280	177	310	432	436	517	1161	
1821	298	204	393	486	485	542	1419	
1831	324	298	369	516	500	597	1571	
1841	314	370	345	492	602	632	1699	
1851	343	445	373	457	586	727	1961	
1861	361	502	350	443	606	708	2191	
1871	373	607	321	378	735	680	2706	
1881	327	608	308	295	624	548	3432	
1891	319	725	352	250	601	470	4738	
							rural/urban	
1901	321	788	325	299	536	429	719	4729
1911	350	748	451	330	479	435	648	5349
1921	328	704	460	337	467	388	656	5218
1931	442	840	568	508	479	455	730	5390
1951	1220	2203	503	478	409	368	1171	8645
1961	2722	3284	693	624	386	400	1289	9190
1971	3746	3709	728	1335	589	348	1308	12826
1981	3941	3817	807	2283	604	346	1278	15466
1991	3825	3411	1183	2333	555	355	1163	17938
1992	*4230*							
1997	*4710*							

Index of Names in the text

With the exception of Appendix 5 names in appendices have not been indexed since they are mostly, in themselves, lists of names. Spelling of names varies. Bowles is, for instance, often Bowels. Normally one spelling is chosen but different spellings of what is essentially the same name have been indexed where this is considered of any historical significance, as, for instance Maliavers and Mollivers or Malherbe and Malherbis.

Abbot, Dr   115-116, 126
Abingdon   5, 70-71, 72
Achemere   136
Achemershfurlong   137
Aethelfled   4
Aethelred (the unready)   5
Akeman street   2
Aldick   134, 135
Aldwick Brook   134
Alfsi   11
Alfwold   11
Allen, WH   97
Allen, WP   97
Alsop, Margaret   36
Alston, Sir Richard   46
Alston, Sir Thomas   69
Ambrosius   4
Ampthill   71
Andrew, St   22
Anglian Water Authority   99-101
Anne, Queen   78-79
Arnolds of Leeds   54
Arnulf of Ardres   12
Arthur   3, 4
Ashburnham, Col.   72
Astey Wood   59
Athelney   4
Aylesbury   70
Ayres   59
Badon (battle of)   4
Bain, Henry   44
Bakery, Old   92, 106
Barker, Gen Sir Evelyn   91
Barton, Dowglasse   45
Barton, John   45
Beachamp, Miles   15
Beachamp, Simon   15
Beard, Paul   60
Beauchamp, Beatrice   18, 19
Beauchamp, Hugh   11-13, 18
Beauchamp, John   16
Beauchamp, William   15, 16
Becks Ash   59
Bedcanford (battle of)   4

Bedford (battles at)   6
Bedford (castle)   6, 13
Bedford (Duke of)   58, 81, 139
Bedford bridge   104
Belchamp – see Beauchamp
Belgic (peoples)   1
Benson   98
Benson, Thomas   38
Benson, William   37
Berne (Canon)   24
Berngate, William   18
Berry Farm   29, 47, 88-89, 107, 135, 141
Beverley   70
Biddenham   2, 35, 76, 82, 94, 102, 103, 105, 135, 136
Big Field   135, 138
Biggs   36, 38
Biggs, Anne   36
Biggs, John   40, 43, 94
Biggs, William   28-29, 94
Birt, Joan   42
Blacknelfield   146
Blahynhyll   137
Blake's Hill   135
Blakynhyll   135
Blakynhythfeld   137
Blartnell Close   137
Blott, Shirley   29
Blyth, Frederick   43, 91
Boelles   17
Bonewode   137
Bosco/Boscum, Wm   19
Boteler   39
Boteler, Elizabeth   141
Boteler, William   19, 27, 65-66, 93, 103, 141, 139
Boudica   2
Bournemouth   81
Bowells Wood   47, 59, 61, 107, 115, 135, 138
Bowels (ors. Bowles)   10, 17
Box End   141
Box, The   108

Brackley   6
Bransome, Frank   42
Braose, William de   16
Bray, Edmund   65
Bray, Sir Reginald   16, 65
Braybrook   6
Brayes (manor of)   17
Breaute, Faulkes de   6-7, 15
Breaute, William de   6-7
Brent, Sir Nathaniel   23
Brett   90
Brewos – see Braose
Brewsters Yate   136
Bridge End   11, 93, 102, 107, 108, 140, 141, 107, 108
Bridgewater   72
Bridport   68
Bristol (Earl of)   23, 67, 68
Bristol (2nd Earl of)   76
Brochiseved   18
Brodemede   134
Bromham (alternatives)   10, 28
Brook, The   61, 101, 134, 135
Brooksbanks, Rev. JA   30
Brookside   58
Brotherputes   136
Brown, Thomas   28
Browne, Thomas   94
Browning (Canon)   24
Bruna   4, 10
Bruty   92
Buckby   89
Buckingham (Duke of)   67
Buckingham   5
Buckinghamshire   4, 65, 80
Bull, Richard   37
Bunny, Simon   37
Bunyan Meeting   29
Burchester   19
Burgh, Hubert de   6, 16
Burghersh (Bishop)   26
Burnt close   134
Burnt Meadow   134, 137
Burr   134

Buryehill   136
Butcher, Charles   24
Butterfield   21, 25
Cambridge   4
Cannon, Richard   36
Canterbury   5
Canvin   135
Carausius   2
Careless, Jane   45
Careless, Robert   44
Carit   24
Carpenter, Miss   93
Carrier, Joseph   55-56
Casse, George   93
Cater, Andrew   24, 37
Cater, Henry   141
Catuvellauni   2
Cauldwell Priory   18, 22, 44, 89
Caversham   70
Cecil (Baroness Dynevor)   78
Chadwick, Sir Edwin   51
Chalet, The   60
Chalverstone, Thomas de   39
Chambers   38
Chandler   21
Charles I   7, 68-77
Chibnall, Anthony   140
Chilvers, Percy   29
Christmas, Thomas   37
Church   38
Church, A   92
Church, Charles   92
Church, George   94
Church, James   40
Church, John   94
Church, Martha   37
Church, Mrs   83
Clapham Dam   18, 69, 91, 96, 99, 108, 111, 134, 137
Clare   24
Clarendon   72
Clark, Thomas   141
Clough, Samuel   40-41
Clyppyscroft   137
Cnut (King)   5
Cochrane   41
Coleman, (widow)   46
Coleman, Cornelius   39
Coleman, William   37
Collins, GF   89
Comberhay   76
Compton, Gregory   44
Conhelm   137
Constantine   3
Conygrave   141
Cooper, Cyril   89
Cooper, John   46

Cople   71
Corrnwallis, Sir Frederick   72
Cow Pasture   135, 137
Cox (widow)   37
Cox   90
Cox, Henry   37
Cramfeud, Avicia   39
Cramfeud, Thomas de   39
Cromwell, Oliver   72, 74, 75
Dainty, Mary   37
Danelaw   4
Danes   4
Dawson, Robert   27
Dedland   136
Denny, Douglas   66
Derby (Earl of)   75
Dickens, Charles   51, 96
Digby, George   67, 68, 69
Digby, Sir John   67, 71
Digby, Sir Kenelm   67
Dixe, Dorothie   45
Dixe, William   44-45
Domesday Book   6, 11
Dorset   72
Drew, William   25
Dunstable   4
Dynevor (Baron)   8, 22, 54, 78, 81-84,96
Dysons   22
Dyve (Lewis, younger)   7, 12, 67-77, 89, 93, 102, 134
Dyve (Lewis, elder)   7, 18, 22, 27, 65-66, 135, 136, 137, 139, 140-141
Dyve, Beatrirce   67
Dyve, Francis   37, 68, 76-77
Dyve, Henry   65
Dyve, Jane   68
Dyve, John (jun.)   68
Dyve, Lewis   77
Dyve, Sir John   39, 65-66, 93, 139, 141
Dyve, William   65
Dyve, John of Quinton   65
Earle, Stephen   37
East Field   137
East, Nicholas   24
Eastmill   47
Eaton (Bray)   16-17
Eaton Socon   58
Edgehill, Battle of   70
Edith (Queen)   11, 12
Edmund (King)   5
Edward (the Confessor)   5
Edward I   16
Edward II   16
Edward the Elder   4-5

Edward VI   27
Elizabeth I   39
Ellis, J (map-maker)   10
Ellison, Andrew   58
Ellison, Francis   37
Ellwood, William   37
Elstow (Abbey)   7
Elstow   95
Elvey, Miss   60
Emmisson   36
English (widow)   37
Essex (Earl of)   72
Eton College   22-23, 25, 47, 89, 110, 139
Eustace (Count)   11, 12
Evelyn (diarist)   76
Evesham (battle of)   7, 16
Faccon, Thomas de   19
Fairfax (Lord)   72-3, 75
Faldo, William de   39
Farrar, Rev. CF   6, 81, 105
Fensome, John   90
Figers, le   137
Flanders   29
Fleming, Dr   39
Flint   77
Flower   70
Fortune, Mathew   37
Forty Acre   138
France   77
Franklin (widow)   37
Franklin, Edward   36
Franklyn, Agnes   37
Franklyn, Henry   36
Franklyn, William   36
Fullake   139
Fullyngmylne   137
Fyssher   103
Galloways   134
Gallows Corner   39
Ganford (widow)   37
Gardner, Jesse   83
Garlic   30
Gaul   1, 3
Gaveston   16
George I   79
Germany   60
Gibbin's Close   135
Gilbert, Rev. E Denby   24, 30
Gildas   4
Gillibrand H   56
Glover, Thomas   28
Godfry, John   37
Godiman, Henry   19
Godwin (Earl)   5, 12
Godwin   11
Golding   42

157

Golding, William   110
Goodall, Rev. JJ   51, 54
Goodhall, Elizabeth   42
Goodhall, Humphrey   42
Goodhall, William   39
Goring (Lord)   72
Grandy, John Thomas   56
Grange Farm   37, 47, 59, 89, 101, 105, 135
Grange Lane   11, 14, 17, 36, 58, 83, 91, 93, 106, 107, 108, 134, 137
Grant, Roger   19
Great Offley   45
Greenwood, cottages   92, 106
Grey, (Earl)   81
Griffiths, Rev. George   30
Guildford   5
Gurney   38
Guthrum   4
Haines (widow)   37
Haines, Lewis   37
Hall, HN   30
Hall, Samuel   28
Hamilton, (Duke of)   75
Hammerton, Joan   44
Hampden (1st Visc.)   26, 52, 105
Hampden (3rd Visc.)   41, 140
Hampden, John   77, 80
Hangers Wood   59, 108
Harald (of Norway)   5
Harding, EPF   92
Harlewene   137
Harold (King)   5
Harper, John   44
Harrison   134
Harrison, Edwin   25
Harrison, Frederick   94
Harrison, Samuel   140
Harrison, Thomas   94
Hart   38
Hart, John   140
Hawford   135
Henman, William   29, 38, 41
Henry I   6
Henry II   15
Henry III   6, 15
Hertford   5
Hill, The   102, 107, 134, 135
Hillyard, Mark   30, 106
Hinde   25
Hinney's   135
Hitchin   50
Hold, Joseph   141
Holland   69
Holm   18
Holt, CJ   79

Honorius   3
Hooton, John   37
Horne (widow)   37
Howden, John   103
Howkins, B   90
Hull   68
Huntingdon   4
Huntingdonshire   115
Hurford, Rev. Frank   30
Hurry, Sir John   71
Hurst, le   137
Hurstpytfeld   135
Huspitt fielde   135
Hykkesholm   137
Ibbott, Thomas   103
Inchiquin (Lord)   75
Inskip   38
Inskip, John   98
Irchester   2
Isle of Man   75
Islip   38, 39
Jarrow, John   46
Jeffries   92
Jeffries, Thomas   92
Jennings ?Jeyes, Richard   94
John (King)   6, 15
Johnstone, Rev. CF   55
Judith (Countess)   11, 12, 17, 18, 43
Julius Ceasar   1
Juvene, Thomas   18
Katherine St   26
Kemeshedd, Henry   43
Kempston -- Church End   2, 56
Kempston Mill   110
Kempston – Moor End   29
Kempston   4, 5, 76, 92, 93, 105, 107, 108, 115, 116
King   38, 40
King, C & WE   89
King, Derek   36
King, Samuel   36, 136
King's Close   134-135, 137, 138
King's Cross station   111
King's Field   135
Kip, Henry   18
Knot, Maurice   39
Knotting   23
Kyng, Dorothy   45
Lake meadow   138
Lake, le   136, 139
Langmadedych   137
Langmede   137
Langport   72
Langton (Stefan)   6, 16
Latimer (Lord)   19, 139
Laud (Archbishop)   23

Lavenden   109, 110
Lawne, The   138
Lawrence   69
Layham, Matthew de   39
Lea (River)   4
Leader   36
Leicester (Thos, Earl of)   16
Leicester   70
Lenthall, Lady   75
Lenthall, Sir John   74
Leofric   11
Lewins   36, 37
Leybrooke   134
Lile Adam   76
Lillburne, John   73, 74
Lilley   39
Lincoln (battle of)   6, 15
Lincoln (Bishop of)   24
Linsford, Sir Thomas   68
Lobbeswick Field   136
Londinim   2
Longehul   137
Longford (Countess of)   53
Longland   136
Longyerde, le   137
Lornd pasture   138
Louis (King)   7
Lowens, Henry   102
Lower Farm Road   91, 107, 136, 137
Luke, Sir Samuel   7, 68, 69, 70, 71
Lumbley, Robert   38
Lyeside   134
Lynchfurlong   137
Madras   43
Magna Carta   6
Maliavers   137
Malcott, John   141
Malerbes   137
Malherbe, Geoffrey   39
Malherbe, John   39
Malherbe, William   18-19, 22
Malherbis   139
Mallerbe, John   18
Mallerbe, Richard   19
Malmede   137
Man, Robert   37
Marche, John le   19
Marcus   3
Margate   28
Mariespoll   136
Markham, Miss Mary   57
Marlborough (Duke of)   79, 82
Marsh, Dr.   98
Marshall, Rev.   30
Marys, St   26
Matilda   6

Matthew of Dunstable 26	Odell, Thomas 37	Rachell, Humphrey 37
Maud, Richard 44	Odell, William 37, 40	Rachell, Lewis 37
Maulden 46	Offa (King) 4	Rachell, Mary 37
Maxey, Thomas 25	Oisse, River 76	Rachell, Thomas 37
Mayhew 38	Old Ned 48	Rachelle, Richard 44
Mayhew, Arthur 42, 81	Old Warren 138	Radulph (of Bedford) 23
Mazarin, Cardinal 76	Olney 109, 111	Ragon Reginald 65
McCullough, Rev. Hugh 30	Onslow (Speaker) 78, 79	Ragon, Agnes 65
Melbourne (Lord) 52	Osborne 38	Ragon, John 65
Melbury 68	Osborne, William 25	Ragon, Sir Reginald 19
Mercia 3, 4-5	Osebern, William 18	Rainsborough 74
Mesham, Rev. 28	Oseberton, John of 27	Ransom, Edwin 110
Middlesex 115	Osgeat 11	Ravensden 37
Mill Close 94	Ouse, River 4, 10, 93, 99, 101, 102, 115, 126, 137	Ravenstone 110
Millard 38		Reading 70
Miller's Holme 94	Owen, St 22	Reed, Rev. Stanley 30
Millfields 102	Pailes, Mrs 60	Reeves, Arthur 60
Millman, Jeff 42	Palestine 91	Rethel 76
Mollivers Farm 47, 90, 107, 135	Palyshul 137	Reynolds 38
Mollivers Lane 17 see also Stevington Lane	Parentyn, Richard 19	Rice Trevor, George 52, 82
	Park Farm 47, 91	Rice, Edward 78
Mollivers Wood 11, 38, 43, 136, 137	Passelowe 17, 19	Rice-Trevor, Elianore 8, 25, 42, 46, 53, 54, 58, 78, 80-84, 96, 110
	Passelowe, Ralph 18	
Monk, General 77	Passelowe, William 14	Rice-Trevor, George 78, 80. 89
Montfort, Simon de 16	Patynson, Rev. John 44	Richard I 18
Montgomery, (Visc.) 75	Paulinus 2	Richards, Mary 37
Moor End 141, see also Kempston	Pavenham 12, 15	Richards, Robert 24
Morgan, Nicholas 44	Pawlin, Ralph 37	Rideout, Julius S 29
Morris, Georgie 134	Peacocke 38	Roadside 136
Naseby, battle of 72	Peacocke, Henry 37	Rochell, Thomas 44, see also Rachell
Negus 36-37	Pell, Alice 37	
Nether Wateland 137	Pepys, Samuel 76	Rogers, Rev. Benjamin 39, 79
Neuman, Robert 18	Perkins, John 99	Rogers 38
Neville (Lord) 19	Perkins, William 40	Rogers, Howanda 67
New Road 107	Pertnall, John 37, 44	Romans 1, 2
Newland & Nash Ltd 140	Pike, William 110	Ros (ors. Rots, Sesto de) 11, 13
Newnham Priory 18	Pixley (widow) 37	Ros, William 19
Newport Pagnell 71, 72, 102, 103, 108, 141	Place, William 27	Rotherham, Sir Thomas 27
	Plumer, Walter le 19	Rous, Richard 19
North Crawley 101	Poole, Pauline 7	Rupert (Prince) 70, 71
Northampton Road 59, 91, 92, 101, 102	Preden (?) 38	Russel 21
	Preston, Edwin 110	Russel, Richard 38
Northampton 111	Prickett, Miss Maud L 57	Rust, James 140
Northampton 4-5, 6	Provis, Henry 104	Rutland 115
Nottingham 70	Prudden 36, 38	Sacerodos, William 23
Nottingham, Henry 37	Prudden, John 38, 39	Salem Thrift 41, 59, 97, 135, 137, 138
Nottingham, John 37	Prudden, Sarah 38	
Nottingham, Robert 37	Pruden, Susan 38	Salmon, Robert 104
Oakley bridge 126	Pruden, William 38	Sampson, Peter 66
Oakley Hunt 58	Pugh, Miss 83	Sampson, Robert 66
Oakley junction 111	Purser, Mrs 98	Sarlefryth 137
Oakley Road 90, 108	Pym, John 71	Saunderson L&B Ltd 31
Oakley 24, 35, 107, 115	Pynkeny, William de 39	Savadge, Robert 36
Oates Close 137, 138	Quenby, George 140	Savadge, Thomas 37
Odell 12, 38	Quenby, Harry 94	Savage 135
Odell, Mrs 98	Quenby, Walter 94	Savages Close 138
Odell, Richard 37	Rachell, Henry 37 or Rochell	Scot, Alex & Mary 18

159

Searle, Elizabeth 79
Senlac Hill (battle of) 5
Sheep Close 138
Sheep Paasture 135, 137
Shefford 4, 24
Sherborne castle 68, 72
Sherington Field 109
Shippen, Sgt.Maj.Gen. 71
Shortfurlong 137
Shorthul 137
Shortmede furlong 136
Simpson (widow) 37
Simpsonne 36
Sinden, John 30, 31, 32
Skinner, Robert 96, 98, 134
Skypwith, Nicholas 103
Slype, The 101, 135
Smith, Geoffrey 26
Smith, William 27
Somers, Lord 78
Spain 76
St Albans 71
St Andrews church 44
St John, Sir John 27
St John's Hospital 137
St John's station 111
St Neots 5, 25
St Owen's Infants Sch. 58
St Pancras station 111
St Peter's hospital 51
Stafferton, Richard 40
Stafford 47
Stagsden Road 11, 91, 93
Stagsden 35, 59, 82, 90, 102, 108, 109, 116
Staines, William 29, 140
Statham 93
Steele, Elizabeth 80
Steffe, Edward 37
Stephen (of Blois, King) 6, 15
Stevintron 12, 18, 59, 76, 102, 105, 115, 126, 138
Stevington Cross 136
Stevington Lane 107, 108
Steyngreve 19
Stokes, John 39
Stokewellelcone 137
Stonyfurlong 137
Stotfold 16
Stowe, William 38
Strafford (Earl of) 68
Strangeways, Sir John 67, 76, 134, 137
Stuart, Bernard 91
Sutor, William 18
Swain 60
Swein (King) 5

Sweyn, William 19
Swineseheved 19
Tallebose, Matilda 13
Tallebose, Ralph 13
Taunton 72
Taylor, John 24
Tempsford 4
Thames, River 70, 75, 76
The Hague 75, 80
Thistley Green 60, 107, 108
Thorkell 5
Thorne, Miss 92-93
Thorowgood, Oliver 23
Thurleigh 60
Towcester 72
Trevallyn 78
Trevanion, Margaret 77
Trevor (1st Baron) 52, 77-80
Trevor (2nd Baron) 25-26
Trevor 41, 96
Trevor, Edward 79
Trevor, Elizabeth 79
Trevor, Eva 22
Trevor, John (elder) 77
Trevor, John 21, 52, 80
Trevor, Lucy 78
Trevor, Richard 79
Trevor, Robert 79, 80
Trevor, Sir Thomas 37, 79, 137, 141
Trotwood, Betsy 81
Tucker, William 25
Turin 80
Turkey, Sultan of 92
Turnham Green, Battle of 70
Turvey 12, 102, 105, 108, 111
Twenty Acre 138
Twinwoods 60
Tysoe, Frank 98
Utrecht, Treaty of 79
Ventris, Francis 27
Verins 136
Verulanium 1, 2
Victoria, Queen 81
Village road 92
Vortigen 3
Vyne, The 137, 140
Wade-Gery, Rev. 48-49, 51
Wake (Manor of) 19
Walcot, Beatrice 66, 67
Walcot, Charles 66
Wales 2
Waller 38, 72
Wallinger 38
Wallingford 5, 72
Walnut Tree Close 135
Walton, Miss F 57

Ward 38
Warnet, John 44
Warnet, Thomas 27
Warwick (Countess of) 66
Warwickshire 2
Wassell, Rev. 30
Waters, Anthony 23
Webbs 135
Webster 83
Wedmore (Treaty of) 4
Weldon, Anne 79
Wellingborough 109, 111
Westphalia, Treaty of 76
Wever, Peter 27
Weymouth 68, 72
Whitbread, Samuel 58
Whitchurch, John 110
White 135
White, Thomas 99
Whitehall 75
Whites Wood 59
Widevile, Thomas 19, 22, 65
Wideville, Elizabeth 19
Wideville, John 17
Wilde, Elizabeth 65
Wilde, Thomas 65
Wiles 25
Willesden 31
William (the Conqueror) 5
William II (Rufus) 13
William III 78
Williams Derek 60
Williams, Ron 60
Willis, Commander 90
Windsor 23
Wing, John 104
Wingfield, Ed Ffolliot 78, 88
Wingfield, George T 88
Wise, Ms Frances E 58
Witney, Mr 93
Woburn Sands 109
Woburn 58
Wodyll, Goditha 103
Wolston, Simon de 26
Woodfield 136
Woolley, Thomas Smith 138
Wooton 24
Worcester 70
Worth, Humphrey 45
Wright, Andrew 66
Wulnescroft 136
Wylden, Roger de 18
Wynemill (widow) 37
Yates, Harry 40-41
Yett, William 37
York (Duke of) 68